CliffsNotes®
Praxis II® Principles of Learning and Teaching

CliffsNotes®

Praxis II® Principles of Learning and Teaching

2ND EDITION

By Diane E. Kern, Ph.D.

WILEY

John Wiley & Sons, Inc.

About the Author

Diane E. Kern, Ph.D. (Wakefield, RI), is associate professor of education at the University of Rhode Island (URI). She teaches courses in education psychology, teaching methods, literacy education, and classroom management. Dr. Kern was a public-school teacher for 14 years and currently coordinates the Secondary English Language Arts teacher-education program in the School of Education at URI.

Author's Acknowledgments

Thanks to my teaching colleagues and former students, as well as my own children and their friends, who provided the memories and inspiration to share my teaching stories and knowledge of teaching. Special appreciation goes to the editorial team of this second edition: Greg, Elizabeth, Cate, and Katherine. This book is dedicated to the many University of Rhode Island teacher candidates, who have told me their test-preparation concerns and have gone on to achieve their dream: to teach.

Editorial

Acquisition Editor: Greg Tubach

Project Editor: Elizabeth Kuball

Copy Editor: Catherine Schwenk

Technical Editor: Katherine Egan

Composition

Proofreaders: Jacqueline Brownstein, Bryan Coyle

John Wiley & Sons, Inc., Composition Services

CliffsNotes® Praxis II® Principles of Learning and Teaching, 2nd Edition

Published by:
John Wiley & Sons, Inc.
111 River Street
Hoboken, NJ 07030-5774
www.wiley.com

Copyright © 2012 John Wiley & Sons, Inc., Hoboken, NJ

Published by John Wiley & Sons, Inc., Hoboken, NJ
Published simultaneously in Canada

Library of Congress Control Number: 2012937945
ISBN: 978-1-118-09046-6 (pbk)
ISBN: 978-1-118-15349-9; 978-1-118-21943-0; 978-1-118-21944-7 (ebk)

Printed in the United States of America

10 9 8 7 6 5 4 3 2 1

Table of Contents

PART II: PREPARING FOR THE FORMAT OF THE PLT

PART III: PREPARING FOR THE CONTENT OF THE PLT

PART IV: FULL-LENGTH PRACTICE TESTS

Introduction

As you know, teaching is a rewarding and challenging profession. One way you will show that you are ready for your teaching license is to pass your state's required Praxis II: Principles of Learning and Teaching (PLT) test. The way you will show that you are ready for your teaching career is to use this book to thoroughly prepare for your teaching licensure test. Successful teachers, like you, do their homework, so let's get started.

Format of the Test

Each of the PLT tests is designed to measure your knowledge of a broad range of teaching-related topics. There is a new numbering system for the PLT, as the PLT tests were recently reviewed by a panel of teaching professionals and updated, or regenerated, to be current on research-based, best practice. The newly revised format also emphasizes additional knowledge of teaching not covered in the previous version of the exam. Your knowledge of the topics measured on the PLT test is usually developed in undergraduate or teacher-certification teaching methods courses, as well as in educational psychology, human development, classroom management, and foundations of education courses. No matter which of the PLT tests you take, you will answer a total of 74 questions—70 multiple-choice questions and 4 short-answer questions (known as *constructed-response questions* on the PLT). There are four different PLT tests, all of which use the same format, broken down by grade (see the following table).

PLT Test	Test Registration Code
Early Childhood	0621
Grades K–6	0622
Grades 5–9	0623
Grades 7–12	0624

Each multiple-choice question includes a question or statement and then four answer choices. There is one credited response. For a preview of the multiple-choice questions, turn to Chapter 5.

The constructed-response questions are short-answer questions that relate to teaching situations (also called *scenarios*) in order to provide real-life teaching context for your responses. For a preview of the constructed-response questions, turn to Chapter 6.

You will have a total of two hours to complete the PLT test. The constructed-response questions that accompany each teaching scenario will require more time per question. You'll want to plan 50 minutes for the four constructed-response questions in order to read each scenario and to write your short-answer responses. It is better to have a bulleted list of key words and examples for the constructed-response questions than to leave any blank. Allow one minute per multiple-choice question, for a total of 70 questions in 70 minutes. There is no penalty for guessing, so be sure to answer every question.

Question Type	Total Number of Questions	Format	Pacing Suggestions
Constructed response	4 short-answer questions	2 teaching scenarios, each followed by 2 constructed-response questions in one section	25 minutes per teaching scenario/2 constructed-response questions, for a total of 50 minutes
Multiple choice	70 multiple-choice questions	70 multiple-choice questions in one section	70 minutes total for one section of 70 questions

On the test, you will first be presented with the 70 multiple-choice questions; then you'll read the first teaching scenario and provide two short-answer constructed responses. Next, you'll read the second teaching scenario and complete the final two short-answer constructed responses.

Content of the Test

Now that you have a general idea of the format and pacing of the test, let's take a closer look at the content of the PLT test. The broad topics Students as Learners and Instructional Process make up at least 57 percent of the test and as much as 69 percent based on the constructed-response questions asked on your version of the exam. Clearly, this is where you'll want to spend the majority of your study time. In addition, the PLT test assesses your understanding of Assessment and Professional Development, Leadership, and Community in at least 30 percent of the test questions and as much as 42 percent of the exam, so these topics also deserve your review time.

Topic	Subjects Covered	Approximate Number of Multiple-Choice (MC) Questions	Approximate Number of Constructed-Response (CR) Questions	Approximate Percentage of Your Score
Students as Learners	Student development and learning processes Diverse learners Motivation and learning environment Analysis of teaching scenarios	21	1–2	22.5% MC 6.25%–12.5% CR
Instructional Process	Instructional strategies Planning strategies Assessment strategies Analysis of teaching scenarios	21	1–2	22.5% MC 6.25%–12.5% CR
Assessment	Analysis of teaching scenarios	14	0–1	15% MC 0–6.25% CR
Professional Development, Leadership, and Community	Reflective practitioners The larger school community Analysis of teaching scenarios	14	0–1	15% 0–6.25% CR

Studying for the Test

Don't wait until the last minute.

Self-assess your strengths and weaknesses as a test taker and student. Also, use this guide to help you determine the content you still need to know. If multiple-choice questions aren't your strong suit, study more of those items. If you're struggling with reading comprehension, writing, or knowing the fundamentals of education psychology, then study and practice more of the constructed-response questions based on teaching scenarios.

Remember: All the practice tests in this book can help you prepare for the content and format of the PLT.

Make a study plan and stick to it. The following tables provide suggested study plans for those with a longer timeline and those with a shorter timeline.

If You Have a Longer Timeline	
When	**What You Need to Do**
3 months (or more) before the PLT	Register for the test. Complete paperwork for accommodations, if applicable. Complete paperwork or speak with your financial-aid officer about the possibility of a fee waiver, if applicable. Read the Introduction and Part I of this book. Dust off your education psychology textbook or borrow one from your library. More recent copies even have references to the Praxis II PLT test! Use your favorite search engine (such as Google or Yahoo!) to search for websites using keywords such as "Praxis II" and "Principles of Learning and Teaching." Look for sites that contain PowerPoint presentations or the names of colleges or universities. Many of these sites are created by professors and offer a wealth of information to shore up your weaknesses and help you prepare for the content of the test. Bookmark these websites for future use.
2 months (or more) before the PLT	Make sure you've already registered for your test. Also, be sure to set aside proof of registration in a safe place—one that you'll remember! Read Parts II and III of this book to help you understand the format and content of the test. Use your favorite PLT websites—the ones you bookmarked last month—to help you prepare for the test. Take a look at the table of contents, the glossary, and the index of your education psychology textbook to provide even more content information for the areas in which you are still learning.
1 month (or more) before the PLT	Do you know where the actual building is for your PLT test day? Take a test drive there leaving your house at the same time you will need to leave when you take the actual test. Time how long it takes and note the traffic conditions. Take the full-length practice tests of the PLT in Part IV of this book to help you simulate test-taking conditions and assess which areas you still need to study. Use your websites and education psychology book to aid you in filling in any missing pieces of content.
1 week before the PLT	Set aside your admission ticket, three or four #2 pencils with erasers, a couple blue or black pens, and two valid forms of identification. Retake any or all of the full-length tests in this book. Review Part III of this book to refresh your memory on the test content.
The night before the PLT	Talk only to people who make you feel good and confident! Pack a water bottle and a small snack bag. Although you can't bring these things into the test session, you'll enjoy the brain refueling after the test! Go to bed early. Don't cram all night. Relax. You've already put in a lot of effort preparing for the PLT test.
The day of the PLT	Eat a good breakfast. Remember to bring your watch, admission ticket, IDs, and writing instruments. Arrive at the test center at least 30 minutes early. Remember: You're confident, wise, and test savvy. In short, you're ready to pass the PLT test!

If You Have a Shorter Timeline	
When	**What You Need to Do**
1 month before the PLT	Register for the PLT test. There is a late registration fee option if you're registering within 1 month of the test. Complete paperwork and submit it to the Educational Testing Service (ETS) if you are eligible for accommodations, although ETS suggests that this may take 4 to 6 weeks to process, so your timeline is tight on this. Perhaps you'll have to take this first exam without accommodations while you process paperwork with ETS to get accommodations the next time you take the test, if you need another opportunity. Talk to your financial-aid officer to learn if your school has a test fee waiver option for you. Read the Introduction and Part I of this book.
3 weeks before the PLT	Read Parts III and IV of this book. Do you know where the actual building is for your PLT test day? Take a test drive there, leaving your house at the same time you will need to leave when you take the actual test. Time how long it takes and note the traffic conditions.
2 weeks before the PLT	Take the full-length practice tests of the PLT in Part IV of this book to help you simulate test-taking conditions and assess which areas you still need to study. Review content outlines in Part III of this book to help you shore up any areas that you are still learning.
1 week before the PLT	Set aside your admission ticket, three or four #2 pencils with erasers, a couple blue or black pens, and two valid forms of identification. Retake any or all of the full-length tests in this guide. Review Part III of this book to refresh your memory on the test content.
The night before the PLT	Talk only to people who make you feel good and confident! Pack a water bottle and a small snack bag. Although you can't bring these things into the test session, you'll enjoy the brain refueling after the test. Go to bed early. Don't cram all night. Relax. You've already put in a lot of effort preparing for the PLT test.
The day of the PLT	Eat a good breakfast! Remember to bring your watch, admission ticket, IDs, and writing instruments. Arrive to the test center at least 30 minutes early. Remember: You're confident, wise, and test savvy. In short, you're ready to pass the PLT test!

Frequently Asked Questions

You've already started on the path to success by orienting yourself to the format of the questions, planning to pace yourself, and becoming familiar with the content covered on this test, but most likely you still have several questions about your licensure test.

Q. How do I register for the PLT?

A. Contact the Educational Testing Service (ETS) on the web at www.ets.org/praxis or by mail. My students and I have found that registering online is easiest, unless you are eligible for accommodations. In that case, you must register by mail. Be sure to know the test code of the Praxis II: PLT test you are required to take. Whether you register online or by mail, you will have to create a Praxis account online.

Q. How do I know which PLT test to take?

A. Contact the department of education for the state in which you seek teacher licensure. I recommend that you use your favorite Internet search engine to locate your state department of education's teaching certification office.

Q. What score do I need to earn my teaching license?

A. Each state department of education sets its passing score. Contact your state's department of education for this answer.

Q. Do all states require the PLT for teacher licensure?

A. No, but several do. Some states have created their own licensure tests. Some states use other Praxis II tests. Again, contact the state department of education for specifics. States that require the PLT will accept your PLT scores no matter where you took the test, provided that you meet the state's passing score requirement and that you did not take the test too long ago (usually five or more years ago).

Q. How long does it take to get my scores back?

A. ETS posts your scores online at your My Praxis personal account in approximately four weeks. Be certain to print a copy of your score report and to save a copy of the file to your hard drive, as your scores expire from your online account after 45 days.

Q. Are any accommodations available to test takers?

A. Yes. Test takers with disabilities, health-related needs, and those whose primary language is not English (PLNE) may apply for test-taking accommodations. More information is available at www.ets.org/disabilities.

Q. What do I need on the day of the test?

A. You need:

- Photo identification with your name, photograph, and signature. Identification must be original and may not be expired.
- Second alternative identification with your name, photograph, and signature—just to be sure! Usually test takers use a valid passport or a student ID.
- Admission ticket, printed from your My Praxis account.
- Three or four sharpened #2 pencils with erasers.
- Two blue or black pens for constructed-response questions.
- A watch without calculator functions (optional, but advised because test sites may not have a clock).
- Layered clothing (optional, but you can't control the temperature of the testing room!).

Q. What's the best way to prepare for the Principles of Learning and Teaching tests?

A. Doing just what you're doing! Become familiar with the format, types of questions, and content of the test. After you're familiar with what will be on the test, it's best to complete several PLT practice tests, self-correct, and study the questions/content you get incorrect.

About This Book

CliffsNotes Praxis II Principles of Learning and Teaching, 2nd Edition, has been revised to reflect the changing nature of information tested on the Praxis II PLT. In addition to minor revisions made to enhance clarity, the following substantial changes have been made to guide your test preparation efforts:

- Sample constructed responses, which provide an actual template to follow when writing your own responses
- Updated diagnostic preview tests and full-length practice tests to reflect changes in questions you might expect on the PLT
- Additional advice and specific examples to help you prepare for both the constructed-response and multiple-choice format questions
- Revised content outlines for each area tested: Students as Learners; Instructional Process; Assessment; and Professionalism, Leadership, and Community

How to Use This Book

CliffsNotes Praxis II Principles of Learning and Teaching, 2nd Edition, offers various levels of support to make your test-preparation efforts successful.

Part I: Diagnostic Preview Tests

This part provides an introductory experience with the constructed-response and multiple-choice formats of the PLT. You can select your specific PLT test version (Early Childhood, Grades K–6, Grades 5–9, or Grades 7–12), complete the sample questions, and self-correct to determine areas you know and areas you need to study. Each item on the preview test has a detailed explanation that leads you to another section of this book to help you gain deeper knowledge of the content covered in each test item.

For additional practice, you also may want to complete all the other preview tests in this section. Although the teaching situations presented are grade specific (for example, the Early Childhood test offers teaching scenarios about a first-grade classroom), the content of any PLT test follows a consistent pattern. In other words, each one tests your knowledge of the four content categories—Students as Learners; Instructional Process; Assessment; and Professionalism, Leadership, and Community—so completing the diagnostic preview tests from other grade levels still pays off!

Part II: Preparing for the Format of the PLT

This part provides specific strategies for answering each of the two question types on the PLT: multiple-choice questions and constructed-response questions.

Part III: Preparing for the Content of the PLT

As you know, the PLT tests have four categories of content: Students as Learners; Instructional Process; Assessment; and Professionalism, Leadership, and Community. In this part, detailed content outlines have been prepared to save you time (no need to scour all those methods and educational psychology textbooks!) and offer a concise overview of the key theories and practices used in teaching today. Each diagnostic preview test question from Part I of this book is linked to a chapter in this section to provide the information you need to learn to be more successful on the actual test.

Part IV: Full-Length Practice Tests

This part offers you the opportunity to apply all you've learned. Complete the practice test for your grade level, self-correct, and then study the detailed explanations. You can even practice your pacing—remember, you have two hours for each practice test. You can make the most of your studying by completing any of the other three full-length practice tests to give yourself additional practice, because the content tested is the same across all the PLT tests; only the grade levels of the students change.

PART I

DIAGNOSTIC PREVIEW TESTS

Chapter 1

PLT Early Childhood Preview Test

This preview of the PLT Early Childhood test (0621) is designed to give you an overall sense of the test's format and to help you determine the content areas you need to focus on in your studies. This preview test will not help you with your pacing on the test; it is approximately half the length of the actual PLT and may not represent the entire scope of the test in either content or difficulty.

After you complete the preview test, score your answers and use the explanations to self-diagnose content areas to study in Part III of this guide. You also may want to complete the other preview tests in Chapters 2, 3, and 4 to aid you in determining which content areas to study. Even though these additional preview tests are written for other PLT test grade levels, the question topics (Students as Learners; Instructional Process; Assessment; and Professional Development, Leadership, and Community) remain the same.

Multiple-Choice Questions

Directions: For each multiple-choice question, select the best answer and mark the corresponding letter space on your answer sheet.

Answer Sheet

1 Ⓐ Ⓑ Ⓒ Ⓓ
2 Ⓐ Ⓑ Ⓒ Ⓓ
3 Ⓐ Ⓑ Ⓒ Ⓓ
4 Ⓐ Ⓑ Ⓒ Ⓓ
5 Ⓐ Ⓑ Ⓒ Ⓓ
6 Ⓐ Ⓑ Ⓒ Ⓓ
7 Ⓐ Ⓑ Ⓒ Ⓓ
8 Ⓐ Ⓑ Ⓒ Ⓓ
9 Ⓐ Ⓑ Ⓒ Ⓓ
10 Ⓐ Ⓑ Ⓒ Ⓓ
11 Ⓐ Ⓑ Ⓒ Ⓓ
12 Ⓐ Ⓑ Ⓒ Ⓓ
13 Ⓐ Ⓑ Ⓒ Ⓓ
14 Ⓐ Ⓑ Ⓒ Ⓓ
15 Ⓐ Ⓑ Ⓒ Ⓓ
16 Ⓐ Ⓑ Ⓒ Ⓓ

1. Mrs. Dougherty's first-grade students work in small groups at the blocks center three days a week. Which of the following provides the best rationale for blocks-center work?

   A. Direct instruction
   B. Discovery learning
   C. Independent practice
   D. Visual learning

2. A reading lesson plan that is organized with direct instruction, guided practice, and independent practice is likely to provide which of the following to students?

   A. Grade-level expectations
   B. Phonemic awareness
   C. Scaffolding
   D. Vocabulary development

Questions 3–4 are based on the following description of a class.

Mrs. Horton teaches a second-grade class of 20 students. She has a diverse group of children, including

- Five students identified as eligible for an IEP and placed in her classroom, which is considered each student's "least restrictive environment"
- Two students whose primary language is not English
- Two students who have been diagnosed with attention deficit hyperactivity disorder (ADHD)
- Two students who are eligible for the gifted-and-talented program

3. One of Mrs. Horton's goals for the class is to have the students take turns and listen attentively to the speaker. Which of the following instructional strategies will best support the students whose primary language is not English?

   A. Practice taking turns and listening in a small group with support from the teacher
   B. Whole-class practice listening and speaking
   C. Listening to a tape-recorded conversation
   D. Brainstorming a list of rules for taking turns and listening

4. Mrs. Horton also has set a goal to teach each student to read at the second-grade level by the end of the school year. Which of the following methods is LEAST likely to support this goal for the diverse group of learners in her class?

   A. Language experience approach
   B. Independent reading of a book on the child's frustration level
   C. Whole-group reading of a quality children's literature book
   D. Guided reading practice in small groups

5. During oral reading, one student reads the word *cape* as *cap*. This child most likely needs help with

   A. concepts about print.
   B. encoding.
   C. comprehension.
   D. phonics.

6. A student in Miss Cindy's kindergarten class loves to repeat the rhymes in poems, visits the listening center often, and has memorized the letters of the alphabet by singing the ABC song. Which of the following best describes this child's intelligence?

   A. Visual/linguistic
   B. Verbal/spatial
   C. Musical
   D. Interpersonal

7. Each of the following teaching activities uses interactive instruction methods, EXCEPT

   A. indirect instruction.
   B. brainstorming.
   C. discussion.
   D. debate.

8. An age-typical moral characteristic of a student in K–2 includes which of the following?

   A. Guilt about misbehaviors that cause obvious harm
   B. Belief that society has a responsibility to help those in need
   C. Interest in pleasing and helping others
   D. Tendency to think of rules and conventions of behavior

9. Mrs. Antosh strives to make accommodations for the students in her kindergarten class who have short attention spans, have difficulty starting a task, and often appear distracted by the busy classroom. Which accommodation is LEAST likely to support these students?

   A. Providing a less visual, quiet area to work
   B. Providing short tasks with immediate positive feedback
   C. Moving the student closer to the teacher
   D. Seating the student in a group

10. As part of the district's assessment plan, Miss Webb gives a criterion-referenced assessment to her first-graders at the end of her Communities social studies unit. Which of the following types of information will Miss Webb most likely get from this assessment?

    A. Each student's grade-level equivalent compared to other first-graders in the district
    B. Each student's attainment of the unit's goals and objectives
    C. A better understanding of the student's attitudes about social studies
    D. Each student's percentile rank in social studies performance on the Communities unit

11. Mrs. Dougherty, a first-grade teacher, utilizes which of the following formal assessments in her classroom?

    A. Observations
    B. Brainstorming
    C. Dolch word list of sight word recognition
    D. Lecture

12. Tory, a 5-year-old girl who hopes to attend kindergarten at her big brother's school next year, is required to register for her placement at the school and to take a series of tests. These tests are most likely which type of assessment?

    A. Analytical
    B. Criterion based
    C. Remediation
    D. Screening

Questions 13–14 are based on the following teaching situation.

   Mrs. Lahiri is a teacher assistant in Mrs. Campbell's primary grade-level resource classroom. During a time when Mrs. Campbell created a lesson plan in which Mrs. Lahiri works with a small group of students drafting a story, the principal asks Mrs. Lahiri to assist in the office because of an absence. Mrs. Campbell and Mrs. Lahiri are discouraged that their plans have been interrupted. Furthermore, their students will not receive the small-group instruction delineated in their Individualized Education Plans (IEPs).

13. Which of the following is a professionally responsible and reflective way for Mrs. Campbell to approach this situation?

    A. Discuss concerns with Mrs. Lahiri and encourage her to file a complaint
    B. Discuss concerns with the school principal and offer alternative solutions to the problem
    C. Support the change in student services in order to be a team member
    D. Discuss concerns with colleagues in the teacher's room and brainstorm solutions to the problem

14. Which of the following best provides guidance to Mrs. Campbell when considering solutions to this teaching situation?

    A. Reading First
    B. Title VI
    C. Individuals with Disabilities Education Act
    D. Title I

15. Mr. Colombino, a second-grade teacher, has a student who has repeated difficulty following class rules. Which of the following approaches can he use to best change this student's behavior?

    A. Corporal punishment
    B. Regular communication with the student's family
    C. Negative reinforcement
    D. Formal operational development

16. The *Brown v. Board of Education* legal case of 1954 struck down which of the following doctrines?

    A. *Carpe diem*
    B. Least restrictive environment
    C. Separate but equal
    D. Separation of church and state

Constructed-Response Questions

Directions: The following questions require you to write short answers, or "constructed responses." You are not expected to cite specific theories or texts in your answers; however, your knowledge of specific principles of learning and teaching will be evaluated. Be sure to answer all parts of the question. Write your answers in the space provided.

Instructional Scenario I

Scenario: Daniel

Daniel is a 7-year-old second-grade student who loves nature, likes classifying and organizing things, and enjoys attention from his peers. His teacher, Miss Whitcomb, uses a science-based, thematic unit approach to instruction but has found that Daniel is having difficulty completing his science log each day. She immerses her students in the lives of many living things by placing a variety of animal tanks around the perimeter of the classroom. She allows the students to move the animals to their desks in order to get close-up views of the animals. She has a variety of information sources about animals in the classroom, including nonfiction books, reference books, children's science magazines, and computer resources such as online encyclopedias and Internet access. Miss Whitcomb asks her mentor to observe Daniel so that she can offer teaching suggestions to help Daniel complete his written work.

Observation: Miss Whitcomb's Class

Pre-observation notes: Miss Whitcomb states, "The purpose of the science log is to make daily observations of a living creature in our classroom and to learn to express thoughts in complete sentences." She continues, "Daniel has not completed his science log for several days now. When Daniel remembers to turn in his log, or when he has not misplaced it, his log entries often have a drawing of the living creature and a few words, not complete sentences. I believe Daniel is capable of higher-level work than this, and I would like you to observe his work to make some suggestions so that I can better help Daniel achieve second-grade standards."

Mentor Classroom Observation Focused on Daniel

Miss Whitcomb begins the whole-group lesson by asking students to share what they wrote in their science logs yesterday. Daniel does not offer to speak. Instead, he whispers to a friend nearby and then looks at the tanks of living creatures near him.

Next, the teacher makes a KWL chart on the chalkboard and asks students to share what they want to know about the living creature they are observing. The teacher writes these facts under the *K* (Know) column. Daniel excitedly contributes that he knows that a hermit crab can move from one shell to another and that he has seen hermit crabs at the beach. After several students share, Miss Whitcomb instructs the students to turn to the next clean page of their logs and write a sentence about what they would like to know. Daniel appears to think during this time and then begins to draw a picture of a hermit crab. After a short time, Miss Whitcomb asks three students to share what they want to know, and then she writes these sentences in the *W* (Want to Know) column. Daniel does not offer to share his sentence, as he does not have a sentence written, only a drawing. He shows his drawing to a girl nearby, and she praises his artistic ability.

Next, Miss Whitcomb asks the second-graders to get their living creature's container, place it on their desk, and observe the creature quietly. After five minutes of individual observation, the students are instructed to spend 10 minutes writing in their science logs about what they observed today. She also asks the students to write what they wanted to know about their living creature.

Miss Whitcomb moves to her desk to correct spelling papers while the students complete their science log entries. Daniel completes his drawing of the hermit crab with careful attention to detail, and then he writes "my hermut crabbe," "bech," and "ates?" on his paper. Once he has finished his work, he talks with a boy near him about the hermit crab and asks the friend if he knows what a hermit crab eats. The boys have a serious conversation about the crab's eating habits until Miss Whitcomb brings the students back together to share their entries.

Miss Whitcomb closes the lesson with time to discuss what the students learned about their living creatures. Once again, Daniel is silent and appears uncomfortable with the written work in his science log. When Miss Whitcomb calls on Daniel to share, he appears nervous and says that he does not want to. Miss Whitcomb reminds the students to place their science logs in the blue bin on their way out to lunch. Daniel puts his log in his desk and hurries to catch up with a friend in the lunch line.

Post-observation notes: Miss Whitcomb shares that she believes Daniel is a bright boy who loves science. She expresses her concern that Daniel does not complete his science log as instructed; instead, he draws, talks to peers, and then labels his page with words, not sentences. Miss Whitcomb also says that Daniel's talking to friends during class may be one reason he does not complete his work. Her mentor suggests, "Perhaps Daniel is completing the assignment to the best of his ability at this time. Let's talk more about strategies to help Daniel be more successful when writing in his science log."

17. Suppose Miss Whitcomb and her mentor discuss alternative ways to open this lesson.

    - Identify TWO alternative ways to open this lesson so that Daniel might be more successful completing his science log.
    - Regarding these two alternatives, explain how each could meet Daniel's learning needs. Base your response on principles of activating and developing prior knowledge before writing.

18. Next, Miss Whitcomb and her mentor discuss ways to support Daniel during the science log observation and writing time.

    - Identify TWO specific ways to actively engage Daniel in this lesson so that he might be more successful.
    - Explain how each way you have identified could meet Daniel's learning needs during observation and writing time. Base your response on best practice and principles of learning and teaching.

Instructional Scenario II

Scenario: Miss Elliott

Miss Elliott is a second-year first-grade teacher in a large urban school district. Miss Elliott's students have diverse learning styles and needs. Of her 25 first-graders, 6 students are English language learners, 5 have learning disabilities, 4 receive gifted-and-talented program services, and 2 have been diagnosed with attention deficit hyperactivity disorder (ADHD). In addition, one of Miss Elliott's students, Susie, was born prematurely with fetal alcohol syndrome. Of all her first-graders, this student is making the least progress academically and socially. As required in her contract, Miss Elliott must complete a professional portfolio that contains clear evidence that she is achieving her professional goals. She also will be evaluated by her principal this month.

Document 1: Professional Goals

The teacher evaluation process requires her to document two ways that she has demonstrated her achievement of three professional goals. Miss Elliott has set the following goals:

- Create effective bridges between students' experiences and the first-grade curriculum goals.
- Improve classroom discussions to help students share thinking in different ways, for different purposes.
- Develop and utilize active partnerships with parents, colleagues, and school leaders.

Document 2: Unit Goals

Miss Elliott plans to collect all six artifacts for her professional development portfolio during the next unit of instruction, which involves the theme of friendship. The following are three curriculum goals for this unit:

- Students will express qualities of a good friend.
- Students will read about friendships to make comparisons/contrasts to their experiences.
- Students will write a story involving friendships with a beginning, middle, and end.

Document 3: Project Assignment: Family Book Bags

A key assignment in Miss Elliott's friendship unit involves the children and their families reading a book at home together in a project called "Family Book Bags." The book bag contains a quality and age-appropriate children's book, a toy or prop that comes from the story, a journal for the student and family to respond in, and a letter to the family explaining the project. Here's a sample letter from the *Baby Animals* book bag:

Dear first-grade friend and family,

Please enjoy reading the book *Baby Animals* with your child. You and your child can read the book together. It's also okay for you to read the whole book to your child. After reading, your child should write and draw on the notebook pages. You should write and draw on the pages labeled "family pages." Your child may want to draw a favorite baby animal, either a real animal or a stuffed animal. You should write down the child's retelling, as well as any comments or questions you have about reading *Baby Animals* with your child.

Good retellings include

- The characters
- The setting
- The main events in the story
- How the story ends

> If your child has a picture of your real animal or would like to bring a stuffed animal to school for the day, please put it in the book bag. Your child can share it with the class! Please have your child return the book bag the next day, if possible. You may have up to two school nights with the book bag, if needed.
>
> Happy reading!
>
> Miss Elliott

Document 4: Project Assessment

When the family book bag is returned to school, the child has the opportunity to show and tell about the book bag experience. The book bag reading experience is assessed on the following criteria:

- Retelling includes characters
- Retelling includes setting
- Retelling includes main events
- Retelling includes conclusion
- Student response includes drawing and words
- Student oral sharing is clearly spoken and connected to *Baby Animals* reading

Document 5: Transcript of Susie Sharing Her Book Bag

Miss Elliott: Susie, it's your turn to share the *Baby Animals* book that you read at home with your grandma.

Susie: Oh, good! I love share time!

Miss Elliott: Tell us about your favorite part of the story.

Susie: My favorite animal is a leopard. My grandma and I went to the zoo, but I could not see the leopard because it was hiding behind the rocks, and then we had an ice cream and I had to go home.

Miss Elliott: Did you see a baby leopard in the *Baby Animals* book?

Susie: No. I did not like this book because it did not have a leopard.

Miss Elliott: Oh, Susie. You will be so happy to know that I saw a baby leopard in the *Baby Animals* book. Look at this picture!

Susie: Yeah! That's a baby leopard. That's my favorite animal. I love the spots and her color.

19. Miss Elliott's first professional goal—to create effective bridges between students' experiences and the first-grade curriculum goals—will require her to consider her students' prior experiences and how these experiences relate to the goals in the friendship unit.

   - Suggest TWO instructional techniques for creating effective bridges between students and curriculum goals.
   - Explain how Miss Elliott can document her use of these techniques as part of her professional evaluation portfolio. Be sure to base your response on best professional practice and principles of learning and teaching.

20. Miss Elliott's third professional goal—to develop and utilize active partnerships with parents, colleagues, and school leaders—requires her to be a reflective practitioner and to connect with the larger school community. Miss Elliott is especially concerned about her student, Susie, who had fetal alcohol syndrome and who is making less than adequate progress in first grade. Miss Elliott would like to concentrate on supporting Susie's educational needs while she documents her achievement of this third professional goal.

- Identify TWO resources Miss Elliott can utilize to help her to achieve this third professional goal.
- Explain how each resource you have identified could benefit Susie's learning needs and could help Miss Elliott meet her professional goal. Base your response on best professional practice and principles of learning and teaching.

Answers and Explanations

Multiple-Choice Questions

Answer Key

Question	Answer	Content Category	Where to Get More Help
1	B	Students as Learners	Chapter 7
2	C	Students as Learners	Chapter 7
3	A	Students as Learners	Chapter 7
4	B	Students as Learners	Chapter 7
5	D	Instructional Process	Chapter 8
6	C	Instructional Process	Chapter 8
7	A	Instructional Process	Chapter 8
8	A	Instructional Process	Chapter 8
9	D	Assessment	Chapter 9
10	B	Assessment	Chapter 9
11	C	Assessment	Chapter 9
12	D	Assessment	Chapter 9
13	B	Professional Development, Leadership, and Community	Chapter 10
14	C	Professional Development, Leadership, and Community	Chapter 10
15	B	Professional Development, Leadership, and Community	Chapter 10
16	C	Professional Development, Leadership, and Community	Chapter 10

Answer Explanations

1. **B** Discovery learning is an instructional approach based on Jerome Bruner's constructivist theory. Students select and transform information, creating hypotheses relying on cognitive structures.

2. **C** Scaffolding is an instructional technique introduced by Lev Vygotsky. The teacher models how to approach a task, breaks complex assignments into smaller parts, and offers scaffolding, or support, for student learning. When the student is ready, the teacher provides independent practice.

3. **A** English language learners benefit from working in small groups, where they can practice speaking in English and listening to peers.

4. **B** Mrs. Horton will least likely achieve her goal of teaching her second-graders to read at grade level if her students read books independently at their frustration level. It is best practice to have students read books at either their independent or instructional level.

5. **D** When a child reads the word *cape* as *cap,* he or she needs help with phonics or decoding. You may have chosen Choice B, encoding, which is synonymous with spelling. However, the question states that the child is reading, not writing, so phonics is the credited response.

6. **C** According to Howard Gardner's theory of multiple intelligences, there are eight different intelligences. Students who possess musical intelligence have sensitivity to pitch, tones, and rhythm. They are the students who like to hum, repeat chants, play instruments, and learn melodies.

7. **A** Indirect instruction is a teaching method that is distinctly different from interactive instruction. Interactive instruction values discussion and sharing between learners. On the other hand, indirect instruction values inquiry, problem solving, and discovery, which can occur within the individual student without discussion and sharing between learners.

8. **A** Children in grades K–2 typically demonstrate guilt about misbehaviors that cause obvious harm; whereas the other moral and social behaviors in choices B, C, and D are those more typically shown in students in grades 6–12.

9. **D** The LEAST effective accommodation for a student who has a short attention span, struggles to begin a task, and appears distracted in the classroom is placing the student in a group. This student would be more successful with added structure and teacher direction until he or she can learn strategies to deal with these attention problems.

10. **B** A criterion-referenced test compares a student's knowledge, as demonstrated on the test, to the goals and objectives in the curriculum.

11. **C** The Dolch word list of sight word recognition is a formal assessment, which is a preplanned assessment used for a specific purpose. Choices A and B are informal assessments. Choice D is a teaching method, not an assessment.

12. **D** Screening tests typically are administered upon entrance to kindergarten and designed to identify and predict students who may be at risk for poor learning outcomes and to match appropriate services for students.

13. **B** Discussing concerns with the school principal and offering alternative solutions to the problem would be the most professional response to this situation. According to the No Child Left Behind Act, teacher assistants assigned to children as part of their IEPs are required to spend instructional time with students. Working professionally and collaboratively with the principal is the most desirable professional option presented.

14. **C** The Individuals with Disabilities Education Act became a public law in 1997 to ensure that students with disabilities and their families have access to a free and appropriate education. This law focuses resources on teaching and learning for students with IEPs.

15. **B** Of the choices offered, regular communication with the student's family has the most potential for supporting the learning needs of a student who struggles to follow class rules. Choice A, corporal punishment—spanking or striking a student—is not an option in public schools today. B. F. Skinner's theory of negative reinforcement (Choice C) states that a student escapes punishment by repeating desired responses, such as following the rules in Mr. Colombino's class. Choice D, formal operational development, does not make sense in the context of this question.

16. **C** The *Brown v. Board of Education* legal case of 1954 struck down the "separate but equal" doctrine in public schools during this time. The Supreme Court determined that state-mandated segregated schools were inherently unequal and discriminatory.

Constructed-Response Questions

Instructional scenarios, or "constructed responses," are graded holistically on a scale of 0 to 2, with 0 being the lowest score. For details on this type of question, be sure to read Chapter 6. In this section, you'll find the content categories and suggested content to include in your constructed responses. For more information about the content category, you can study Part III. The suggested content is designed to help you get a sense of the type of response required, but it may not cover all the correct options in such an open-ended question. You also may find it helpful to share your constructed responses with an education professor, adviser, or educator.

Instructional Scenario I

17. **Suggested content:** Two alternatives that Miss Whitcomb could try to help Daniel complete his work are <u>direct instruction</u> and <u>benchmark papers</u>. Miss Whitcomb could use direct instruction methods to specifically teach Daniel and his classmates how to complete a science log entry. Steps in direct instruction include <u>establishing an anticipatory set</u>, <u>setting clear and measurable objectives</u>, <u>providing modeling and guided practice</u>, and <u>checking for understanding</u> throughout the lesson and in the <u>closing</u>. The second alternative Miss Whitcomb could try is to share benchmark papers to demonstrate exemplary, acceptable,

and unacceptable examples of the assignment. Miss Whitcomb could save samples of previous students' science logs and help Daniel and his classmates see what scores each sample earned, explaining to the students her rationale for scoring.

Each of these alternative strategies provides a higher level of scaffolding, or support, for this assignment. Daniel may be choosing to draw observations and write words because he is not clear on the assignment's expectations or because his level of literacy development is below the level expected by Miss Whitcomb. One key to success is finding out what Daniel knows and is able to do and then providing specific, supportive and corrective instruction.

18. **Suggested content:** Two strategies to use during this lesson might include: breaking the task into smaller chunks and providing more frequent, positive feedback to Daniel. Students such as Daniel benefit from differentiated instruction. Daniel may need to build his confidence by working on smaller chunks of the assignment to help him feel he has accomplished his work successfully. In the past, he often may have been one of the last students done, which may have frustrated or demotivated him. Chunking the task not only helps Daniel feel more confident, but also provides him with more frequent feedback from the teacher. Daniel's level of literacy development may be at an earlier stage than his peers. His behavior may be age-appropriate for his knowledge level. Daniel would benefit from positive guidance and timely feedback. These changes in the learning environment will likely help Daniel develop self-motivation. Encouraging Daniel to explain his thinking probes for his understanding and may encourage his divergent thinking, which sends a message of caring and respect.

Instructional Scenario II

19. **Suggested content:** Based on principles of learning and teaching, there are several ways to bridge students and curriculum, including the following: modeling, guided practice, independent practice, appropriate homework, activating prior knowledge, and teaching predicting and verifying. For more information about this content, turn to Chapter 8.

Teachers must actively teach students to connect prior knowledge to new curriculum content. Schema theory, scaffolding, and teaching to a student's zone of proximal development are three theories that provide a rationale for the techniques.

20. **Suggested content:** Miss Elliott might turn to the professional literature, the school nurse, or the child's family to help her make instructional decisions for her student who was born with fetal alcohol syndrome.

Building partnerships to solve educational problems provides an opportunity for shared ownership and shared decision making of the problem. Susie may need to repeat first grade or receive evaluation for special education services. When school and home are working collaboratively, a student's needs are met more effectively.

Chapter 2

PLT Grades K–6 Preview Test

This preview of the PLT Grades K–6 test (0622) is designed to give you an overall sense of the test's format and to help you determine the content areas you need to focus on in your studies. This preview test will not help you with your pacing on the test; it is approximately half the length of the actual PLT and may not represent the entire scope of the test in either content or difficulty.

After you complete the preview test, score your answers and use the explanations to self-diagnose content areas to study in Part III of this guide. You also may want to complete the other preview tests in Chapters 1, 3, and 4 to aid you in determining which content areas to study. Even though these additional preview tests are written for other PLT test grade levels, the question topics (Students as Learners; Instructional Process; Assessment; and Professional Development, Leadership, and Community) remain the same.

Multiple-Choice Questions

Directions: For each multiple-choice question, select the best answer and mark the corresponding letter space on your answer sheet.

Answer Sheet

1 Ⓐ Ⓑ Ⓒ Ⓓ
2 Ⓐ Ⓑ Ⓒ Ⓓ
3 Ⓐ Ⓑ Ⓒ Ⓓ
4 Ⓐ Ⓑ Ⓒ Ⓓ
5 Ⓐ Ⓑ Ⓒ Ⓓ
6 Ⓐ Ⓑ Ⓒ Ⓓ
7 Ⓐ Ⓑ Ⓒ Ⓓ
8 Ⓐ Ⓑ Ⓒ Ⓓ
9 Ⓐ Ⓑ Ⓒ Ⓓ
10 Ⓐ Ⓑ Ⓒ Ⓓ
11 Ⓐ Ⓑ Ⓒ Ⓓ
12 Ⓐ Ⓑ Ⓒ Ⓓ
13 Ⓐ Ⓑ Ⓒ Ⓓ
14 Ⓐ Ⓑ Ⓒ Ⓓ
15 Ⓐ Ⓑ Ⓒ Ⓓ
16 Ⓐ Ⓑ Ⓒ Ⓓ

1. B. F. Skinner and other behavior theorists recommend teachers first identify the student behavior they are trying to change, reward the positives, and then

   A. provide consequences for the negative behavior.
   B. reward the negative behavior.
   C. ignore the negative behavior.
   D. contact the parent/guardian about the negative behavior.

2. A fourth-grade teacher gives a spelling pretest for which of the following reasons?

   A. Lev Vygotsky's zone of proximal development
   B. David Ausubel's theory of advance organizers
   C. Bernice McCarthy's 4MAT with the pretest as the first of four activities
   D. Lawrence Kohlberg's theory of moral development

3. Glen is a fifth-grader who appears to learn best through visual learning experiences. Which of the following techniques might help him learn best in his social studies class?

   A. Activity exploration
   B. Tape-recording teacher's lessons
   C. Using the overhead projector
   D. Completing questions and answers at the end of the chapter

4. A sixth-grade teacher offers "prizes" such as homework passes and pencils for quality work and good behavior. The primary rationale for such rewards is to improve students' behavior through

   A. humanistic motivation.
   B. internal motivation.
   C. intrinsic motivation.
   D. extrinsic motivation.

5. When planning a sixth-grade social studies unit on immigration to the United States, the teacher hopes to introduce his or her students to primary source documents as required by state and national standards. Which of the following primary source documents will best support this unit on immigration?

   A. A letter from a soldier at Pearl Harbor
   B. An Army recruiting poster
   C. A medical screening form from Ellis Island
   D. A short story on coming to America at the turn of the century

6. Which of the following questions is an example of a "knowledge" question in Bloom's Taxonomy of the cognitive domain?

   A. What do you think is the author's message?
   B. Who can tell us the setting of the story?
   C. Where did the boy go to school?
   D. How would you rate this story and why?

7. Students who have difficulty working in cooperative groups and expect the teacher to provide answers to questions may be experiencing differences in

   A. mood.
   B. cultural expectations.
   C. intrapersonal skills.
   D. attention to directions.

8. Which of the following in an INCORRECT way to respond to a student's incorrect response?

   A. "What do you mean by . . . ?"
   B. "What are your reasons for saying this?"
   C. "Can you be more specific?"
   D. "No, that's incorrect."

9. A teacher-made multiple-choice test is an example of which of the following?

   A. Criterion-referenced assessment
   B. Norm-referenced assessment
   C. Performance assessment
   D. Embedded assessment

10. Which of the following is NOT an example of peer assessment?

    A. Using a checklist to rate another's paper
    B. Guided reading measure while buddy reading
    C. Conferencing with a classmate
    D. Evaluating the word problems of a friend

11. Which of the following is a formative assessment?

    A. Observation of students' work
    B. California Achievement Test
    C. Final exam
    D. Culminating project

12. What is the difference between an achievement test and an aptitude test?

    A. Achievement tests measure understanding or an ability to learn that an individual has prior to taking the test; aptitude tests measure understanding of acquired skills and content.
    B. Achievement tests measure understanding of acquired skills and content; aptitude tests measure general mental ability.
    C. Achievement tests measure general mental ability; aptitude tests measure understanding of acquired skills and content.
    D. Achievement tests measure understanding of acquired skills and content; aptitude tests measure understanding or an ability to learn that an individual has prior to taking the test.

Questions 13–14 are based on the following passages, which are from a debate about the advantages and disadvantages of using published school reading program materials.

Why Published School Reading Program Materials Are Effective

Published school reading program materials are based on scientifically based best practice in reading instruction and are written by well-known researchers in the field. In order to receive federal funding in our K–6 school, we must use proven instructional methods as required by the No Child Left Behind Act (NCLB). Published school reading program materials offer an easy and effective solution to difficult curriculum revision decisions. Our school does not have the time or the resources to write a curriculum given all the other demands on our teaching staff. Published reading programs provide a detailed teacher's manual and a variety of instructional support materials that are very helpful to beginning teachers and those teachers who do not know how to use scientifically based reading best practices in classrooms today.

Why Published School Reading Program Materials Are Ineffective

Teachers should teach with a variety of materials and methods to meet the diverse needs of learners in classrooms today. Children should learn to read and read to learn with authentic works in order to achieve real, purposeful, and meaningful literacy tasks. Children have little opportunity to select their own reading, an important literacy strategy. The skills-based approach of these programs usually presents skills in isolation and becomes boring and meaningless for many children. Furthermore, the extraordinary expense of purchasing a published reading program and maintaining these materials usually prohibits inclusion of quality children's literature, big books, and trade books in the budget. Perhaps the most damaging effect of published reading programs is the disempowerment of the teacher as decision maker in the classroom. The teachers' manual is designed to be teacher-proof—anyone can teach reading to any child because all the decisions are research based.

13. The first passage advances the idea that published reading programs are scientifically based and contain ideas for best practice. In the view of the author of the second passage, if your district requires the use of such materials, which of the following is essential when teaching K–6 in schools today?

    A. Lesson plans are done for you.
    B. Well-known leaders in literacy wrote these materials.
    C. Teachers modify lessons to meet the diverse needs of students.
    D. These materials are teacher-proof.

14. The author of the second passage believes that

    A. teachers should take three or more courses in reading methods.
    B. teachers benefit from the teachers' manuals in published reading programs.
    C. teachers need to learn to teach reading well.
    D. teachers are decision makers.

15. Which of the following is the name of the published reading program introduced in 1841 that had themed lessons on honesty, truthfulness, and promptness?

    A. Dick and Jane series
    B. Spot and Dot Basals
    C. McGuffey Readers
    D. Exploration series

16. Special education and related services specifically designed to meet the special needs of students are called which of the following?

    A. No Child Left Behind Act
    B. American with Disabilities Act
    C. Interdisciplinary Education Plan
    D. Individualized Education Plan

Constructed-Response Questions

Directions: The following questions require you to write short answers, or "constructed responses." You are not expected to cite specific theories or texts in your answers; however, your knowledge of specific principles of learning and teaching will be evaluated. Be sure to answer all parts of the question. Write your answers in the space provided.

Instructional Scenario I

Scenario: Miss Webb

Miss Webb knows that she is facing a challenging school year, so she is getting started on long-range and short-range planning in early August. Her neighborhood school has closed as part of a redistricting and consolidation plan, so her third-graders will not attend the same school their older siblings attended. In addition, the district has adopted a new mathematics series that promotes problem solving, higher-level thinking, and the use of manipulatives. Her principal has decided that she will be comparing last year's third-grade student performance in mathematics basic understanding and mathematics problem solving to this year's student performance in the same areas, so Miss Webb is feeling a bit anxious about her students' mathematics performance with all these changes in the district. The following documents provide samples of Miss Webb's short-term goals, long-term goals, and lesson plans for the start of the school year.

Document 1: Short-Term Goals

- My third-grade students will know the location of important places in the school building (such as the nurse's office, main office, emergency exits, restrooms, water fountains, and cafeteria).
- My third-grade students will meet weekly with a sixth-grade "buddy" for two main reasons: 1) to share mathematics problem-solving strategies and 2) to establish student relationships in order to build a positive school community.
- My third-grade students will explain "how they know" during mathematics problem solving in order to demonstrate a variety of approaches to solving problems.

Document 2: Long-Term Goals

- My third-grade students will meet or exceed third-grade mathematics standards for problem solving.
- Each of my third-grade students will have an older buddy or friend to make them feel a part of the school community.
- My third-grade students will show what they know about mathematics through written and oral work.

Document 3: Lesson Plan

Objective

Each third-grade student will learn the names of two sixth-grade students and be able to identify one interest of each older student.

Resources

Name cards, crayons, color pencils, photographs of sixth-grade buddies

Motivation

Today, we are going to meet our sixth-grade "buddies"! Before we do, let's think about three things you like to do. Perhaps you have a hobby, a talent, or a special interest that you like to do in the summer or after school.

Procedures

Warm-up: I really like to attend my children's basketball games, so basketball is one of my interests. What do you like to do? (Teacher asks for volunteers and then writes down contributions on chart paper.) On this name card, you can see that I wrote my name in large, dark letters so that others can read my name from a distance. I have also drawn a picture of a basketball because it is one of my interests. I've also drawn a picture of my pet dog and another picture of flowers. I have three interests—basketball, pets, and gardening. Now I'd like you to write your name on your name card and draw pictures of three interests you have.

Preview

Your name cards look great, and it's so exciting to learn about all your interests! Now, let's bring our name cards and walk down the hall to our buddy classroom. Our sixth-grade buddies have made name cards, too. You are going to have a chance to meet several sixth-graders and learn about their interests. By the end of our time in our buddy classroom, I'd like you to be able to tell us the name of two sixth-grade buddies and one interest that you learned about each sixth-grader. Our goal is to get to know older students who can be our buddies this year, help us learn more about our school, and help us solve both school problems and mathematics problems.

Teach

Miss Webb greets the buddy classroom teacher, Miss Orr, and both teachers discuss their interests, which are drawn on their name cards. After the teachers model the task, Miss Webb matches each of her third-grade students with a sixth-grade student and asks the students to introduce them and share interests. After a few minutes, Miss Webb asks the students to greet another student and repeats this procedure one more time.

Assessment

Third-grade students return to their own classroom and, using the photographs of the sixth-grade buddies that are posted on a classroom bulletin board, state the student's name and one interest. If more than one student has met this sixth-grader, more interests may emerge. Miss Webb uses a checklist with her students' names and writes in the sixth-grade buddy's name and interests as stated. She then reviews the name cards from the sixth-graders to verify accuracy of names and interests. In future lessons, Miss Webb will use this checklist to match up third-graders and sixth-graders who have common interests or appear to have made personal connections.

Independent Work

Students will be encouraged to look for and greet their buddies on the school bus, in their neighborhoods, in the hallways, and on the playground. When students find their buddies in school and in the local community, they can return to class and share this buddy connection by writing the places they saw the buddies on stickers and posting the stickers next to the sixth-grader's photographs.

17. Consider Miss Webb's long-term goal "My third-grade students will meet or exceed third-grade mathematics standards for problem solving." Offer THREE suggestions to help Miss Webb attain this goal. Be sure to base your response in principles of instruction and assessment, as well as teacher professionalism.

18. Suggest TWO ways in which Miss Webb can assess her third-grade students' growth as mathematical problem solvers during their work in the classroom and during sixth-grade buddy sessions. Be sure to base your response in principles of assessment and communication techniques.

Instructional Scenario II

Scenario: Stafford

The Teacher Support Team (TST) is designed to support teachers' attempts to resolve instructional problems for their students with academic, emotional, social, or behavioral issues. The team is comprised of the school principal, the team guidance counselor, a reading specialist, a special education teacher, a school psychologist, a classroom teacher, and the teacher who requests the TST's assistance regarding a particular student. Caregivers, a school social worker, and the school nurse are invited to attend when appropriate. The goal of the TST is to offer instructional strategies to classroom teachers in an effort to provide education services in a student's least restrictive environment. For students who are not making adequate yearly progress, the TST may recommend further testing by specialists.

Mrs. King is an experienced second-grade teacher who has requested a meeting of the TST to discuss her student, Stafford. The TST reviewed the background information prepared by Mrs. King on Stafford, an 8-year-old second-grader in her classroom. Stafford lives with both his mother and father, as well as his two older sisters. His primary language is English, and he appears to be in good physical health based on records from the nurse's office. Stafford did not attend preschool. He stayed home with his mother while his two older sisters attended school. He attended the public school district's half-day kindergarten, where he had limited success learning the alphabet, had trouble with concepts about print, and experienced difficulty with appropriate social and emotional behaviors when he faced academic or social challenges in the classroom. In first grade, Stafford lagged behind his peers in reading and writing development. Now in second grade, Stafford loves listening to stories read aloud but rarely reads independently. He enjoys the listening center and chooses the building or blocks center every opportunity he gets. He enjoys recess time where he can demonstrate his advanced gross motor skills and enjoys being chosen as the teacher's helper.

At the TST meeting, Mrs. King described the problems Stafford is experiencing in second grade. He is becoming a classroom bully; he has frequent outbursts when asked to complete his reading or writing work. In addition, Mrs. King has noticed that Stafford has difficulty hearing rhythm, rhyme, and syllables in poetry or language arts exercises. Mrs. King added that she has met with Stafford's parents, who share her concerns about Stafford's lack of reading progress and his increasing outbursts during homework time at home. Stafford's parents mentioned that they recently purchased a phonics-based home-study program to help their child with reading and would appreciate any support Mrs. King can give them.

Mrs. King has tried the following strategies to support Stafford's reading and writing development:

- Moved his seat to the front of the classroom, near the teacher's instruction.
- Placed him in a reading group at his instructional level. Stafford is alone in this group and receives one-on-one instruction from Mrs. King for 15 minutes each day.
- Provided opportunities to read along with books on tape in the listening center.
- Asked Stafford to make signs for the blocks and building center.

After meeting with the TST and Stafford's parents, Mrs. King would like suggestions for new strategies to try in the classroom, but she also would like the support of her colleagues' expertise. She has requested that a reading specialist or a special educator conduct an in-depth evaluation of Stafford's strengths and weaknesses.

19. Identify TWO strategies Mrs. King hasn't tried to support Stafford's diverse learning needs. Be sure to base your response in principles of student learning and instruction.

20. Suggest TWO reasons that Stafford may benefit from an evaluation for reading intervention or special education. Be sure to base your rationale in principles of learning, instruction, and assessment.

Answers and Explanations

Multiple-Choice Questions

Answer Key

Question	Answer	Content Category	Where to Get More Help
1	A	Students as Learners	Chapter 7
2	A	Students as Learners	Chapter 7
3	C	Students as Learners	Chapter 7
4	D	Students as Learners	Chapter 7
5	C	Instructional Process	Chapter 8
6	C	Instructional Process	Chapter 8
7	B	Instructional Process	Chapter 8
8	D	Instructional Process	Chapter 8
9	A	Assessment	Chapter 9
10	B	Assessment	Chapter 9
11	A	Assessment	Chapter 9
12	D	Assessment	Chapter 9
13	C	Professional Development, Leadership, and Community	Chapter 10
14	D	Professional Development, Leadership, and Community	Chapter 10
15	C	Professional Development, Leadership, and Community	Chapter 10
16	D	Professional Development, Leadership, and Community	Chapter 10

Answer Explanations

1. **A** According to Skinner's behaviorist theory, providing consequences for negative behavior is the best response. Choices B and C are ways to provide consequences for the negative behavior but are too narrow and may not be best for certain behaviors and situations.

2. **A** Vygotsky's zone of proximal development is based on a teacher finding the best information to teach a student next. The spelling pretest is one way for the teacher to find out which words to teach his or her students to spell next.

3. **C** Visual learners learn by seeing information. In addition to using the overhead projector, the teacher could use graphic organizers, facial expressions, body language, and digital media to convey new content.

4. **D** Extrinsic motivation is outside the learner. Intrinsic motivation is from within and is the most desirable type of motivation. Teachers sometimes use small rewards or tokens to motivate students, but teachers should strive to help students realize the intrinsic rewards for learning. Choice A, humanistic motivation, is a distracter.

5. **C** Primary source documents enable teachers and students to get as close as possible to an actual historical event or time period. The best primary source document related to U.S. immigration is the medical screening document from Ellis Island.

6. **C** Knowledge-level questions require students to recall specific facts and terms from the material. Choice A is a comprehension-level question. Choice B requires analysis. Choice D is at the evaluation level of Bloom's Taxonomy of cognitive development.

7. **B** In some cultures, teachers are seen as the primary source of knowledge, and students expect the teacher to be the only one in the classroom to present information. Cooperative learning groups require students to rely on one another as sources of information and expect the teacher to facilitate, not lead, instruction. This disconnect between home and school cultures is the best reason presented for why the student is having difficulty working in the group.

8. **D** It is important to acknowledge a student's response with a positive tone and body language without saying "no" or "not correct," which may shut down a student's thinking or willingness to take risks in the classroom. Often, if a student is redirected to examine his or her response, he or she may be able to self-correct. Choices A, B, and C are all appropriate ways to respond to a student's incorrect answer.

9. **A** A criterion-referenced test is made up of questions based on predetermined criteria, such as the teacher's lesson objectives or unit plan goals.

10. **B** Choice B, guided reading measure while buddy reading, is a distracter. This choice lacks specificity and does not make it clear that the measure is being used as a self-assessment or peer assessment. Choices A, C, and D are all examples of peer assessment.

11. **A** Observation of student work is a formative assessment; formative assessments are ongoing reviews or observations in a classroom. Choices B, C, and D are examples of summative assessments, which are used to evaluate the effectiveness of instruction and judge students' attainment of goals and objectives after the instruction is complete.

12. **D** Achievement tests measure understanding of acquired skills and content; aptitude tests measure understanding or an ability to learn that an individual has prior to taking the test. Choice A is not correct because the definitions have been inverted. Choices B and C are not correct because the definition of intelligence tests (which measure general mental ability) has been inserted.

13. **C** Even if required to use district-mandated materials, teachers must remember that they are instructional decision makers who should modify lessons to meet the diverse needs of students.

14. **D** The author of the second passage states, "Perhaps the most damaging effect of published reading program materials is the disempowerment of teachers." A person with this view sees teachers as decision makers who know the needs of their students.

15. **C** The McGuffey Readers, published in 1841 and very moralistic in tone, were among the earliest published school reading program materials.

16. **D** An Individualized Education Plan (IEP) is a document written for an individual learner who has documented learning differences. The IEP plans for all areas of difference, related services to support the child, and needed accommodations in regular and special education settings.

Constructed-Response Questions

Instructional scenarios, or "constructed responses," are graded holistically on a scale of 0 to 2, with 0 being the lowest score. For details on this type of question, be sure to read Chapter 6. In this section, you'll find the content categories and suggested content to include in your constructed responses. For more information about the content category, you can study Part III. The suggested content is designed to help you get a sense of the type of response required, but it may not cover all the correct options in such an open-ended question. You also may find it helpful to share your constructed responses with an education professor, adviser, or educator.

Instructional Scenario I

17. **Suggested content:** Three suggestions for attaining the long-term goal "Third-grade students will meet or exceed third-grade mathematics standards for problem solving" include, but are not limited to, reading professional literature on mathematics problem solving and using manipulatives to solve problems, setting grade-level benchmarks for exemplary problem solving, and attending professional development offered by the district or local colleges.

18. **Suggested content:** Two ways Miss Webb can study her students' growth as mathematical problem solvers, include the following: <u>teacher action research</u>, <u>comparing benchmark papers</u>, <u>examining student work</u> from this year and last, and <u>keeping a professional journal</u> with reflections on student performance and problem-solving processes.

Instructional Scenario II

19. **Suggested content:** Strategies Mrs. King can employ to support Stafford's learning needs include, but are not limited to, trying a <u>targeted intervention</u> in phonics or phonemic instruction, asking the <u>reading specialist</u> to assess Stafford's literacy strengths and weaknesses, listening to Stafford <u>read aloud</u> and <u>noting his miscues and strategies</u>, and including <u>more kinesthetic experiences</u> when teaching literacy, including <u>role play</u> and <u>tactile experiences</u> with letters.

20. **Suggested content:** Stafford might benefit from an <u>evaluation by a reading specialist</u> or <u>special educator</u> for the following reasons: he may have a <u>learning disability</u>; he may have <u>attentional difficulty</u>; or he may not have had the <u>prior experiences</u>, such as being read aloud to as a child or having life experiences such as going on educational trips, to prepare him academically for reading and writing in second grade.

Chapter 3

PLT Grades 5–9 Preview Test

This preview of the PLT Grades 5–9 test (0623) is designed to give you an overall sense of the test's format and to help you determine the content areas you need to focus on in your studies. This preview test will not help you with your pacing on the test; it is approximately half the length of the actual PLT and may not represent the entire scope of the test in either content or difficulty.

After you complete the preview test, score your answers and use the explanations to self-diagnose content areas to study in Part III of this guide. You also may want to complete the other preview tests in Chapters 1, 2, and 4 to aid you in determining which content areas to study. Even though these additional preview tests are written for other PLT test grade levels, the question topics (Students as Learners; Instructional Process; Assessment; and Professional Development, Leadership, and Community) remain the same.

Multiple-Choice Questions

Directions: For each multiple-choice question, select the best answer and mark the corresponding letter space on your answer sheet.

Answer Sheet

1 Ⓐ Ⓑ Ⓒ Ⓓ
2 Ⓐ Ⓑ Ⓒ Ⓓ
3 Ⓐ Ⓑ Ⓒ Ⓓ
4 Ⓐ Ⓑ Ⓒ Ⓓ
5 Ⓐ Ⓑ Ⓒ Ⓓ
6 Ⓐ Ⓑ Ⓒ Ⓓ
7 Ⓐ Ⓑ Ⓒ Ⓓ
8 Ⓐ Ⓑ Ⓒ Ⓓ
9 Ⓐ Ⓑ Ⓒ Ⓓ
10 Ⓐ Ⓑ Ⓒ Ⓓ
11 Ⓐ Ⓑ Ⓒ Ⓓ
12 Ⓐ Ⓑ Ⓒ Ⓓ
13 Ⓐ Ⓑ Ⓒ Ⓓ
14 Ⓐ Ⓑ Ⓒ Ⓓ
15 Ⓐ Ⓑ Ⓒ Ⓓ
16 Ⓐ Ⓑ Ⓒ Ⓓ

1. Mrs. Basel asks her seventh-graders to complete a collage titled "Who Am I?" during the first weeks of middle school. She is most likely supporting which of the following human development stages from Erik Erikson's theory?

   A. Autonomy vs. doubt
   B. Integrity vs. despair
   C. Risk vs. safety
   D. Identity vs. role confusion

2. Mary, a student in a fifth-grade mathematics class, relies on her 100s chart to help her complete multiplication problems. She is most likely working at which of the following stages of Jean Piaget's theory of cognitive development?

   A. Concrete operational
   B. Formal operations
   C. Preoperational
   D. Hierarchical

Questions 3–4 are based on the following passage.

Mr. DePasquale has three bilingual students in his eighth-grade social studies class and one student who is an English language learner. He works to build on students' language and cultural "funds of knowledge." He seeks the advice of the teacher of English language learners (TELL) to ensure that he is meeting the needs of his student still learning to learn in English.

3. Mr. DePasquale most likely sees the cultural and language differences of his students as

   A. teaching differences.
   B. sources of enrichment.
   C. sources of difficulty.
   D. an added challenge.

4. One important consideration for Mr. DePasquale to be mindful of when teaching English language learners according to the TELL is that ELL students may

   A. be absent frequently.
   B. be required to speak only English in his classroom.
   C. be silent or contribute less to class discussion.
   D. need frequent breaks.

5. Mrs. Shackleton, a ninth-grade English teacher, has set the following objective for her students:

   Students will demonstrate appreciation of the author's message and use of language in *Night,* by Elie Weisel, in a written essay.

   Mrs. Shackleton's objective is best categorized by which domain of objectives?

   A. Affective
   B. Cognitive
   C. Deductive
   D. Psychomotor

6. Mrs. Munroe, a fifth-grade teacher, holds class meetings to discuss conflicts that come up in the classroom. She focuses on behaviors rather than students to help her students resolve conflicts. Her classroom management philosophy is based on which of the following theories?

   A. Canter's assertive discipline
   B. Glasser's control theory
   C. Kounin's management plan
   D. Hunter's direct instruction

7. Prior to calling on a student to respond to his questions about the Crusades, Mr. Edmonds asks students to think, pair with another student to discuss ideas, and then raise hands to share responses. Mr. Edmonds is using which of the following modifications to his lesson to help all students succeed?

   A. Inquiry, response, inquiry
   B. Hands-on experiences
   C. Direct instruction
   D. Cooperative learning

8. Response to Intervention (RTI) includes all the following EXCEPT

   A. high-quality instruction.
   B. assessment.
   C. due process.
   D. evidence-based intervention.

9. Miss Weeks, a sixth-grade social studies teacher, teaches a unit on the Medieval period in which her students are assigned the task of creating a village from this period that includes activities, dress, food, and occupations. She provides a rubric that includes criteria for achieving acceptable, exemplary, or unsatisfactory success on this assignment. This project can be described as which of the following assessments?

   A. Local assessment
   B. Self-assessment
   C. Performance assessment
   D. Standardized assessment

10. Progress monitoring involves each of the following EXCEPT

   A. assessing student performance.
   B. quantifying the rate of student responsiveness to instruction.
   C. evaluating the effectiveness of instruction.
   D. evaluating the effectiveness of curriculum.

11. The screening level of assessment is used to

   A. identify or predict students who may be at risk for poor learning outcomes.
   B. establish a trend line on a data chart of students' performance.
   C. determine the level of instructional intensity.
   D. describe the effectiveness of an intervention program.

12. A collection of student work representing a selection of performance is known as a

   A. showcase.
   B. portfolio.
   C. dossier.
   D. report card.

13. After teaching her lessons, Miss Hoyt spends a lot of time thinking about her students' interactions and considers both the intended and unintended consequences of her instruction. One would best describe Miss Hoyt as a

   A. novice teacher.
   B. cooperating teacher.
   C. master teacher.
   D. reflective teacher.

14. Mrs. Friedman's eighth-grade class is working on writing a poem when she notices that Jimmy is not working and is looking frustrated and angry. She offers to brainstorm ideas to include in the poem, and Jimmy says that doing so will not help because he's not good at rhyming anyway. Which of the following responses by Mrs. Friedman best demonstrates her ability as a reflective practitioner and teacher of writing?

   A. "Everyone needs to write a poem for his or her portfolio. You can use the dictionary, but you need to get started."
   B. "You can work with Mary, who is good at writing, Jimmy, but you need to get something written before the end of class."
   C. "It is difficult to find the right words when writing poetry, Jimmy. I suggest we first brainstorm ideas together and then find a type of poetry that best matches your ideas. Not all poems need to rhyme."
   D. "You can help me correct math papers now, and we will find another assignment for you to complete after school during detention."

15. Mrs. Smith is planning to meet with her students' caregivers for sixth-grade parent/teacher conferences. Which of the following is NOT something Mrs. Smith should plan to do?

   A. Be positive.
   B. Share information about the rest of the students.
   C. Be prepared.
   D. Highlight students' strengths.

16. This education leader organized annual education conventions and helped create the first U.S. schools for training teachers.

   A. Horace Mann
   B. John Dewey
   C. Jean Piaget
   D. Edward Thorndike

Constructed-Response Questions

Directions: The following questions require you to write short answers, or "constructed responses." You are not expected to cite specific theories or texts in your answers; however, your knowledge of specific principles of learning and teaching will be evaluated. Be sure to answer all parts of the question. Write your answers in the space provided.

Instructional Scenario I

Scenario: Mr. Enright and Mr. Toll

Two middle-level social studies teachers at Plainville School couldn't be further apart in their approaches, but both teachers are well respected for their eighth-grade students' success. Mr. Enright involves students actively in learning content through history simulations, WebQuests, dramatic reenactments, and project-based learning. Mr. Toll uses lectures, worksheets, and textbook questions and answers to teach the same history content. Mr. Toll sees himself as an "explainer" of important historic events. He often uses an advance organizer to start a lesson and study guides to help students prepare for tests. The following documents show recent lesson plans on the Civil War written by each teacher.

Document 1: Mr. Enright's Civil War Lesson Plan

Objective

The student will discuss the primary causes of the Civil War from a variety of perspectives.

Resources

Costumes from Civil War period, music from the Civil War, primary source documents, chart paper, markers

Motivation

Mr. Enright opens the class dressed as President Abraham Lincoln and introduces his "guests," Robert Barnwell Rhett of South Carolina (the principal dressed as this political leader of the South) and Henry Ward Brown of Connecticut (the physical education teacher dressed as this abolitionist leader of the North). The three adults lead a dramatic reenactment of a discussion on the causes of the Civil War.

Warm-up

Mr. Enright thanks his "guests" to the students' applause and leads the students in creating a KWL chart to elicit their prior knowledge of the Civil War and to help students set purposes for learning more about the Civil War's causes from multiple perspectives.

Preview

Mr. Enright tells the students that they will learn about the causes of the Civil War and will be able to discuss the causes from various perspectives, specifically from Abraham Lincoln's view and from the view of leaders from the North and South.

Teach

Mr. Enright divides his class into three heterogeneous groups to read and discuss the primary documents found at their table. One group studies Abraham Lincoln's view of the war's causes; one studies Northern leaders' views; and the third studies Southern leaders' views. The students use chart paper and markers at the table to complete the following graphic organizer as a group:

Abraham Lincoln's view	Northern leaders' views	Southern leaders' views

Students discuss the quotes, who said each one, and meanings. Then, after giving them time to write at least three ideas on the chart paper, Mr. Enright has the groups change tables and read the information and contribute additional information to the other charts.

After the three groups have moved to all three information tables and have had a chance to make a contribution to the charts, Mr. Enright gathers the students as a whole group and the class reviews the charts. Mr. Enright closes the lesson by impersonating President Lincoln again. He summarizes what the students have learned so far and then assigns homework.

Assessment

Mr. Enright observes the students' participation in the group discussion and evaluates students' individual contributions in the closing discussion. He also individually assesses the homework for content accuracy.

Independent Work

The homework requires students to write three paragraphs summarizing the three different views on the causes of the Civil War as a review of the day's class work.

Document 2: Mr. Toll's Civil War Lesson Plan

Objective

The student will discuss and write about the primary causes of the Civil War.

Resources

- Social studies textbook
- Online resources

Motivation

Mr. Toll provides an advance organizer with an outline of the textbook chapter on the causes of the Civil War.

Warm-up

Mr. Toll uses a computer projector to show the class a credible source website that discusses the causes of the Civil War. The students take turns reading the information from the website aloud and discuss important or difficult material as they go.

Preview

Mr. Toll tells the students that they will learn about the primary causes of the Civil War and will be able to discuss and write about those causes.

Teach

Mr. Toll asks the students individually to read the social studies text chapter section on the causes of the Civil War and use the advance organizer to guide their reading. After the students finish reading, Mr. Toll leads a lecture on the causes of the Civil War and asks students questions to check for understanding. To close the lesson, Mr. Toll summarizes the primary causes of the Civil War and assigns homework.

Assessment

Mr. Toll observes student involvement in reading the online text and individual reading of the textbook. He informally assesses students' contributions to the discussion. He individually grades the homework for content accuracy.

Independent Work

For homework, the students individually write their answers to the four questions at the end of the chapter.

17. Identify ONE student learning style that may find success in Mr. Enright's room and ONE student learning style that may find success in Mr. Toll's room. Be sure to base your response in principles of student learning and instruction.

18. Suggest ONE way Mr. Enright can modify his instruction to meet the needs of all learners. Suggest ONE way Mr. Toll can modify his instruction to meet the needs of all learners. Be sure to base your response in principles of students as learners and instruction.

Instructional Scenario II

Scenario: Mrs. Pendola

Mrs. Pendola is thrilled to have the opportunity to teach in the town in which she was educated more than 20 years ago. A few of her former teachers at Lincoln Middle School are still teaching, the building looks the same, and the principal is the same, but the school's student body has changed over the years—racially, ethnically, linguistically, and economically.

Approximately 50 percent of the student body is Hispanic; 13 percent is white; 31 percent is African American; 5 percent is Asian; and 1 percent is Native American. Roughly 15 percent of the student body receives English language learner or bilingual education services. The students in Mrs. Pendola's seventh-grade class speak more than 10 different languages besides English. Approximately 16 percent of the student body receives special-education services; 46 percent of the student body at Lincoln School receives free or reduced lunch.

Mrs. Pendola has set three professional goals for the school year:

- To create a positive, respectful learning environment in which all of her students can achieve high standards
- To get to know each student and his or her family
- To actively engage students in meaningful learning experiences

Her first unit is called "That Was Then, This Is Now." The students will read S. E. Hinton's novel *That Was Then, This Is Now* in her reading/language arts class. The following activity demonstrates how Mrs. Pendola has chosen to kick off the unit and to begin to achieve her professional goals.

That Was Then, This Is Now

Mrs. Pendola shares her seventh-grade class picture when she attended Lincoln School two decades ago. She tells a bit about her "favorites"—friends, subjects, activities, and teachers. She also explains a bit about the makeup of her nuclear family and some of their traditions. As she shares this information, she allows students to ask questions and adds the information to a large chart paper. This provides a model for her students. Next, she asks her students to think back to their lives one decade ago, to when they were around 3 years old. She smiles and adds that they weren't born two decades ago! She asks the students to write down information about friends, activities, teachers (if they attended preschool), or caregivers who taught them something, who they lived with, and what some of their traditions were. For homework, she asks the students to speak with adults at home and review baby books or photo albums to add more information to their visuals. She also asks each student to bring a photo or drawing from this period. The students share their work the next day, and Mrs. Pendola posts their photos next to each student's first-day-of-school photograph she has taken.

19. Suggest TWO ways Mrs. Pendola can achieve her first goal: to create a positive, respectful learning environment in which all students can achieve high standards. Be sure to base your response in principles of learning and teaching.

20. Suggest TWO ways Mrs. Pendola can achieve her third goal: to actively engage students in meaningful learning experiences. Be sure to base your response in principles of learning and teaching.

Answers and Explanations

Multiple-Choice Questions

Answer Key

Question	Answer	Content Category	Where to Get More Help
1	D	Students as Learners	Chapter 7
2	A	Students as Learners	Chapter 7
3	B	Students as Learners	Chapter 7
4	C	Students as Learners	Chapter 7
5	A	Instructional Process	Chapter 8
6	B	Instructional Process	Chapter 8
7	D	Instructional Process	Chapter 8
8	C	Instructional Process	Chapter 8
9	C	Assessment	Chapter 9
10	D	Assessment	Chapter 9
11	A	Assessment	Chapter 9
12	B	Assessment	Chapter 9
13	D	Professional Development, Leadership, and Community	Chapter 10
14	C	Professional Development, Leadership, and Community	Chapter 10
15	B	Professional Development, Leadership, and Community	Chapter 10
16	A	Professional Development, Leadership, and Community	Chapter 10

Answer Explanations

1. **D** Erikson suggests that the stage of identity vs. role confusion is typically addressed during adolescence (ages 12 to 18) and is the single most significant conflict a person faces. Choices A and B also are stages in Erikson's theory. Choice C is a distracter—a choice not based on any theory.

2. **A** Children 7 to 11 years of age typically operate in the concrete operational stage of cognitive development, in which they reason logically with familiar situations. Choices B and C also are stages of Piaget's theory. Choice D is a distracter.

3. **B** According to Luis Moll, when a teacher considers students' culture and language as "funds of knowledge," he sees this diversity as enriching to a classroom community of learners.

4. **C** Many English language learners experience a period of silence in the English-speaking classroom and may be less vocal in class discussions. English language learning takes time—usually up to two years for conversational literacy and five to seven years for academic English literacy.

5. **A** The affective domain of objectives includes teaching and assessing students' values, attitudes, and beliefs.

6. **B** Glasser's control theory suggests that teachers discuss behaviors, not students, in class meetings. In this constructivist approach, students listen to one another and arrive at compromises to resolve conflicts.

7. **D** Cooperative learning instructional methods, such as think-pair-share, offer opportunities for students to talk to one another and to support one another's higher-level thinking.

8. **C** Due process is an established course of formal proceedings using established rules and procedures. This term is typically used in special education procedures related to the Individuals with Disabilities Act, not Response to Intervention. Response to Intervention involves providing high-quality instruction (Choice A),

using assessment (Choice B) to inform instruction, and using evidence-based interventions (Choice D) to provide all students with the opportunity to learn in school and to assist in the identification of learning or other disabilities.

9. **C** A performance assessment is an authentic task that requires analysis and synthesis of information. Students must create a meaningful and purposeful response to demonstrate understanding of the course content. Students are given a rubric that delineates task criteria, and they often are asked to assess their own progress.

10. **D** Progress monitoring does not aim to measure the effectiveness of curriculum (Choice D); this is too broad of an answer choice. The other three choices—assessing student performance (Choice A), quantifying the rate of student responsiveness to instruction (Choice B), and evaluating the effectiveness of instruction (Choice C)—all capture the primary purposes of progress monitoring, which is targeted at the individual student and instruction level, not the curriculum level.

11. **A** Screening assessments usually are the first stage of an assessment system in which students are tested to identify or predict those who may be at risk for poor learning outcomes. Choices B (establish a trend line on a data chart of students' performance) and C (determine the level of instructional intensity) are too narrow, which means that screening assessment could be used to create a trend line or determine the level of intensity of instruction a student might need, but this is not the overarching purpose of screening assessments. Choice D (describe the effectiveness of an intervention program) is the definition of a summative assessment, not a screening assessment.

12. **B** Is the definition of a portfolio. Choice A (showcase) is one type of portfolio and is a distracter. Choice C (dossier) is a file or collection of papers giving detailed records on a person, usually in a professional setting, not a classroom setting. Choice D (report card) is a short record of a student's performance that contains grades and/or narrative, not a collection of student work samples.

13. **D** A reflective teacher or practitioner engages in thoughtful reconsideration of their students' behaviors and his or her instruction.

14. **C** Mrs. Friedman responds reflectively by acknowledging Jimmy's difficulty emotionally and content-wise. She offers support and an alternative form of poetry as a possible solution to Jimmy's problem.

15. **B** It is important for teachers to prepare for conferences with caregivers and to be positive and focus on students' strengths. Mrs. Smith should refrain from sharing information about other students in the classroom.

16. **A** Horace Mann (1796–1859) attended Brown University, served as the first secretary of education in Massachusetts, and made significant contributions to teacher education in his lifetime.

Constructed-Response Questions

Instructional scenarios, or "constructed responses," are graded holistically on a scale of 0 to 2, with 0 being the lowest score. For details on this type of question, be sure to read Chapter 6. In this section, you'll find the content categories and suggested content to include in your constructed responses. For more information about the content category, you can study Part III. The suggested content is designed to help you get a sense of the type of response required, but it may not cover all the correct options in such an open-ended question. You also may find it helpful to share your constructed responses with an education professor, adviser, or educator.

Instructional Scenario I

17. **Suggested content:** Students who may find more success in Mr. Enright's social studies class may have a kinesthetic or tactile learning style, may have bodily-kinesthetic multiple intelligence, or may have limited background knowledge of this content, which is further developed through the social experiences in this classroom.

Students who may find more success in Mr. Toll's social studies class may have a verbal linguistic multiple intelligence, may have an auditory learning style, or may have lots of background knowledge in this content area.

18. **Suggested content:** Mr. Enright's students might benefit from <u>frequent check-ins</u> (especially during long-term projects), <u>guided discovery questions</u> and <u>discussion</u>, and <u>individual accountability</u> during group work to ensure that students are retaining content objectives.

    Mr. Toll's students might benefit from more <u>frequent check-ins</u>; <u>step-by-step instructions</u>; <u>graphic organizers</u> on which to take notes; or additional kinesthetic, or <u>hands-on, experiences</u> with the content, such as <u>concrete examples</u>, <u>making a mock TV show</u>, or creating a <u>visual representation</u>.

Instructional Scenario II

19. **Suggested content:** Two ways to create a positive, respectful learning environment with high standards for all include, but are not limited to, <u>cooperative learning</u>; <u>responsive classroom class meetings</u>; <u>conflict resolution modeling and discussion</u>; and Glasser's, as well as Canter's, <u>assertive discipline model</u>.

20. **Suggested content:** Two ways Mrs. Pendola can actively engage her diverse learning include the following: <u>project-based learning</u>, <u>simulations</u>, <u>cooperative learning</u>, and <u>discovery learning</u>. Be sure to then describe and provide examples of project-based learning, simulations, cooperative learning, and/or discovery learning.

Chapter 4

PLT Grades 7–12 Preview Test

This preview of the PLT Grades 7–12 test (0624) is designed to give you an overall sense of the test's format and to help you determine the content areas you need to focus on in your studies. This preview test will not help you with your pacing on the test; it is approximately half the length of the actual PLT and may not represent the entire scope of the test in either content or difficulty.

After you complete the preview test, score your answers and use the explanations to self-diagnose content areas to study in Part III of this guide. You also may want to complete the other preview tests in Chapters 1, 2, and 3 to aid you in determining which content areas to study. Even though these additional preview tests are written for other PLT test grade levels, the question topics (Students as Learners; Instructional Process; Assessment; and Professional Development, Leadership, and Community) remain the same.

Multiple-Choice Questions

Directions: For each multiple-choice question, select the best answer and mark the corresponding letter space on your answer sheet.

Answer Sheet

1 Ⓐ Ⓑ Ⓒ Ⓓ
2 Ⓐ Ⓑ Ⓒ Ⓓ
3 Ⓐ Ⓑ Ⓒ Ⓓ
4 Ⓐ Ⓑ Ⓒ Ⓓ
5 Ⓐ Ⓑ Ⓒ Ⓓ
6 Ⓐ Ⓑ Ⓒ Ⓓ
7 Ⓐ Ⓑ Ⓒ Ⓓ
8 Ⓐ Ⓑ Ⓒ Ⓓ
9 Ⓐ Ⓑ Ⓒ Ⓓ
10 Ⓐ Ⓑ Ⓒ Ⓓ
11 Ⓐ Ⓑ Ⓒ Ⓓ
12 Ⓐ Ⓑ Ⓒ Ⓓ
13 Ⓐ Ⓑ Ⓒ Ⓓ
14 Ⓐ Ⓑ Ⓒ Ⓓ
15 Ⓐ Ⓑ Ⓒ Ⓓ
16 Ⓐ Ⓑ Ⓒ Ⓓ

1. Carol Gilligan was a student of Lawrence Kohlberg who derived her own theories of moral development in people. Her theory is best known as

   A. feminist theory.
   B. the ethic of care.
   C. gender equity.
   D. cognitive development.

2. Mr. Robinson's twelfth-grade student Danielle often demonstrates a genuine interest in the welfare of others in her classroom discourse, her involvement in community service, and her written work. Danielle may have achieved which level of Kohlberg's stages of moral development?

   A. Conventional
   B. Anti-conventional
   C. Post-conventional
   D. Pre-conventional

Questions 3–4 are based on the following passage.

Theresa is an eleventh-grade student who has been at South High School for a year. Her parents recently filed bankruptcy because of a failed small-business investment and plan to move again next month in order to find work. Theresa's grades have begun to decline, and she is often alone at lunch and in the hallways.

3. According to Abraham Maslow's hierarchy of needs, which of the following may be affecting Theresa?

   A. Self-actualization
   B. Esteem
   C. Safety
   D. Synthesis

4. Theresa's new teachers have been informed by her former teachers that Theresa's family has a pattern of migration in pursuit of work opportunities. An accommodation that may best support Theresa is

   A. involving parents in planning and decision making for Theresa.
   B. more time on tests.
   C. cooperative learning.
   D. independent study.

5. Which of the following is NOT teacher-centered instruction?

   A. Direct instruction
   B. Mastery learning
   C. Expository instruction
   D. Discovery learning

6. According to Lee and Marlene Canter's model, which of the following statements is true?

   A. Teachers must show their students they are "with it."
   B. Teachers must maintain a positive, caring, and productive classroom.
   C. Teachers must try to keep the whole class involved.
   D. Teachers must be aware of the "ripple effect."

7. A teacher with a laissez-faire approach to classroom management

   A. uses discussion to determine rules with students.
   B. uses rewards and punishments to change student behavior.
   C. establishes no rules, and students do what they want.
   D. establishes rules, and students do what they want.

8. Which of the following is NOT a level in the cognitive domain of Bloom's Taxonomy?

   A. Creating
   B. Judging
   C. Remembering
   D. Analyzing

9. A test that measures what it is designed to measure is considered

   A. reliable.
   B. valid.
   C. usable.
   D. normative.

10. A written record of a learner's progress, written in a positive tone about learning milestones, is known as a(n)

    A. diagnostic assessment.
    B. analytical checklist.
    C. continuum.
    D. anecdotal record.

11. A well-written lesson objective contains which of the following?

    A. Behavior
    B. Criterion
    C. Conditions
    D. All of the above

12. The breadth and the depth of the curriculum is known as

    A. standards for learning.
    B. common core and state standards.
    C. scope and sequence.
    D. formative and summative.

Questions 13–14 are based on the following passages, which are from a debate about student-centered vs. teacher-centered instructional methods.

Student-Centered Instruction Is More Effective

Student-centered instruction involves more student input, self-monitoring, and responsibility. If teachers' primary goal is to teach students to learn to be reflective, responsible adults, then teachers should use student-centered methods. When students have opportunities to give input into what is taught and how, they develop more ownership, which motivates them intrinsically. Students who know how to self-monitor learning know what learning strategies work for them and know how to use information in a variety of ways. Responsibility for learning should be transferred to students by high school to help them learn how to learn without the direct guidance of an adult. Student-centered instruction methods are the most effective teaching methods in secondary schools today.

Teacher-Centered Instruction Is More Effective

Teacher-centered instruction methods are the most effective in secondary schools today. Students benefit when teachers use direct instruction, mastery learning, and meaningful homework. Direct instruction is scientifically research based and has been proven to be the best approach when a student has limited background on a skill or concept being taught. Mastery learning is systematic instruction that requires mastery

of one concept before moving on to the next. Meaningful homework is essential to help students learn that they will be held accountable for their work. Teacher-centered instructional methods make the most of academic learning time and hold students to high standards of academic excellence.

13. The first passage advances the idea that student-centered instruction is more effective. The author of this passage most highly values which of the following?

    A. Students' areas of cognition, interest, and social adjustment
    B. Students' grades from last quarter
    C. Students' teachers from last year
    D. Students' completion of homework

14. Which of the following is LEAST likely to be used in the classroom of the author of the second passage?

    A. Discussions
    B. Homework
    C. Lecture
    D. Guided discovery learning

15. Donald Schön describes teacher reflection-in-action as

    A. looking back on experience or action in order to change future teaching.
    B. observing action and thinking as they occur in order to adjust teaching.
    C. analyzing teaching after a lesson observation by an administrator.
    D. discussing teaching with a colleague to improve future lessons.

16. John Dewey established which of the following periods of education, which fostered individuality, free activity, and learning through experience?

    A. Common School period
    B. Early National period
    C. Modern period
    D. Progressive period

Constructed-Response Questions

Directions: The following questions require you to write short answers, or "constructed responses." You are not expected to cite specific theories or texts in your answers; however, your knowledge of specific principles of learning and teaching will be evaluated. Be sure to answer all parts of the question. Write your answers in the space provided.

Instructional Scenario I

Scenario: Jason

Jason is an eighth-grade student in Mr. Pope's health class. Jason shows great interest in the course content, actively participates in class, and responds well to Mr. Pope's enthusiastic and positive teaching style. Jason does very well with an assignment that Mr. Pope designed for a test grade and then repeats once a month throughout the marking period. Following is a brief synopsis of the assignment.

> Use the Internet or a magazine to find an article related to health and fitness. Write a summary of the article that includes at least three main health-related points, and then make one connection between the article and your knowledge/experiences. Be sure to include the proper citation of your article and its source.

Mr. Pope introduced the assignment by providing a model and then offering direct instruction on how to write the summary. He also gave examples of personal connections between the article and his knowledge and experiences and showed the students how to add this information to the end of the summary. Mr. Pope modeled his writing process by thinking aloud and actually demonstrating his writing using the overhead projector. Mr. Pope's eighth-grade English teaching colleague teamed with Mr. Pope and planned to carefully teach how to cite Internet sources and periodicals. The two devised a guide sheet, which they provided to students and turned into a poster for both of their classrooms.

Jason earned a B on his first health summary because he misunderstood or did not read some of the directions carefully. In addition, the assignment was one day late. Jason got discouraged that he forgot his homework on his desk, which is a problem he often has with schoolwork. Mr. Pope has noticed that Jason's health binder is usually disorganized and Jason frequently forgets to bring a pencil to class. Mr. Pope reviewed the second health summary assignment individually with Jason and checked with Jason to be sure he had an appropriate article a week before it was due. He also had his class work in pairs to discuss real-life connections to the topics of their articles during class time a few days before the next summaries were due. On the second assignment, Jason earned an A. He continued to earn A's on his other summary assignments, with the exception of one, which was submitted late. Jason became an active class contributor and appeared to be confident in his abilities to find health-related information on the Internet and in magazines, as well as in his ability to write a summary.

17. Identify TWO strengths of Mr. Pope's health assignment. Explain how each strength demonstrates aspects of effective planning. Be sure to base your response on principles of planning instruction.

18. Identify TWO ways to make accommodations for a student with Jason's learning style. Be sure to base your response on principles of teaching students with diverse needs.

Instructional Scenario II

Scenario: Ms. Brousseau

Ms. Brousseau is a tenth-grade mathematics teacher of geometry. Her class has been grouped with average-achieving students, although, as one might imagine, her students have a wide range of knowledge, skills, and dispositions in mathematics. Several of her students have been identified as having diverse learning needs, such as attention deficit hyperactivity disorder (ADHD) and learning disabilities. She also has English language learners in her class.

For a lesson on points, lines, and planes, she has the following objectives:

- The student will state whether an object suggests a point, a line, or a plane.
- The student will define the following terms: *segment, intersection,* and *union.*

She gathers the following materials and resources before her lesson begins: a replica of the Empire State Building, an art poster that involves lots of geometric shapes and repetition, a geometry textbook, an overhead projector, transparencies, and an overhead pen.

Opening of lesson: Ms. Brousseau shows a replica of the Empire State Building. She states, "We see geometry in the structures in which people live and work. Architects use geometry to create buildings. Artists use geometry to create art. Some of you may plan careers in these areas. Geometry is all around us. Let's take a look at the Empire State Building here." She asks students about their background knowledge related to this famous building and then asks them to identify points, lines, and planes using the replica. She continues the discussion and accessing of prior knowledge by sharing an art poster that involves lots of repetition of geometric shapes. She asks the students to identify points, lines, and planes in the art poster.

Middle of lesson: Ms. Brousseau uses direct explanation of points, lines, and planes as they relate to line segments, intersections, and unions. She uses the overhead projector to display examples from the geometry textbook and provides a definition of each term for students to write down in their notebooks. After trying a few problems together with teacher guidance, her students work alone to complete problems that require the application level of knowledge for each of these geometric terms.

Close of lesson: Ms. Brousseau asks students to review what they have learned today and how these terms are found in everyday life, besides her math class. She assigns homework that includes answering more application questions and finding a picture or replica of three real-life examples that suggest a point, a line, and a plane.

She assesses her students' participation in the lesson discussion and grades homework individually, making corrections as needed.

19. Identify TWO strengths of Ms. Brousseau's geometry lesson. Explain how each strength demonstrates aspects of effective planning. Be sure to base your response on principles of planning instruction.

20. Suggest TWO ways Ms. Brousseau can assess students' understanding of the lesson. Be sure to use the class experience and homework and to base your response on principles of assessment.

Answers and Explanations

Multiple-Choice Questions

Answer Key

Question	Answer	Content Category	Where to Get More Help
1	B	Students as Learners	Chapter 7
2	C	Students as Learners	Chapter 7
3	C	Students as Learners	Chapter 7
4	A	Students as Learners	Chapter 7
5	D	Instructional Process	Chapter 8
6	B	Instructional Process	Chapter 8
7	C	Instructional Process	Chapter 8
8	B	Instructional Process	Chapter 8
9	B	Assessment	Chapter 9
10	D	Assessment	Chapter 9
11	D	Assessment	Chapter 9
12	C	Assessment	Chapter 9
13	A	Professional Development, Leadership, and Community	Chapter 10
14	D	Professional Development, Leadership, and Community	Chapter 10
15	B	Professional Development, Leadership, and Community	Chapter 10
16	D	Professional Development, Leadership and Community,	Chapter 10

Answer Explanations

1. **B** Gilligan's theory of moral development, known as "the ethic of care," is based on Kohlberg's, Piaget's, and Freud's theories but reframes these theories for women. Like Kohlberg, she defines three stages: pre-conventional, conventional, and post-conventional.

2. **C** Kohlberg's theory of moral development suggests that the third stage, post-conventional, is not always reached by all adults. At this stage, people demonstrate understanding of social mutuality and show a genuine interest in the welfare of others.

3. **C** The migration of Theresa's family in pursuit of work may be affecting her sense of safety. According to Maslow's theory, safety needs relate to establishing stability and consistency in a chaotic world. Theresa also may have physiological needs that are not being met, such as food and sleep, but this was not an answer choice.

4. **A** Involving parents in planning and decision making in schools where migration is common provides greater opportunity for effectiveness of instructional methods and students' academic achievement.

5. **D** Discovery learning is a student-centered approach in which students construct their own understanding of a concept. This approach is based on the work of Jerome Bruner and John Dewey.

6. **B** This choice is central to Canter's assertive discipline model. Choices A, C, and D all are hallmarks of Kounin's classroom-management plan.

7. **C** There are three basic approaches to classroom-management styles: authoritarian, laissez faire, and authoritative. A teacher with a laissez-faire style of classroom management does not set rules and behavior expectations.

8. **B** The levels in the cognitive domain of Bloom's Taxonomy is comprised of remembering (Choice C), understanding, applying, analyzing (Choice D), evaluating, and creating (Choice A). Although judging is a behavior associated with evaluating, it is not one of the six levels.

9. **B** Test validity is related to measuring what it is meant to measure. Test reliability is related to whether the test remains consistent across testing times and settings. Choice C, usable, is not a term used with education assessment. Although it may be considered correct—the test is usable—this is too broad of a choice in a multiple-choice test. This is a good example of why it is important to read all multiple-choice response options because sometimes one choice may be "correct," but another choice is better and will be the credited response. Choice D is a distracter in that the term *norm* is often associated with testing, which may make you fall for this one if you do not understand the definition of *test validity*.

10. **D** An anecdotal record is written by the teacher to capture a student's progress using a positive tone, highlighting strengths and accomplishments toward milestones in the child's social, emotional, physical, or cognitive development. Choice A, diagnostic assessment, tells teachers what the student needs to learn and is a more formal assessment than the anecdotal record. Choice B, analytical checklist, is comprised of a list of learning behaviors or performance expectations. Choice C, continuum, is a list of developmental behaviors that the teacher can use during observations of students.

11. **D** A well-written lesson objective statement contains all three elements listed. When properly written, the objective statement is measurable and contains the behavior (Choice A) to be measured or observed (also known as a measurable verb, often from Bloom's Taxonomy), the conditions (Choice C), which describes how the students will do the behavior, and the criterion (Choice B), which is degree of accuracy the teacher expects.

12. **C** Scope and sequence in a curriculum help teachers know how much information they will cover (scope) and in what order they will teach (sequence). Choice A, standards for learning, reflects state standards that set expectations for the knowledge and skills expected in a school program. Choice B, common core and state standards, is a distracter; it alludes to the Common Core State Standards, a set of standards currently adopted by 44 states to define the knowledge and skills students should have during their K–12 education. Choice D, formative and summative, is also a distracter; it refers to terms related to assessment, not curriculum.

13 **A** A teacher who uses a student-centered approach considers students' areas of cognition, interest, and social adjustment when planning lessons.

14. **D** Guided discovery learning is a student-centered approach in which the teacher "guides" students through questions and directions.

15. **B** Schön's notion of reflection-in-action describes the ability of a teacher to "think on her feet" and to change instructional practice while in the lesson. Choice B, observing action and thinking as they occur in order to adjust teaching, is the only choice in which the reflection is happening during instruction. Each of the other responses occurs either before or after the lesson.

16. **D** The Progressive period (1880–1920) was based on the educational philosophy first advanced by Dewey.

Constructed-Response Questions

Instructional scenarios, or "constructed responses," are graded holistically on a scale of 0 to 2, with 0 being the lowest score. For details on this type of question, be sure to read Chapter 6. In this section, you'll find the content categories and suggested content to include in your constructed responses. For more information about the content category, you can study Part III. The suggested content is designed to help you get a sense of the type of response required, but it may not cover all the correct options in such an open-ended question. You also may find it helpful to share your constructed responses with an education professor, adviser, or educator.

Instructional Scenario I

17. **Suggested content:** Strengths include <u>exploring real-life connections</u> between content and learners, <u>using computer technology</u>, <u>collaborating</u> with the English teacher, and providing <u>modeling and direct instruction</u>.

18. **Suggested content:** Appropriate accommodations include, but are not limited to, <u>supporting organization</u> of the binder, <u>probing for Jason's understanding</u> before sending him off to do his homework, offering <u>frequent check-ins</u> with Jason, and <u>communicating with guardians</u> through the school's website or via e-mail.

Instructional Scenario II

19. **Suggested content:** Strengths of Ms. Brousseau's lesson include both <u>student-centered</u> and <u>teacher-centered</u> techniques to meet the needs of a wide range of learners, <u>real-life purposes</u> for content, and using a <u>concrete example</u> to open the lesson, all of which build <u>background knowledge</u> and motivate learners.

20. **Suggested content:** Ways to assess students in this lesson include, but are not limited to, <u>formative assessment</u>, such as students sharing examples using the overhead projector; <u>thinking aloud responses</u>; and having a <u>partner check</u> problems in class. Summative assessment ideas include creating a <u>performance assessment</u> using the student-generated pictures of geometry-related replicas.

PART II

PREPARING FOR THE FORMAT OF THE PLT

Chapter 5

Multiple-Choice Questions

In this chapter, you will learn about the format and types of multiple-choice questions on the PLT test. Multiple-choice questions require you to analyze situations, synthesize information, and apply knowledge, all of which takes time. Knowing the format of the questions will get your mind ready to recognize the patterns of these questions. This chapter also includes helpful tips to help you achieve your goal—a passing score on the PLT!

Multiple-Choice Question Types

There are a total of 70 discrete multiple-choice questions on the PLT. These questions are unrelated to the constructed-response questions and the instructional scenarios (see Chapter 6). Multiple-choice questions require strong critical reading skills and content knowledge of three of the four PLT areas tested:

- Students as Learners
- Instructional Process
- Assessment
- Professional Development, Leadership, and Community

There are five types of multiple-choice questions:

- Complete the statement
- Which of the following
- Roman numeral
- LEAST/NOT/EXCEPT
- Graphs/tables/reading passages

The following sections give you an example of each type of question.

Complete the Statement

In a complete-the-statement question, you are asked to read the question stem and to determine which of the four answer choices best concludes the sentence.

During oral reading, one student reads the word *cape* as *cap*. This child most likely needs help with

A. concepts about print.
B. encoding.
C. comprehension.
D. phonics.

Answer: **D.**

Which of the Following

With this multiple-choice question type, you read a short question that ends with the phrase *which of the following*. This is the most frequent question type on the PLT.

> A mathematics lesson plan that is organized with direct instruction, guided practice, and independent practice is likely to provide which of the following to students?
>
> **A.** Grade-level expectations
> **B.** Phonemic awareness
> **C.** Scaffolding
> **D.** Vocabulary development

Answer: **C.**

Roman Numeral

Roman-numeral multiple-choice questions require you to read a short passage that includes several options to consider. The answer choices are presented as a list of Roman numerals. You must use your critical reasoning to determine which of the answer choices contain all the correct options. These questions take more time than most multiple-choice questions and appear infrequently on the PLT.

> Mrs. Humbyrd, the principal of Calfee Corner Middle School, wants to convene an IEP meeting for Jeffrey, a sixth-grader with learning disabilities. The Individuals with Disabilities Act (IDEA) requires Mrs. Humbyrd to invite the following participants:
>
> I.   Jeffrey's regular education teachers
> II. Special educators who may work with Jeffrey
> III. The school nurse
> IV. Jeffrey's parents
>
> **A.** I, II, III, IV
> **B.** I, II, III
> **C.** I, II, IV
> **D.** I, II

Answer: **C.**

LEAST/NOT/EXCEPT

The LEAST/NOT/EXCEPT multiple-choice questions require more time and analysis than other types of questions. In responding to this type of question, you must carefully read the questions stem, consider all four of the response options, and carefully analyze which of the choices are relevant. Last, you need to remember if you are looking for the LEAST likely choice, the response that is NOT relevant, or the one that is the EXCEPTION to the other three choices.

> Mrs. Antosh strives to make accommodations for the students in her kindergarten class who have short attention spans, have difficulty starting a task, and often appear distracted by the busy classroom. Which accommodation is LEAST likely to support these students?
>
> **A.** Providing a quiet, less visual area to work
> **B.** Providing short tasks with immediate positive feedback
> **C.** Moving the students closer to the teacher
> **D.** Seating the students in a group

Answer: **D.**

Graphs/Tables/Reading Passages

This type of multiple-choice question presents a longer passage, a graph, or a table for you to read and interpret. Be careful to read headings on the graphs and tables. Of course, the longer reading-passage questions may take longer for you to answer, so be ready for this. Fortunately, this question type does not appear very frequently on the PLT.

> Mrs. Lahiri is a teacher assistant in Mrs. Campbell's primary grade-level resource classroom. Mrs. Campbell has provided a lesson plan for Mrs. Lahiri to implement with a small group of students who need additional support with their writing. While Mrs. Lahiri works with the small group of students drafting a story, the principal asks her to assist in the office because of an absence. Mrs. Campbell and Mrs. Lahiri are discouraged that their plans have been interrupted. Furthermore, their students will not receive the small-group instruction delineated in their Individualized Education Plans.
>
> Which of the following is a professionally responsible and reflective way for Mrs. Campbell to approach this situation?
>
> A. Discuss concerns with Mrs. Lahiri and encourage her to file a complaint.
> B. Discuss concerns with the school principal and offer alternative solutions to the problem.
> C. Support the change in student services in order to be a team member.
> D. Discuss concerns with colleagues in the teacher's room and brainstorm solutions to the problem.

Answer: **B.**

Strategies for Answering Multiple-Choice Questions

Now you know that there are 70 multiple-choice questions that are unrelated to the constructed-response questions and instructional scenarios, and you know to look for five basic types of multiple-choice questions. In this section, you will review a systematic approach to the multiple-choice questions and then practice the strategy.

1. **Read the question stem.** The bold part of the question below is the question stem:

> **Mrs. Dougherty's first-grade students work in small groups at the blocks center three days a week. Which of the following provides the best rationale for blocks center work?**
>
> A. Direct instruction
> B. Discovery learning
> C. Independent practice
> D. Visual learning

Answer: **B.**

2. **Read all the answer choices.** Don't be too quick to select the answer choice you think is correct without carefully considering all the answer choices. Remember, one key area this test assesses is your critical reasoning skills, so each test question has at least one "distracter." This is an answer choice that appears correct in some way—it's related to the topic, it has a similar spelling or meaning, or it's almost correct but not as good as the credited response. The credited response is the answer choice that will get you the points on the PLT, so clearly this is the one you want!

3. **Use the process of elimination.** Cross out any answers that you know are incorrect. It's fine to write in your test booklet. Underline key phrases and words if you find it helpful. Analyze the situation and apply your knowledge to the question. If you do not clearly know the correct answer, your goal is to find the best two choices of the four. If you can use the process of elimination to get this close to the credited response, you have a 50 percent chance of choosing the right one. If you simply guess, you have only a 25 percent chance. Your odds are clearly better when you use the process of elimination.

4. **Insert the answer choices into the question stem.** Try out the best two answer choices to find the credited response.

5. **Mark your answer sheet carefully.** Because you can skip questions or start at any point on the PLT that you would like, it is important for you to mark your answer sheet carefully so that each answer choice refers to the correct question. You also want to completely fill in the answer and not make any stray marks on the sheet because a computer is scoring your multiple-choice question responses.

Apply the Strategies

Now it's your chance to practice the strategies for the multiple-choice questions. Remember to read the question stem first, skim all the answer choices, and use the process of elimination to get to the credited response. In this practice section, you will work on 12 multiple-choice items made up of all five types of multiple-choice questions: complete the statement, which of the following, Roman numeral, LEAST/NOT/EXCEPT, and graphs/tables/reading passages.

After you complete these 12 questions, review the answers and explanations, paying particular attention to the types of questions you got correct and the types of questions that you got incorrect. You may find that one type of question is harder for you, in which case you'll want to spend more time practicing that type of question in the full-length tests that appear in Part IV of this book.

In addition, to help you diagnose any strengths or weaknesses in your knowledge of the principles of teaching and learning, I have included the categories Students as Learners; Instructional Process; Assessment; and Professional Development, Leadership, and Community. You will find Part III of this book particularly helpful in closing any gaps you discover.

Practice

Directions: For each question, select the best answer and mark the corresponding letter space on your answer sheet.

Answer Sheet

1 Ⓐ Ⓑ Ⓒ Ⓓ
2 Ⓐ Ⓑ Ⓒ Ⓓ
3 Ⓐ Ⓑ Ⓒ Ⓓ
4 Ⓐ Ⓑ Ⓒ Ⓓ
5 Ⓐ Ⓑ Ⓒ Ⓓ
6 Ⓐ Ⓑ Ⓒ Ⓓ
7 Ⓐ Ⓑ Ⓒ Ⓓ
8 Ⓐ Ⓑ Ⓒ Ⓓ
9 Ⓐ Ⓑ Ⓒ Ⓓ
10 Ⓐ Ⓑ Ⓒ Ⓓ
11 Ⓐ Ⓑ Ⓒ Ⓓ
12 Ⓐ Ⓑ Ⓒ Ⓓ

1. Researchers have found patterns of learning differences between girls and boys. Girls tend to rely on

   A. self-esteem.
   B. mathematics.
   C. memorization.
   D. physical activity.

2. Which of the following multiple intelligences involves a student's ability to understand people and relationships between people?

   A. Intrapersonal intelligence
   B. Introspective intelligence
   C. Intergeneral intelligence
   D. Interpersonal intelligence

3. In your teaching career, you will create a classroom atmosphere that fosters which of the following:

   I. Love
   II. Assistance
   III. Prior knowledge
   IV. Respect

   A. I, II, IV
   B. II, III, IV
   C. I, III
   D. II, III, IV

4. Auditory learners tend to approach learning in all these ways EXCEPT

   A. exploration.
   B. listening.
   C. lecture.
   D. read-aloud.

Question 5 is based on the following passage.

Mr. Behr, a first-grade teacher, has an interactive, constructivist view of education based on his teacher-education program and his successful experiences as a preschool teacher. He provides a variety of meaningful activities for his students, including listening to quality children's literature read aloud, opportunities for creative expression and dramatic play, and hands-on experiences with mathematics situations.

5. His principal can best describe Mr. Behr's practice as

   A. teacher directed.
   B. emergent literacy.
   C. leader centered.
   D. developmentally appropriate.

6. Teachers who establish the rules and expect students to follow them, as well as use a set of rewards and punishments for following or breaking the rules, are considered

   A. authoritative teachers.
   B. authoritarian teachers.
   C. Arthurian teachers.
   D. laissez-faire teachers.

7. Which of the following is an example of an informal assessment used in education settings?

   A. Metropolitan Achievement Test
   B. State licensure exam
   C. Running records
   D. Rorschach inkblot assessment

8. Bloom's taxonomy is a classification system for organizing the level of abstraction of educational objectives and questions that teachers may ask. This taxonomy is made up of three domains, including the following:

   I. Cognitive
   II. Evaluative
   III. Affective
   IV. Psychomotor

   A. I, II, IV
   B. I, III, IV
   C. II, III, IV
   D. I, II, III

9. Which of the following is NOT a provision of the Americans with Disabilities Act (ADA) (1990)?

   A. Prohibits discrimination on the basis of disability
   B. Describes the special services designed to meet the unique needs of individuals
   C. Sets clear and enforceable standards that address discrimination
   D. Invokes the power of congressional authority and the U.S. Constitution

Question 10 is based on the following table.

The History of American Education		
Time Period	**Key Contributor**	**Description**
Late 1800s	McGuffey Readers	Moralistic books
Early 1900s	Dewey	"Progressive" schooling
1908	Montessori	Multi-aged grouping
1950s	Sputnik and the space race	Essentialist schooling
1965	Johnson Administration	Elementary and Secondary Education Act
1970s	Goodman	Whole language
1980s	Reagan Administration	A Nation at Risk Report
Early 2000s	George W. Bush Administration	No Child Left Behind Act

10. Those educators in the essentialist movement have a view opposite to progressive education. Which of the following would an essentialist educator value the most?

   A. Discovery learning
   B. Observations of students
   C. Student-centered curriculum
   D. Achievement test results

11. The intent of Public Law 94-142 is to provide

   A. a free and appropriate education to all handicapped students.
   B. directions on assessing students with learning disabilities.
   C. appropriate education in the "least restrictive environment."
   D. transition services for high-school students.

12. Which of the following is true about teachers' rights and responsibilities?

   A. Teachers may be dismissed for belonging to a radical religious group.
   B. Teachers may be dismissed for conduct "unbecoming to an educator."
   C. Teachers may be sued and held liable for negligence.
   D. Teachers may be asked to provide information unrelated to employment.

Answers and Explanations

Answer Key

Question	Answer	Content Category	Where to Get More Help	Question Type
1	C	Students as Learners	Chapter 7	Complete the Statement
2	D	Students as Learners	Chapter 7	Which of the Following
3	A	Students as Learners	Chapter 7	Roman Numeral
4	A	Students as Learners	Chapter 7	LEAST/NOT/EXCEPT
5	D	Instructional Process	Chapter 8	Graphs/Tables/Reading Passages
6	B	Instructional Process	Chapter 8	Complete the Statement
7	C	Assessment	Chapter 9	Which of the Following
8	B	Instructional Process	Chapter 8	Roman Numeral
9	B	Professional Development, Leadership, and Community	Chapter 10	LEAST/NOT/EXCEPT
10	D	Professional Development, Leadership, and Community	Chapter 10	Graphs/Tables/Reading Passages
11	A	Professional Development, Leadership, and Community	Chapter 10	Complete the Statement
12	C	Professional Development, Leadership, and Community	Chapter 10	Which of the Following

Answer Explanations

1. **C** Girls tend to emphasize memorization, whereas boys tend to emphasize physical activity and hands-on learning. *(See Chapter 7.)*

2. **D** In Howard Gardner's theory of multiple intelligences, people with interpersonal intelligence are people-smart. These students tend to be the leaders on the playground and understand people and relationships to a higher degree than others. Choice A is the opposite of interpersonal intelligence; it serves as the "distracter" in this question. Those who possess intrapersonal intelligence have a good sense of who they are, their inner feelings, and their moods. Choices B and C are made up, so I hope that you crossed them out and were able to use the process of elimination to get to the credited response. *(See Chapter 7.)*

3. **A** Love, assistance, and respect are three important aspects of creating a positive classroom atmosphere. Although tapping into students' prior knowledge is important, it is not an aspect of the classroom atmosphere; therefore, it serves as the "distracter" in this question. Love may seem like a less important aspect of creating a positive classroom, especially as you move up the grade levels, but a teacher's love of his or her subject, enthusiasm about working with students, and pleasure in teaching add considerably to the classroom environment at any grade level. *(See Chapter 7.)*

4. **A** Auditory learners have a learning style that emphasizes listening. Exploration is not connected to an auditory learner, although providing opportunities for exploration may be a successful approach with an auditory learner. Exploration is the "distracter" and requires you to reason critically to find the credited response, not the plausible-but-not-as-good answer. *(See Chapter 7.)*

5. **D** The passage describes hallmarks of developmentally appropriate practice according to guidelines established by the National Association for the Education of Young Children (NAEYC). Choice A is not a part of the instructional scenario in Mr. Behr's classroom. Choice B is a term that may be used in a developmentally appropriate classroom, but this term is used to describe students' literacy development, not a teacher's practice. Choice C is not a term used in education to describe a teacher's practice. *(See Chapter 8.)*

6. **B** Authoritarian teachers use a teacher-centered approach to classroom management. The teacher sets the rules; the teacher monitors the breaking or following of the rules and metes out punishments or rewards as he or she sees fit. Choice A is a close response, but not as precise as authoritarian because teacher-directed methods relate to the way in which a teacher plans and delivers lesson, not classroom management. Choice C is not a term used when discussing classroom management. Choice D may be "correct" but is not the credited response because the question stem is the definition of an authoritarian approach. *(See Chapter 8.)*

7. **C** Running records are used in reading assessment to note a student's oral reading, word recognition, fluency, comprehension, and self-correction behaviors. The state licensure exam and the Metropolitan Achievement Tests are norm-referenced and formal assessments. The Rorschach inkblot assessment is used primarily by clinical psychologists and is a projective test. *(See Chapter 9.)*

8. **B** Bloom's taxonomy is made up of the cognitive, affective, and psychomotor domains. The cognitive domain involves knowledge and development of educational attitudes and skills. The affective domain involves development of emotional areas and attitudes. The psychomotor domain involves manual or physical skills. Evaluation or evaluative questions are a part of Bloom's taxonomy of the cognitive domain. Because II, Evaluative, serves as a distracter, choices A, C, and D are all incorrect. *(See Chapter 8.)*

9. **B** Choice B describes the purpose of an Individualized Education Plan (IEP), not the basic tenets of the Americans with Disabilities Act (ADA). All the other choices are important features of this act, which prohibits discrimination on the basis of disability. *(See Chapter 10.)*

10. **D** Those in the essentialist schooling movement would more highly value teacher-centered instruction, subject-oriented curriculum, and the results of achievement tests. *(See Chapter 10.)*

11. **A** The essence of Public Law 94-142 is to provide a free and appropriate education to all handicapped students. Choice B is not related to any public law. Choice C relates to PL 99-457. Choice D relates to PL 98-199. *(See Chapter 10.)*

12. **C** Teachers may be sued and held liable for negligence. Successful lawsuits against teachers generally have found that the teacher reasonably could have foreseen the event or that the teacher acted differently than a reasonable teacher would have acted in a similar situation. Choice A violates a teacher's right to religious or political freedom. Choice B is a distracter in that "conduct unbecoming to a teacher" is widely open to interpretation. If a teacher has broken the law, then the teacher could be dismissed after a due-process hearing. Choice D is also incorrect; teachers may not be asked to provide information about their age, marital status, sexual orientation, religious affiliation, political affiliation, or any other information unrelated to employment. *(See Chapter 10.)*

Final Tips for Answering the Multiple-Choice Questions

- Remember, your goal is to pass the PLT, not to compete with another person's score or to set PLT test-taking records. Norm-referenced tests are designed for you not to know all the answers. Be prepared for several difficult questions.

- Know that you can work on the multiple-choice questions in any order. In other words, you can skip the ones you're having difficulty with. If you do so, be sure to mark your answer sheet carefully and accurately.

- Write in your test booklet if it helps you. Underline, circle key words, and make note of any items you skipped. Just be sure to mark your final choice on the answer sheet. Your test booklet is not scored, but it is collected at the end of the test session.

- Remember that there are no patterns to the order in which questions are posed or to their credited answers.

- Be mindful that there is no penalty for guessing. Don't leave any multiple-choice questions blank! Remember to use the process of elimination if you have the time to do so.

- Monitor your testing time. Don't rely on the proctor or your sense of time. Bring a watch, and make sure that you are working quickly but carefully.

- Read all the answer choices before choosing the credited response.

- Check your answers if time permits. Remember, it's okay to change your answer if you have taken the time to analyze the question stem and realize that your initial thought was incorrect.

Chapter 6

Constructed-Response Questions

This chapter will help you approach the constructed-response questions in a systematic way in order to save time on the actual test. The strategies you practice here will also help you respond to these questions in a clear, accurate, and concise way. That's exactly what the Educational Testing Service (ETS) is looking for in your constructed responses.

How to Approach the Constructed-Response Questions

Let's look back at a instructional scenario and a sample constructed-response question based on a scenario from Chapter 4.

Sample Scenario: Jason

EXAMPLE:

Jason is an eighth-grade student in Mr. Pope's health class. Jason shows great interest in the course content, actively participates in class, and responds well to Mr. Pope's enthusiastic and positive teaching style. Jason does very well with an assignment that Mr. Pope designed for a test grade and repeats once a month throughout the marking period. Below is a brief synopsis of the assignment:

> Find an article related to health and fitness on the Internet or in a magazine. Write a summary of the article that includes at least three main health-related points of the article, and then make one connection between the article and your knowledge/experiences. Be sure to cite your article and its source properly.

Mr. Pope introduced this assignment by providing a model and then offering direct instruction on how to write the summary. He also gave examples of personal connections between the article and his knowledge and experiences and showed the students how to add this information to the end of the summary. Mr. Pope modeled his writing process by thinking aloud and actually demonstrating his writing using the overhead projector. Mr. Pope teamed up with his eighth-grade English teaching colleague and planned to teach how to cite Internet sources and periodicals carefully. The two devised a guide sheet that they provided to students and turned into a poster for both of their classrooms.

Jason earned a B on his first health summary because he misunderstood or did not read some of the directions carefully. In addition, the assignment was one day late. Jason was discouraged that he forgot his homework on his desk at home, which is a problem he often has with homework. Mr. Pope has noticed that Jason's health binder is usually disorganized and Jason frequently forgets to bring a pencil to class.

Mr. Pope reviewed the second health summary assignment individually with Jason, checking with Jason to make sure that he had an appropriate article one week before the assignment was due. He also had his class work in pairs to discuss real-life connections to the topics of their articles during class time a few days before the next summaries were due. On the second assignment, Jason earned an A. He continued to earn A's on his other summary assignments, with the exception of one, which was late. Jason became an active class contributor and appeared confident in his abilities to find health-related information on the Internet and in magazines, as well as in his ability to write a summary.

Sample Constructed-Response Question

> Identify TWO strengths of Mr. Pope's health assignment. Explain how each strength of the assignment demonstrates aspects of effective planning. Be sure to base your response on the principles of planning instruction.

As you can see, the constructed-response questions are made up of a instructional scenario for you to read, followed by a question that requires you to provide a short answer. In this next section, I have some suggested approaches for you to use with the constructed-response questions on your PLT test.

Strategies for Approaching Constructed-Response Questions

Here are some suggested strategies for answering constructed-response questions:

1. **Read the question first, not the instructional scenario.** Remember, you are reading each scenario in order to get the answers to the questions right. Before you spend time reading the instructional scenario, think about why you are reading it.

2. **Actively read each instructional scenario.** Take notes, underline, keep your mind on the questions, and think as you read. You'll find more on this a bit later in this chapter.

3. **Reread each question and make a brief plan or sketch of your response points.** For example, a brief plan for the sample question about the strengths of Mr. Pope's lesson might look like this:

    Point ONE

    Specific example

    Explanation

    Point TWO

    Specific example

    Explanation

4. **Review the instructional scenario.** Make sure that you can refer specifically to the scenario and know what the question is asking for and that you can provide specific examples and details.

5. **Write your constructed response using the following format.** Write an opening sentence that states what the instructional scenario is about and what you are going to write about. By restating the question in the opening sentence of your response, you demonstrate that you know what the question is asking you to do.

- Point #1
    - Specific example from instructional scenario
    - Explanation using key terms from Part III of this book
- Point #2
    - Specific example from instructional scenario
    - Explanation using key terms from Part III of this book

6. **Review your response.** Were you clear, concise, specific, and accurate? Did you base your response on the principles of learning and teaching? Did you answer all parts of the question? Beware of the two-part constructed-response question! These questions ask about two points rather than just one. The length of your response will vary on the question. It is okay for you to use bulleted lists or brief examples. You do not need to have perfectly written paragraphs to earn a high score. The most important aspect of your response is the content you write and the accuracy of the examples you provide. If you have remembered key terms, methods, or approaches, be sure to underline them. This will help the scorers more easily see that you have answered the question concisely and accurately.

7. **Be mindful of your testing time.** You have two hours total to answer 70 multiple-choice questions, read two instructional scenarios, and answer four constructed-response questions. Each test-taker will need a different amount of time to respond to a constructed-response question accurately and completely, so I cannot give you a specific time to spend on each instructional scenario, but most people should strive to spend 25 minutes reading one instructional scenario and responding to the two questions that follow. You'll have to practice your timing before the actual test. Constructed-response questions are likely to take a large amount of your testing time, so practice the full-length tests with your watch in hand. Be sure to check your watch at the start of the test and then every 30 minutes. You want to be halfway through the full-length test after one hour.

How to Read an Instructional Scenario

Now that you better understand how to approach the constructed-response questions, you're ready to look more closely at the instructional scenario itself. All scenarios on the test are approximately the same length (800 to 850 words), and each one is followed by two constructed-response questions. None of the scenarios requires knowledge from specific content areas, such as science, physical education, social studies, mathematics, or English language arts; instead, the questions seek your knowledge of the four categories on the PLT:

- Students as Learners
- Instructional Process
- Assessment
- Professional Development, Leadership, and Community

Types of Instructional Scenarios

The next important thing you need to remember is that there are two types of instructional scenarios on the PLT test:

- Teacher-based scenarios
- Student-based scenarios

Teacher-Based PLT Scenarios

Teacher-based instructional scenarios examine the teaching practice of one or more teachers. This type of scenario will include enough information about the teaching context, lesson goals, objectives, lesson plans, teaching strategies, and interactions with students to help you identify issues of teaching and learning involved in the situation so that you can respond to the questions about the teacher's practice. It is never acceptable to respond that there is not enough information for you to answer the question. There is always enough required information included for you to come up with an answer. You also need to be able to offer new examples or suggestions, and not just repeat an example or teaching idea presented in the instructional scenario.

You can rest assured that the teaching examples are positive, and you will not be asked to make value judgments about a teacher's practice. An instructional scenario may ask you to provide an additional teaching idea or another way of looking at the teaching and learning discussed in the scenario.

Student-Based PLT Scenarios

Student-based instructional scenarios examine one student and include specific information about the student's background, strengths, or weaknesses. These scenarios may include examples of student work, excerpts of classroom conversations, and descriptions of the student's classroom learning. As with the teacher-based scenarios, the instructional scenarios will provide all the information you need to respond to the question. Remember, too, that there is nothing "wrong" with the student. Teachers must demonstrate positive approaches to teaching all children, even those who have difficulty learning in a classroom setting.

Formats of Instructional Scenarios

Both teacher-based instructional scenarios and student-based instructional scenarios can be presented in one of two formats: document-based or narrative.

Document-Based

Document-based instructional scenarios consist of three or more documents that relate to the teacher- or student-based scenario. Teacher-based scenarios might include lesson plans; assignments; student work; notes from a principal, parent, or mentor; or teacher journals. Student-based scenarios might include excerpts from class discussions, conversations between teachers and colleagues, student records, student work samples, or notes from parents, counselors, or colleagues.

Narrative-Based

Narrative-based instructional scenarios present a nonjudgmental account of a teaching or learning situation—in a school, in a set of classrooms, or in a class. This type of instructional scenario provides an excerpt of a situation. You do not know everything that is happening in this teaching or learning situation. When answering the questions, you can assume that the information about the teacher or student that is included is valuable.

Strategies for Reading Instructional Scenarios

Remember to read the constructed-response questions first and then:

1. **Read the instructional scenario carefully, closely, and actively.** By carefully, I mean read slowly enough to comprehend what you've read. By closely, I suggest that you keep the major content categories in mind (Students as Learners; Instructional Process; Assessment; and Professional Development, Leadership, and Community). By actively, I mean to make margin notes, underline key points, and think about why this information is included. Although it's okay to write on your test booklet, only your responses on the score sheet will be examined by reviewers.

2. **Ask questions as you read.** What issues about teaching and learning does this instructional scenario raise? How might the teacher help the student(s) in this situation? How else might the teacher or student resolve the issues presented?

3. **Keep in mind that all information is there for a reason.** This is why you read the constructed-response questions before reading the instructional scenario. As you read the instructional scenario, ask yourself how the information presented in the instructional scenario addresses each question.

Scoring Guide

This section of the chapter helps you focus on how to earn the highest score. It also can help you better understand what makes a less-effective response. You'll see that your answers need to be complete, relevant, appropriate, thorough, and specific to the principles of teaching and learning. Although an appropriate response must be legible and accurate content-wise, note that you are not required to use perfect spelling, grammar, or handwriting.

Criteria for Scoring

Constructed-response questions are scored on a scale ranging from 0 to 2 points. The ETS offers the following general framework for scoring constructed responses:

A response that earns a score of 2:

- Demonstrates complete understanding of the parts of the scenario that are relevant to the question
- Responds appropriately to all parts of the question
- Provides a thorough explanation that is well supported by relevant examples when an explanation is required
- Demonstrates a strong knowledge of pedagogical concepts, theories, facts, procedures, or methods relevant to the question

A response that earns a score of 1:

- Demonstrates a basic understanding of the parts of the scenario that are relevant to the question
- Responds appropriately to one portion of the question
- Provides a weak explanation supported by relevant evidence when an explanation is required
- Demonstrates some knowledge of pedagogical concepts, theories, facts, procedures, or methods relevant to the question

A response that earns a score of 0:

- Demonstrates misunderstanding of the parts of the scenario that are relevant to the question
- Does not respond appropriately to the question
- Provides an explanation that is not supported by relevant evidence
- Demonstrates little knowledge of pedagogical concepts, theories, facts, procedures, or methods relevant to the question

Note: No credit is given for blank or off-topic responses.

How Is an "Appropriate Response" Determined?

The ETS uses the term *appropriate* in its scoring guide. It's important that you consider how the ETS scorers determine "appropriate responses":

- Two or three education experts are asked to read instructional scenarios and answer the questions.
- Benchmark papers are selected from individuals who have agreed to participate in a pilot test. In other words, your test is not used to train scorers!
- The test writer uses the experts' "model answers" to develop a specific scoring guide for each instructional scenario and its questions. These models become examples of correct answers, not *the* correct answers.
- Next, the specific scoring guide is used to select model answers that serve as "benchmark papers" for training scorers for your exam.
- During the training session and when reading benchmark papers, scorers can add new answers to the scoring guide as they see fit.
- Training sessions are designed to train scorers to use benchmark papers and the specific scoring guide, not their own opinions or preferences.

How to Use the Scoring Criteria to Assess Your Own Responses

You can share your preview test or one of the upcoming full-length practice tests with an experienced teacher or educator and ask him or her to use the scoring guide to provide feedback to you. You also may want to assess your own responses and make sure you are addressing all the important aspects of each question.

Although the ETS has set up a reliable and valid way to score test-takers' written responses, you may have concerns about how your own constructed responses are scored. You can request and pay for your score to be verified. Go to www.ets.org/praxis for more information.

Apply the Strategies

In this section, you'll have a chance to try out the strategies I've gone over in this chapter. It's important to practice the suggested strategies to make sure that you feel comfortable approaching the constructed-response questions in this way. If you find an approach that works better for you and you're getting the credited responses, you should use it.

Try the suggested strategies with the following instructional scenario and its two constructed-response questions. If you'd like more practice reading instructional scenarios and answering constructed-response questions, turn to any of the full-length practice tests in Part IV of this book.

Practice

Directions: The following questions require you to write short answers, or "constructed responses." You are not expected to cite specific theories or texts in your answers; however, your knowledge of specific principles of learning and teaching will be evaluated. Be sure to answer all parts of the question. Write your answers in the space provided.

Scenario: Justin

Justin is an 11-year-old boy in the fifth grade. He is taller and heavier than most children in his age group, but socially and emotionally he appears to be less mature. He recently moved with his three older sisters, father, and mother, who is a naval officer, to a school district that largely serves a Navy community because there is a military base within walking distance of the school. Justin has moved five times in his life and is very quiet on the first days of school. After those first few days, he has more overt difficulties. Mr. Hole is concerned that Justin may not be adjusting well to his new classroom, school, and community.

Mr. Hole does not have a cumulative record for Justin because it takes the school system several days, sometimes weeks, to request and obtain records through the central administration department in this large district that serves many transient students. This is a common problem in the school system and one that Mr. Hole has learned to work around. He has planned several "get-to-know-you" activities during the first weeks of school. Based on early observations and pre-testing, Mr. Hole has the following assessments to report to the Multi-Disciplinary Team (MDT) in late September:

- On the first few days of school, Justin wore his hood over his head and face and was very quiet. He seemed to observe the happenings in the classroom with interest but did not participate in any discussions or activities. He was compliant when it came time to go to lunch, recess, and specialists' classes, such as Art, Music, and Physical Education. At lunch and recess, he sat alone.

- Justin has difficulty following class rules, especially raising his hand, taking turns, and remaining in his own personal space during work time and when walking in the hallway.

- On September 10, Justin initiated an argument in the coatroom that escalated to shouts and Justin throwing his backpack at a fellow student.

- Justin's instructional reading level is at the beginning of grade 3. His comprehension appears to be very weak, yet his vocabulary and word-recognition skills are strong.

- Justin is also below grade-level expectations in mathematics. He has difficulty with multiplication and division as well as problem solving that requires two or more steps.

- On September 15, Justin and another boy were observed taking candy from the teacher's desk. The other boy admitted his part in the incident, but Justin adamantly denied that he took the candy.

- Justin enjoys drawing and music.

- On September 23, Justin took a new set of crayons from a boy in class, broke each one in half, and left them on the student's desk.

- On the same day, Justin had a fistfight on the playground and was suspended from school.

Mr. Hole is concerned about Justin's adjustment to his new school. He knows that students who move a lot, such as those like Justin who come from military families, often have gaps in academics, low self-esteem, or difficulty behaving. Mr. Hole has thought carefully about Justin's learning situation and has tried the following strategies to support Justin's transition to his new school and classroom before requesting the MDT meeting on Justin's behalf:

- **"Classroom buddy":** A student who also has moved frequently and is high-achieving and polite has been assigned to help Justin as needed.
- **Individual attention:** Mr. Hole has allowed Justin to do special jobs for the teacher and has spent one-on-one time with him during a special "lunch with the teacher."
- **Authentic praise:** Mr. Hole has made it a point to recognize Justin's positive contributions to the classroom and in his individual work.
- **Lower-than-grade-level tasks:** Mr. Hole has given Justin mathematics problems and reading materials at his instructional level. This has led to some social difficulties, though, because Justin is the only student performing this far below grade level.
- **Home/school communication:** Mr. Hole has communicated with Justin's family by phone and in one parent-teacher conference. Justin's family appears to be concerned about and involved in Justin's educational progress, although his mother has recently left the United States for a six-month tour in the Persian Gulf. The parents reported that Justin has had difficulty with behavior at other schools and has frequent outbursts at home, although he has not received any specialized services or testing for his behavior difficulties.

The MDT reviewed this information and samples of Justin's work and determined that Justin should be evaluated by the school psychologist and an educational diagnostician to determine the cause of his behavioral difficulties and his below-grade-level performance.

1. Identify TWO additional strategies that Mr. Hole could use to support Justin's learning in his fifth-grade classroom while he waits for results from the school psychologist and the educational diagnostician. Be sure to base your response on the principles of instruction.

2. Suggest TWO additional ways that Mr. Hole and Justin's parents can work together to support Justin's behavior and academic performance in school. Be sure to base your response on the principles of professionalism, leadership, and community.

Answers and Explanations

1. This question requires you to read carefully about Mr. Hole's attempts to help Justin and to describe two new ideas that Mr. Hole has not tried. These ideas must be grounded in principles of learning and teaching. You may have other "reasonable responses" that would be considered exemplary responses by the ETS. The following points are potential examples, so you'll want to ask an experienced educator to read your response for specific feedback and suggestions regarding the content you provide in your response.

   Here are a couple suggestions you could offer Mr. Hole:

   - **Clearly review the classroom <u>rules and expectations</u> that the class as a group has determined and then start a <u>behavior plan</u> for Justin that includes natural consequences for his choices.** William Glasser's "choice theory" suggests that students must have choices, clear expectations, and natural consequences for their actions.

   - **Try placing Justin in a <u>heterogeneous cooperative group</u> for reading or math work instead of providing individual work.** Students working in effective cooperative groups develop a sense of camaraderie, and peer support often provides intrinsic motivation for students to make positive contributions to the group.

   Once you think of the two specific suggestions that do not duplicate any of the ideas Mr. Hole has already tried, it's time for you to write an opening sentence and then provide your two points with specific examples and details. The sample response shows you the format to use, so that you are clear and concise, using your strategic reading and responding. This approach has saved my students lots of time on the actual test!

   Sample response: Mr. Hole is a fifth-grade teacher who has a new student, Justin, who is having difficulty adjusting to his new school placement. Mr. Hole has tried many strategies, such as individual attention and authentic praise, with little success so far. Here are TWO additional suggestions Mr. Hole might try:

   - **Clear expectations and classroom rules:** Justin may not be able to fully understand the norms that have been established in this fifth-grade classroom. He also may be experiencing a cultural mismatch between his home rules, his former classroom rules, and the new rules for this classroom. In <u>Glasser's choice theory</u>, students need clear expectations, choices, and natural consequences for their actions. Justin may have an improved <u>sense of belonging</u> and feel more <u>empowered</u> after the unsettling feeling of moving so often in his life. He also may need more <u>explicit expectations</u> and <u>natural consequences</u> to help Justin improve his <u>self-control</u>.

   - **Cooperative learning groups:** In cooperative learning groups, the teacher creates heterogenous groups of four to six students to work together to complete school assignments. It's important that Mr. Hole assigns roles, <u>such as facilitator or summarizer</u>, and designs the assignment so that students must be interdependent to successfully complete the task. For example, Justin could play the role of the group gatekeeper to ensure that the group's work begins and ends on time. Each student would be responsible for a subsection of the whole task. All assignments also would be turned in to Justin, who would be responsible for compiling them into a completed whole. Without the gatekeeper, the group's work could not be accomplished and Justin would be held <u>individually accountable</u> for the group's productive use of class time.

2. Mr. Hole has had one parent-teacher conference and one parent phone call. In this question, you are to suggest two additional ways Mr. Hole and Justin's parents can work together to support Justin. For all students, but particularly those who move a lot, it is very important for the teacher and the student's caregivers to be involved in the student's school life. Because they know the child best, the caregivers may be in a better position to "teach" the student in each transition between schools and communities. Your suggestions must be grounded in principles of learning and teaching. You may have other "reasonable responses" that would be considered exemplary responses by the ETS.

   Here are a couple of ideas to help Mr. Hole and Justin's family work together to support his education:

   - **Establish a home/school log between teacher and parents.** Each day Mr. Hole writes a brief note to Justin and his parents about Justin's accomplishments as well as one difficulty, if there was one. He also asks for ways to help Justin at school and suggests ways to help Justin at home. Justin's parents write back to

Mr. Hole, and Justin signs his name at the end of the journal entry to signify that he has read his teacher's and his parents' entries. If Justin would like to contribute to the journal, he can. Note that this log highlights the many positive contributions Justin is making and de-emphasizes his poor choices or difficulties.

- **Mr. Hole and Justin's parents can communicate via e-mail and the Internet using a school web page that Mr. Hole creates.** This page identifies each homework assignment, lists the class rules and expectations, and shows examples of student work. In addition, Mr. Hole could post suggested reading and websites to enrich or remediate the week's lessons. Mr. Hole and Justin's parents could communicate more specifically and privately about Justin's daily or weekly progress via e-mail.

Sample response: Mr. Hole has communicated with Justin's family by phone and in one parent-teacher conference. Justin's family appears to be concerned about and involved in Justin's educational progress. The parents reported that Justin has had difficulty with behavior at other schools and has frequent outbursts at home, although he has not received any specialized services or testing for his behavior difficulties. Here are TWO additional ways that Mr. Hole and Justin's parents can work together to support Justin's behavior and academic performance in school:

- **Home/school daily log:** Each day Mr. Hole writes a brief note to Justin and his parents about Justin's accomplishments, as well as one main difficulty, if there was one. He also asks for ways to help Justin at school and suggests ways to help Justin at home. Justin's parents write back to Mr. Hole, and Justin signs his name at the end of the journal entry to signify that he has read his teacher's and his parents' entries. If Justin would like to contribute to the journal, he can. This gives Justin a choice and may empower him to make better behavior choices in the classroom. It is important that this log highlights the many positive contributions Justin is making and communicates only the observable behaviors Justin may be exhibiting. Glasser defines Mr. Hole's role in this classroom as a lead teacher, not a boss teacher. Justin and his family need to interpret that Mr. Hole is a teacher who is there to support Justin and to encourage him to learn as best he can.

- **E-mail or Internet communication:** Justin's mother was recently deployed for a six-month tour in the Persian Gulf. Communicating via e-mail or through a teacher web page may help both his mother and his father to take an active interest and involvement in Justin's education. Justin may be missing his mother or worried about her safety, so the use of technology may be part of the solution to motivating Justin to work on his self-control while at home and at school.

PART III

PREPARING FOR THE CONTENT OF THE PLT

Chapter 7

Students as Learners

The Students as Learners category of questions on the PLT test requires that you know the key theories, theorists, and terms in the areas of psychology of learning and student differences. You will be expected to apply your knowledge in this category to both the multiple-choice and constructed-response questions. We know that students learn and develop in a variety of ways. You will recognize many of the names of the theorists and theories from your education psychology or psychology of learning coursework. If you are like my students (and me when I was in your shoes), you will find the outline format of this section helpful as you prepare to answer questions about how people learn and learning theory on the PLT. If you are completely unfamiliar with a term, theory, or theorist, in addition to reviewing the outlines I have provided in this chapter, I suggest that you review a current edition of an education psychology textbook or search the Internet for reliable sources on this topic.

Student Development and the Learning Process

Learners construct knowledge, not receive knowledge, based on what they already know and believe. In this section, we will review the five theoretical approaches to the study of learning. In addition, we will examine the patterns of human cognitive, physical or psychomotor, affective, and social and moral development that can inform our work with students. On the PLT test, you may be asked to discuss one or more of the five theoretical perspectives on how people learn and describe the characteristics of a typical child in each stage in the cognitive, physical, social, and moral domains. You will be expected to know what is both typical and atypical within each stage. In addition, you should be able to use the names of key theorists, use the names of their theories, and describe the theory in action in a classroom setting.

Theoretical Approaches to Understanding How People Learn

Psychologists have studied the learning process for over a hundred years, and their findings guide our instructional practices. There are five theoretical perspectives to help us better understand how our students learn, each of which you should be able to define and identify in an instructional context. In addition, you should know key terms and the psychologists who have advanced these theories.

Behaviorism

Behaviorists view learning as a process of accessing and changing associations between stimuli and responses. We see behaviorist theory in action in approaches to classroom management and establishing positive contexts for learning. B. F. Skinner, Edward Thorndike, and Ivan Pavlov are key contributors to our understanding of how people learn from a behaviorist perspective.

Social Cognitive Theory

Social cognitive theorists focus on the ways people learn from observing one another. The key theorist you should know from the social cognitive theoretical perspective is Albert Bandura.

Information Processing Theory

Information processing theorists focus more on what happens inside the learner's mind, considering the processes of learning, memory, and performance. Some theorists believe that the human mind works a lot like a computer processor; therefore, they contributed terms such as *storage, retrieval, working memory,* and *long-term memory.* In addition, information processing theorists advanced the idea of building students' declarative, procedural, and conditional knowledge. There are no key theorists whose names you should know on the PLT test, but you should be able to define and provide examples of several terms to know that involve what happens inside a learner's mind. The "Terms to Know" section follows the "Theorists" section in this chapter.

Constructivism

Constructivist theorists suggest that people construct or create knowledge (as opposed to absorb knowledge) based on their experiences and interactions. Some theorists focus on *individual constructivism* (how one person makes meaning); others focus on *social constructivism* (how people gain knowledge by working together). You should understand the work of Jean Piaget and Jerome Bruner, whom you will learn about in the next section of this chapter.

Sociocultural Theory

Sociocultural theorists posit that the combination of social, cultural, and historical contexts in which a learner exists have great influence on the person's knowledge construction and the ways teachers must organize instruction. A key theorist to study is Lev Vygotsky and his theory on the zone of proximal development.

Theorists and Theories

In this section, you will find the names of key theorists and their contributions to our understanding of how people learn. Each theorist helps us to better understand the patterns of human development in one or more of the following domains: cognitive, physical or psychomotor, affective, social, or moral development.

Bloom, Benjamin

Theories: Bloom's Taxonomy of learning domains

Bloom is a key theorist you should know. His taxonomy of three learning domains—cognitive, performance or psychomotor, and affective—impact the way educators write lesson objectives, plan learning activities, and assess student performance. I address writing objectives in Chapter 8 and assessing student performance in Chapter 9, but you should remember these categories and examples of verbs organized by domain:

- **Cognitive domain (knowledge):** The cognitive domain involves the mind and skills or strategies one uses, and is organized into six levels from lowest order to higher order:
  - **Knowledge:** To recall information or data; key words: *defines, lists, locates, recites, states*
  - **Comprehension:** To understand meaning of instruction and problems; key words: *confirms, describes, discusses, explains, matches*
  - **Application:** To use a concept in a new situation; key words: *applies, builds, constructs, produces, reports*
  - **Analysis:** To separate concepts into parts; key words: *analyzes, categorizes, compares, debates, investigates*
  - **Synthesis:** To build a pattern from diverse elements; key words: *composes, designs, hypothesizes, implements, revises*
  - **Evaluation:** To make judgments; key words: *assesses, concludes, critiques, justifies, solves*
- **Performance or psychomotor domain (skills):** The performance domain involves manual or physical skills one uses, which are divided into seven subdivisions:
  - **Perception:** To use senses to guide motor activity; key words: *chooses, describes, identifies, selects*
  - **Set:** To be ready to act; key words: *begins, moves, proceeds, shows, states*
  - **Guided responses:** To use trial and error, imitation to learn (early stage); key words: *copies, traces, follows, reproduces, replicates*
  - **Mechanism:** To respond in a habitual way with movements performed with some confidence and proficiency (intermediate stage); key words: *assembles, calibrates, displays, manipulates*
  - **Complex overt responses:** To perform complex movement patterns skillfully (skillful stage); key words (same as mechanism, but adverbs or adjectives are added to indicate proficiency): *assembles quickly, calibrates accurately, displays proficiently, manipulates quickly and accurately*

- **Adaptation:** To use well-developed skills and be able to modify to fit special requirements; key words: *adapts, alters, changes, rearranges, revises*
- **Origination:** To create new movement patterns to fit a specific problem or situation; key words: *arranges, builds, composes, constructs, initiates, originates*
- **Affective domain (attitude):** The third learning domain in Bloom's Taxonomy is the affective domain. There are five subdivisions in the affective domain:
  - **Receiving phenomena:** To be aware, to have selected attention; key words: *asks, follows, gives, locates, uses.*
  - **Responding to phenomena:** To actively participate; key words: *answers, discusses, helps, tells*
  - **Valuing:** To determine worth; key words: *demonstrates, differentiates, explains, invites, joins*
  - **Organization:** To organize values into priorities; key words: *arranges, alters, modifies, relates, synthesizes*
  - **Internalizing values:** To control behavior using own value system; key words: *acts, discriminates, listens, modifies, verifies*

Bandura, Albert

Theory: Social (or observational) learning theory

Children learn by observing others. In a classroom setting, this may occur through modeling or learning vicariously through others' experiences. One important concept from social learning theory is **distributed cognition,** in which a person is able to learn more with another or in a group than he or she might be able to do alone.

Bruner, Jerome

Theories: Discovery learning and scaffolding

Bruner thought learning was an active process in which learners construct new ideas or concepts based on knowledge or past experiences. Discovery learning teaching techniques feature methods to allow a student to discover information by himself or herself or in a group. Scaffolding involves instructional supports provided to a student by an adult or a more capable peer in a learning situation. The more capable a student becomes with a certain skill or concept, the less instructional scaffolding the adult or peer needs to provide. Scaffolding might take the form of a teacher reading a portion of the text aloud and then asking the student to repeat read the same sentence, for example.

Dewey, John

Theory: Learning through experience

Dewey is considered the father of progressive education practice that promotes individuality, free activity, and learning through experiences, such as project-based learning, cooperative learning, and arts-integration activities. He theorized that school is primarily a social institution and a process of living, not an institution to prepare for future living. He believed that schools should teach children to be problem solvers by helping them learn to think as opposed to helping them learn only the content of a lesson. He also believed that students should be active decision makers in their education. Dewey advanced the notion that teachers have rights and must have more academic autonomy.

Erikson, Erik

Theory: Eight stages of human development

Erikson was a psychologist who suggested the following eight stages of human development, which are based on a crisis or conflict that a person resolves.

Stage	Age Range	Crisis or Conflict	Key Event
Stage 1: Infancy	0–1	Trust vs. mistrust	Feeding
Stage 2: Toddler	1–2	Autonomy vs. doubt	Toilet training
Stage 3: Early childhood	2–6	Initiative vs. guilt	Independence
Stage 4: Elementary and middle school	6–12	Competence vs. inferiority	School
Stage 5: Adolescence	12–18	Identity vs. role confusion	Sense of identity
Stage 6: Young adulthood	18–40	Intimacy vs. isolation	Intimate relationships
Stage 7: Middle adulthood	40–65	Generativity vs. stagnation	Supporting the next generation
Stage 8: Late adulthood	65–death	Integrity vs. despair	Reflection and acceptance

Gilligan, Carol

Theory: Stages of the ethic of care

Gilligan's work questions the male-centered personality psychology of Freud and Erikson, as well as Kohlberg's male-centered stages of moral development. She proposed the following stage theory of the moral development of women:

Approximate Age Range	Stage	Goal
Not listed	Pre-conventional	Individual survival
Transition from selfishness to responsibility to others		
Not listed	Conventional	Self-sacrifice is goodness
Transition from goodness to truth that she is a person, too		
Maybe never	Post-conventional	Principle of nonviolence

Kohlberg, Lawrence

Theory: Theory of moral development

Elementary-school-aged children are generally at the first level of moral development, known as "Pre-conventional." At this level, some authority figure's threat or application of punishment inspires obedience.

The second level, "Conventional," is found in society. Stage 3 is characterized by seeking to do what will gain the approval of peers or others. Stage 4 is characterized by abiding the law and responding to obligations.

The third level of moral development, "Post-conventional," rarely is achieved by the majority of adults, according to Kohlberg. Stage 5 shows an understanding of social mutuality and genuine interest in the welfare of others. Stage 6 is based on respect for universal principles and the requirements of individual conscience.

Age Range	Stage	Social Orientation
Birth to 9	Pre-conventional	1. Obedience and punishment 2. Individualism, instrumentalism, and exchange
9–20	Conventional	3. "Good boy/good girl" 4. Law and order
20+ or maybe never	Post-conventional	5. Social contract 6. Principled conscience

Maslow, Abraham

Theory: Hierarchy of needs

Maslow is known for establishing a theory of a hierarchy of needs in which certain lower needs must be satisfied before higher needs can be met.

1. **Physiological needs:** These very basic needs include air, water, food, sleep, and sex.
2. **Safety needs:** These needs help us establish stability and consistency in a chaotic world, such as a secure home and family. Safety needs sometimes motivate people to be religious, ensuring the promise of safety after we die.
3. **Love and belongingness needs:** This next level of the hierarchy occurs when people need to belong to groups: churches, schools, clubs, gangs, families, and so on. People need to be needed at this level.
4. **Esteem needs:** At this level, self-esteem results from competence or the mastery of a task and the ensuing attention and recognition received from others.
5. **Self-actualization:** People who have achieved the first four levels can maximize their potential. They seek knowledge, peace, oneness with a higher power, self-fulfillment, and so on.

Montessori, Maria

Theory: Follow the child

Montessori was an Italian physician whose philosophy and teaching practice still affect many early-childhood programs and charter schools today. She believed that childhood is divided into four stages, which are divided into six-year intervals:

- Birth–6
- 6–12
- 12–18
- 18–24

This belief led to multi-aged groupings of students based on their period of development. Montessori also believed that adolescence can be divided into two levels:

- 12–15
- 16–18

She believed that there are three stages of the learning process:

- **Stage 1:** Introduce a concept by lecture, lesson, experience, book read-aloud, and so on.
- **Stage 2:** Process the information and develop an understanding of the concept through work, experimentation, and creativity.
- **Stage 3:** "Knowing," which Montessori described as possessing an understanding of something that is demonstrated by the ability to pass a test with confidence, teach the concept to another, or express understanding with ease.

Montessori established her school Casa Bambini in 1908. Modified versions of her approach to education are found in some U.S. schools today.

Piaget, Jean

Theory: Stages of cognitive development

Piaget, a cognitivist theorist, suggested four stages of cognitive development:

Stage	Age Range	Behavior
Sensorimotor	Birth to 2	Explore the world through senses and motor skills.
Preoperational	2–7	Believe that others view the world as they do. Can use symbols to represent objects.
Concrete operational	7–11	Reason logically in familiar situations. Can conserve and reverse operations.
Formal operational	11 and up	Can reason in hypothetical situations and use abstract thought.

Skinner, B. F.

Theory: Operant conditioning

Skinner is thought of as the grandfather of behaviorism, as he conducted much of the experimental research that is the basis of behavioral learning theory. His theory of operant conditioning is based on the idea that learning is a function of change in observable behavior. Changes in behavior are the result of a person's response to events (stimuli). When a stimulus-response is reinforced (rewarded), the individual becomes conditioned to respond. This is known as *operant conditioning*.

Vygotsky, Lev

Theory: Zone of proximal development

Vygotsky is credited with the social development theory of learning. He suggested that social interaction influences cognitive development. His learning theory, called the zone of proximal development, suggests that students learn best in a social context in which a more able adult or peer teaches the student something he or she could not learn on his or her own. In other words, teachers must determine what a student can do independently and then provide the student with opportunities to learn with the support of an adult or a more capable peer. I think of this as finding the "just right" next lesson to teach a student and provide an appropriate level of educational support.

Terms to Know

In addition to knowing the key theories and theorists, you should know specific terms to both include in your constructed-response questions and identify in the multiple-choice questions. In this section, you will find several common terms from this area of content, along with the definition of the term.

Accommodation

Responding to a new event or object by changing an existing scheme or creating a new scheme. For example, after my refrigerator leaked the sixth time, I called the repairperson again, but referred to my paperwork to see when my repair contract would end and began to search sales circulars for new refrigerators.

Assimilation

Responding to a new event or object that is consistent with an existing scheme. For example, when my refrigerator leaked water for the third time, I called the repairperson, because I have a repair contract.

Classical Conditioning

A process of behavior modification by which a person comes to respond in the desired manner to what was once a neutral stimulus. In classical conditioning the neutral stimulus has been repeatedly presented along with an *unconditioned stimulus* (a natural, inherent stimulus, such as the smell of food) that eventually elicits the desired response. For example, in the classroom, the teacher creates a positive, supportive classroom environment that eventually conditions a student with anxiety or fears about speaking in front of the class to find this experience enjoyable.

Also see "Operant Conditioning," in this section.

Conservation

Knowing that a number or amount stays the same even when rearranged or presented in a different shape. For example, a child understands that there has been no change when 6 ounces of milk is poured into a short, round glass in which the glass appears half-full and when the same 6 ounces of milk is poured in a tall, cylindrical glass that appears only a quarter of the way full.

Constructivism

A philosophy of learning based on the premise that people construct their own understanding of the world they live in through reflection on experiences.

Convergent Thinking

A process of gathering several pieces of information together to solve a problem.

Creativity

New and original behavior that creates a culturally appropriate product.

Declarative, Procedural, and Conditional Knowledge

We know that knowledge is constructed, not absorbed. In order to acquire knowledge, one must develop declarative knowledge (knowledge of what is), procedural knowledge (knowledge of how to), and conditional knowledge (knowledge of when again). Teacher can use these types of knowledge to develop lesson plans that explicitly help students know what they are learning (declarative knowledge), how to complete the thinking procedure or to acquire the content (procedural knowledge), and when students can transfer or use this new knowledge in another situation or experience (conditional knowledge).

Discovery Learning

Teaching methods that enable students to discover information by themselves or in groups.

Disequilibrium

One's inability to explain new events based on existing schemes, which is usually accompanied by discomfort.

Disposition

A person's natural tendency to approach learning or problem solving in certain ways. A student's disposition is an important factor to consider and to attempt to shape, if needed, so that the student can succeed in complex or challenging learning tasks.

Distributed Cognition

A process in which two or more learners share their thinking as they work together to solve a problem.

Divergent Thinking

The process of mentally taking a single idea and expanding it in several directions.

Equilibration

Movement from equilibrium to disequilibrium and then back to equilibrium again.

Equilibrium

One's ability to explain new events based on existing schemes.

Long-Term Memory

The part of memory that holds skills and knowledge for a long time.

Metacognition

A person's ability to think about his or her own thinking. Metacognition (*meta* = between; *cognition* = thinking) requires self-awareness and self-regulation of thinking. A student who demonstrates a high level of metacognition is able to explain his or her own thinking and describe which strategies he or she uses to read or to solve a problem.

Operant Conditioning

Operant conditioning is a form of psychological learning in which the learner modifies his or her own behavior based on the association of the behavior with a stimulus. For example, operant conditioning is at work when a teacher sets up a system of punishments and reinforcements for classroom behaviors. Operant behavior involves one's interaction with the environment and the behavior that is maintained by its consequences; whereas, classical conditioning deals with the conditioning of "reflexive behaviors," which are evoked by *antecedent conditions* (those that came before the event). Instructional objectives, contingency contracts, computer-assisted instruction, and mastery learning all have theoretical foundations that are based on operant conditioning.

Also see "Classical Conditioning," in this section.

Problem Solving

To use existing knowledge or skills to solve problems or complex issues.

Readiness to Learn

A context within which a student's more basic needs (such as sleep, safety, and love) are met and the student is cognitively ready for developmentally appropriate problem solving and learning.

Response

A specific behavior that a person demonstrates.

Scaffolding

Instructional supports provided to a student by an adult or a more capable peer in a learning situation. The more capable a student becomes with a certain skill or concept, the less instructional scaffolding the adult or peer needs to provide. Scaffolding might take the form of a teacher reading aloud a portion of the text and then asking the student to repeat the same sentence, for example.

Schema

A concept in the mind about events, scenarios, actions, or objects that have been acquired from past experience. The mind loves organization and must find previous events or experiences with which to associate the information, or the information may not be learned.

Self-Efficacy

A belief that one is capable.

Self-Regulation

The process of taking control of one's own learning or behavior.

Stimulus (Stimuli)

A specific object or event that influences (positively or negatively) a person's learning or behavior.

Transfer

The ability to apply a lesson learned in one situation to a new situation. For example, a student who has learned to read the word *milk* in a book about cows and then goes home and reads the word *milk* successfully in a note that a parent left on the counter. *Positive transfer* occurs when something is learned at one point that facilitates learning or performance in another situation. *Negative transfer* occurs when something learned interferes with the learning or performance in another situation.

Working Memory

The part of memory that holds and actively processes a limited amount of information for a short amount of time.

Zone of Proximal Development

This is a key concept in Vygotsky's theory of learning. The zone of proximal development suggests that students learn best in a social context in which a more-able adult or peer teaches the student something he or she could not learn on his or her own.

Students as Diverse Learners

In this section, review the content outline to ensure that you understand the number of variables that affect how students learn, recognize areas of exceptionality in learner behavior, understand the implication and application of legislation related to diverse learners, know a variety of approaches for accommodating students with exceptionalities, and recognize the traits of learners such as intellectually gifted learners, English language learners, and learning disabled learners.

Theorists and Theories to Know

In this section, I review key theorists and theories relevant to the diversity of students as learners.

Gardner, Howard

Theory: Multiple intelligences

Gardner developed his theory of multiple intelligences in the early 1980s. These multiple intelligences are as follows:

- **Verbal/linguistic intelligence:** Students who have verbal/linguistic intelligence learn best by saying, hearing, and seeing words.
- **Logical/mathematical intelligence:** Students who have logical/mathematical intelligence are conceptual thinkers, compute arithmetic in their heads, and reason problems easily.
- **Visual/spatial intelligence:** Students who have visual/spatial intelligence think in mental pictures and visual images.
- **Bodily/kinesthetic intelligence:** Students who have bodily/kinesthetic intelligence are athletically gifted and acquire knowledge through bodily sensations.
- **Musical intelligence:** Students who have musical intelligence have sensitivity to pitch, sound, melody, rhythm, and tones.
- **Interpersonal intelligence:** Students who have interpersonal intelligence have the ability to engage and interact with people socially; these students have a strength in making sense of their world through relationships.
- **Intrapersonal intelligence:** Students who have intrapersonal intelligence have the ability to make sense of their own emotional lives as a way to interact with others.
- **Naturalist intelligence:** Students who have naturalist intelligence have the ability to observe nature and see patterns.

Hidalgo, Nitza

Theory: Three levels of culture

- **Concrete:** This is the most visible and tangible level of culture. It includes surface-level aspects, such as clothes, music, games, and food.
- **Behavioral:** This level of culture is defined by our social roles, language, and approaches to nonverbal communication and helps us situate ourselves organizationally in society (for example, gender roles, family structure, and political affiliation).
- **Symbolic:** This level of culture involves our values and beliefs. It is often abstract yet is key to how one defines himself or herself (for example, customs, religion, and mores).

Moll, Luis

Theory: Funds of knowledge

Moll's research into the lives of working-class Mexican-American students and their families revealed that many families had abundant knowledge that the schools did not know about. His view that multicultural families have funds of knowledge contends that these families can become social and intellectual resources for a school. Moll urges teachers to seek out and use these funds of knowledge and to gain a more positive view of these capable, but misjudged, students and their families.

Variables That Affect How Students Learn

In addition to knowing the key theories and theorists, you should know that there are a number of variables that affect how students learn, including learning style, gender, culture, socioeconomic status, prior knowledge and experiences, motivation, self-confidence, self-esteem, cognitive development, and maturity and language development or acquisition. In this section, you will find several common terms organized by variable, along with the definition of the term. Study these terms and approaches to help you respond to multiple-choice and constructed-response questions about the ways these variables affect how individual students learn and perform tasks.

Learning Style

Students have specific cognitive or learning styles, which are ways the student tends to approach classroom tasks and cognitive activities. Following are three learning styles you will want to be familiar with for the PLT and classroom success:

- **Auditory (or aural) learner:** Auditory learners process information through listening. They learn through lectures, discussions, listening to audio files, repeating information, and reading aloud.
- **Kinesthetic or tactile learner:** Kinesthetic or tactile learners process information through moving, touching, and doing. They learn through acting out scenes, using manipulatives, putting on plays, moving to the beat, pacing out measurements on the sidewalk, and so on.
- **Visual learner:** Visual learners process information through seeing. They learn through visual displays, films, illustrated books, handouts, graphic organizers, bulletin boards, and so on.

Gender

Gender plays an important role in students' sense of self, learning, and emotions. When children are between ages 3 and 6, they become aware of physical gender differences. As children grow, we find that males tend to read less for pleasure than girls do, and males are more likely to have difficulty with handwriting, reading, and stuttering. Females tend to have stronger verbal skills, and males tend to have strength in visual-spatial reasoning. In the classroom, we may find that females prefer to tell us about something and males prefer to show us. Research has demonstrated that males are more prone to engage in an argument in a class discussion than females are.

Culture

Students come from a wide variety of cultures, and successful teachers help students define and understand their own cultures to deal with mutual misconceptions and to inform future lesson planning. Hidalgo's three levels of culture—concrete, behavioral, and spiritual—can be discussed to build a sense of relatedness and respect in the classroom. Sometimes a family's expectations may differ from a teacher's expectations for a student. Making positive connections between schoolwork and home life can support students' success.

Acculturation is a process of learning and adopting the customs and values of another culture. This is particularly important as we consider how student's culture is similar to or different from the culture of the educational setting. Children who are not from the dominant culture may have difficulty adjusting to or understanding the implicit rules that will gain them access and power in mainstream educational setting, which may result in cultural mismatch. For example, children may come from a culture that expects them to be seen and not heard; therefore, they may present themselves as quiet or particularly obedient and may need explicit help in learning to contribute ideas to a class discussion. Some children may have been taught to not make eye contact with an adult who is talking or disciplining; instead, they are to cast their eyes downward as a sign of respect. In some cultures, people speak with and over one another when making a point; in other cultures, people are to take turns one at a time, listening quietly to the speaker.

Teachers must take the time to understand the family and community values that a child may be bringing to the classroom, so that each child can be respected for his or her cultural ways and not disciplined or devalued for any cultural differences. Families can provide valuable funds of knowledge (Moll) for teachers to tap into and utilize for successful lessons. Communicating with families, knowing the school community, and appreciating the differences and similarities of family cultures will help teachers offer instruction that meets the needs of all children.

Motivation

Teachers need to understand that motivation is an important factor in how students learn and perform in the classroom. Ways teachers can enhance student motivation include the following:

- Arrange the classroom to minimize disruptions and maximize student attention.
- Use authoritative teaching techniques, which includes communicating respect, acceptance, and caring while giving students choices and a sense of self-determination in the classroom.
- Establish and promote a sense of community and belongingness for all students.
- Establish rules and procedures that are clear and meaningful.
- Enforce classroom rules equitably and consistently.
- Organize for simultaneous management of activities and smooth transitions.

- Engage students in meaningful, authentic, and productive work that deemphasizes grades and highlights students' strengths.
- Monitor class activities continually, providing meaningful, authentic feedback to students.

See the section "Student Motivation and the Learning Environment," later in this chapter, for more information.

Socioeconomic Status (SES)

Research indicates that children from low-SES households and communities develop academic skills more slowly than children from higher SES groups do. Young children from low-SES households tend to have lower pre-academic skills. School systems in low-SES communities often are under-resourced, which negatively affects students' academic progress. Low-SES children tend to have fewer resources to help with their academic achievement, such as materials and someone to help with homework or to read to them. In addition, they tend to suffer from the effects of their families' unemployment, a high level of migration of the best qualified teachers in their schools, and the effects of limited access to healthcare.

School and education systems can make a difference for children from SES households and communities. When children from lower-SES households were involved in programs that paired them with adults to help them with academics, the children reported higher effort in their academic achievement. Schools have shown significant gains for their low-SES students when they focus on improving teaching and learning, create an information-rich environment, build learning communities, provide continuous professional development, involve parents and caregivers, and increase funding and resources.

Prior Knowledge and Experiences

Teachers must understand their students' physical, social, emotional, and cognitive development. Student progress is seen on a developmental continuum, and growth, or lack of progress toward age-appropriate growth, must be recorded and reported to parents. A student whose knowledge or behavior is outside the norm for the age group may need differentiated instruction or other supports. For example, a 10-year-old student who has a well-developed understanding of working with fractions may need more challenging work with fractions than his or her grade-level peers. Likewise, a student who is unable to form the letters of the alphabet in second grade may need supports for fine motor skill development.

Self-Concept and Self-Esteem

As Maslow's theory reminds us, students whose most fundamental needs (nutrition, emotional care, and so on) are not met may experience social or emotional issues in school until those needs are met. Teachers can report observations to families, the principal, school social workers, nurses, or mental-health professionals to advocate for the child's basic needs. Differences in SES among students and between the teacher and the students can lead to misunderstandings about students' social and emotional needs. For example, a student from a low or high SES may act out or demand excessive attention. A teacher must consciously set high expectations for all students regardless of SES and modify instructional methods to help each student achieve a sense of success in the classroom. Some students have physical or mental-health issues that lead to social or emotional issues in the classroom. Collaborating with families and colleagues who know the child's needs can help the teacher create a successful learning environment for the student. Students who have low self-esteem, have anxiety, or are easily distractible also may present social or emotional behavioral issues in school.

Cognitive Development

Students create or construct meaning in a variety of ways. According to Piaget's theory, children move from the preoperational to the concrete operational and then the formal operational stage during their school years. One student can make sense more easily through listening, while another prefers visual information. Successful teachers understand their students' thinking styles—especially for those with learning disabilities and those who are accelerated—and plan lessons to accommodate a wide variety of ways to make meaning.

It's important to know each of Piaget's cognitive develop stages and to be able to give examples of what a learner can do at each stage:

- **Concrete operational stage:** Children approximately ages 7 to 11 think in logical terms, not in abstract terms. Students in this age range require hands-on experiences to learn concepts and manipulate symbols logically.

- **Formal operational stage:** Children approximately ages 11 to 15 develop hypothetical and abstract thinking. Students at this stage can use logical operations to work abstract problems. For example, students at this stage are better able to complete algorithms when working math problems as opposed to using math manipulatives to understand the problems.

- **Preoperational stage:** Children show evidence of thinking in the preoperational stage sometime from the age of 2 through the age of 6 or 7. In this stage, children are able to make mental representations of unseen objects, but they cannot use deductive reasoning. In other words, the child is unable to draw conclusions from a set of premises or use logic to solve problems.

- **Sensorimotor stage thinker:** This stage begins at birth and typically lasts until a child is 2 years old. The most important feature of thinking at this stage involves making sense of the world through the senses. For example, a child in the sensorimotor stage likes to pick up objects and then drop them or put them in his or her mouth. Children in this stage do not understand that once an object is hidden, such as in a game of peek-a-boo, the object is still there, just hidden; this is known as the concept of object permanence.

Maturity

Teachers must understand their students' physical, social, emotional, and cognitive development. Student progress is seen on a developmental continuum, and growth or lack of progress toward age-appropriate growth must be recorded and reported to parents. A student whose knowledge or behavior is outside the norm for the age group may need differentiated instruction or other supports.

Language Development and Acquisition

Many students' first language is not English; furthermore, students within the same school district may speak in various dialects. Students whose first language is not English or who use a dialect that is not standard American English (SAE) benefit when a teacher views these differences as sources of enrichment in the classroom. Students who are new to speaking English may experience a period of silence and may prefer listening in the classroom, which is to be expected and respected. Language is always used in a social context; therefore, students who have linguistically diverse language patterns may "code-switch." In other words, a student may use a certain dialect on the playground and another in the classroom. One dialect, African American English Vernacular (AAEV), or Ebonics, is spoken by many African Americans. Which teaching methods are best for children who speak AAEV became a political controversy in the 1990s. Teaching techniques similar to those used with children whose primary language is not English appear to be most successful for children who speak with dialects of SAE.

Physical Issues

Successful teachers communicate with the school nurse, families, school mental-health professionals, teacher assistants, and the student to understand how the student's physical issues can be supported so that the child can learn at an optimal level. Physical issues common among students include vision, hearing, and mobility problems. Some students suffer from asthma, seizures, and allergies. A teacher should be aware of any physical issues and procedures to ensure the child's safety, especially during field trips, fire drills, and other emergencies.

Areas of Exceptionality and Impact on Student Learning

Although we know that learners have patterns of cognitive, physical, social, and moral development, we also know that people have exceptions that vary from the norm, which may have an impact on student learning. In this next section, study the terms and definitions to help you identify areas of exceptionality and explain how there are a variety of ways these exceptionalities may impact student learning in the classroom.

Terms to Know

In addition to knowing the key theories and theorists, you should know specific terms to identify in the multiple-choice questions and include in your constructed responses. Below, you will find several common terms from this area of content, along with the definition of the term.

Acculturation

Process of learning and adopting the customs and values of another culture.

Attention deficit disorder (ADD)

Attention deficit disorder may be found to impact student learning. Students with ADD may have difficulty focusing, following directions, organizing, making transitions, completing tasks, and so on. The diagnosis is made by a medical professional, not by school personnel.

Attention deficit hyperactivity disorder (ADHD)

Attention deficit hyperactivity disorder may be found to impact student learning. Students with ADHD may have many of the same difficulties as students with ADD (difficulty focusing, organizing, and so on) but may also have difficulty with impulsivity, sitting still, and taking turns. The diagnosis is made by a medical professional, not by school personnel.

Auditory (or Aural) Learner

Auditory learners process information through listening. They learn through lectures, discussions, listening to tapes, repeating information, and reading aloud.

Autism Spectrum Disorders

Autism spectrum disorders may include autism, Asperger's syndrome, and other pervasive developmental delays (PDD). Students with these disorders have difficulty socializing and communicating. Asperger's syndrome is a form of autism in which the person has normal intelligence and language development, yet has marked difficulties with social skills and social cognition.

Behavior Disorder (BD)

Behavior disorder (also known as conduct disorder) is a type of disruptive behavior disorder in children and adolescents. Students with behavior disorder may violate rules, show aggression toward people or animals, destroy property, or practice deceitfulness.

Cognitive Style

A person's way of perceiving and remembering information; the way the person thinks or solves problems.

Concrete Operational Thinker

Children approximately ages 7 to 11 think in logical terms, not in abstract terms. Students in this age range require hands-on experiences to learn concepts and manipulate symbols logically.

Developmental Delays

Developmental delays are identified by a medical professional in a person before the age of 22. The student may have one or more of the following difficulties: self-care, expressive or receptive language, learning, mobility, self-direction, capacity for independent living, or economic self-sufficiency.

Disposition

A person's overall approach and temperament when solving problems, learning, and thinking.

English Language Learner (ELL), English as a Second Language (ESL), or Primary Language not English (PLNE)

ELL, ESL, and PLNE are terms used to describe students who are learning English as a second (or third or fourth) language. Teachers of bilingual and multilingual students can support English language acquisition and learning in several important ways, including building on students' culture, supporting students' proficiency in their native language, giving students time to learn English (two years for conversational English, seven years for academic English), and offering opportunities for students to work and talk in small groups.

Formal Operational Thinkers

Children approximately ages 11 to 15 develop hypothetical and abstract thinking. Students at this stage can use logical operations to work abstract problems. For example, students at this stage are better able to complete algorithms when working math problems as opposed to using math manipulatives to understand the problems.

Functional Mental Retardation (MR)

Functional MR is a diagnosis determined by a medical professional for a child who exhibits difficulties with the following: age-specific activities (for example, playing), communication, daily living activities, and getting along with others.

Giftedness

Significantly higher than usual ability or aptitude in one or more areas.

Kinesthetic Learner

Kinesthetic learners process information through moving and doing. They learn through acting out scenes, putting on plays, moving to the beat, pacing out measurements on the sidewalk, and so on.

Learning Disabilities (LDs)

Learning disabilities are determined by a multidisciplinary team or a physician. Students with learning disabilities are not learning to their potential in one or more areas, such as reading, writing, oral language, or mathematics. There are three main types of learning disabilities: reading, mathematics, and writing. Common characteristics of students with learning disabilities include the following:

- Poor coordination
- Poor depth perception
- Short attention span
- Impulsivity
- Difficulty following simple directions

- Hyperactivity
- Perseveration (getting stuck on one thought or idea or repeating a behavior)
- Distractibility
- Delayed speech
- Limited vocabulary
- Difficulty recalling what is heard
- Dislike of being touched or cuddled
- Inappropriate use of words
- Low or high pain threshold
- Overreaction to noise

Physical or Sensory Difficulties

Physical or medical conditions that affect school performance significantly, such as health, visual, or hearing impairments.

Tactile Learner

Tactile learners process information through touching. They learn through active involvement with the physical world—hands-on experiences.

Visual Learner

Visual learners process information through seeing. They learn through visual displays, films, illustrated books, handouts, graphic organizers, bulletin boards, and so on.

Legislation to Know

You should study the following key laws that have impacted teaching and learning in U.S. public schools.

American with Disabilities Act (ADA)

The ADA is a federal law, enacted in 1990, that prohibits discrimination on the basis of a person's disability for all services, programs, and activities provided or made available by state and local governments. The ADA is not dependent on the receipt of federal funds.

Due Process

Due process is a set of procedures or safeguards that give students with disabilities and their parents/guardians extensive rights. Those rights include notice of meetings, opportunities to examine relevant records, impartial hearings, and a review procedure.

Family Educational Rights and Privacy Act (FERPA)

Legislation passed in 1974 that gives students and parents access to school records and limits others' access to those records.

Individuals with Disabilities Act (IDEA)

The IDEA is a federal statute, enacted in 1990, that has resulted in several grant programs to states in educating students with disabilities. The IDEA specifically lists types of disabilities and conditions that render a child entitled to special education.

Individualized Education Plan (IEP)

An IEP is a written plan for a student with disabilities developed by a team of professionals (teachers, special educators, school psychologists, and so on) and the child's parents or caregivers. An IEP is based on an evaluation by the child's multidisciplinary team (MDT) and describes how the child is doing presently, what the child's learning needs are, and what services the child will need. IEPs are reviewed and updated yearly. They are required under Public Law 94-142, the IDEA.

Inclusion

Although there is no official legal definition, inclusive education practices strive to educate a child with disabilities in his or her neighborhood school and in the regular education classroom as much as possible. The key goal is to foster a sense of belonging and full acceptance of the learner within the school and classroom community.

Least Restrictive Environment (LRE)

The LRE is the educational setting that, to the maximum extent appropriate, allows students with disabilities to be educated with nondisabled peers.

Section 504 of the Rehabilitation Act

Section 504 of the Rehabilitation Act of 1973 is a civil rights law prohibiting discrimination against individuals with disabilities by federally assisted programs or activities. Eligibility for protection under Section 504 is not restricted to school-age children; it covers individuals from birth to death.

Accommodations and Modifications

Of course, students have diverse learning needs. Teachers must learn to make accommodations (adjustments to the student's task, learning environment, or supports provided without changing academic achievement expectations) and modifications (changes to curriculum expectations because the curriculum is beyond the student's level of ability). Following are several common accommodations and modifications teachers make to help meet the needs of all their students.

Alternative Assessments

Alternative assessments include anecdotal records of student behavior, portfolios, checklists of student progress, and student/teacher conferences. Alternative assessments can be contrasted with traditional assessments. Alternative assessments provide a view of a student's process and product, which is closely related to the instructional activity. Traditional assessments usually provide a view only of the product of the learning, such as the score on a test, and may not be as closely related to classroom instruction.

Differentiated Instruction

According to Tomlinson (1995), differentiated instruction involves a flexible approach to teaching. A teacher plans and implements varied approaches to teaching content, process, and product in an effort to respond to student differences in readiness, interests, and learning needs.

Testing Accommodations

Common testing accommodations provided to students include, but are not limited to, providing longer testing times, giving untimed tests, having someone write or type for the student (scribe), offering Braille or large-print reading materials, allowing for short breaks during testing, and providing sign-language interpretation for directions. Offering approved testing accommodations for students who qualify for those accommodations is a desirable differentiation of assessment and is especially important on higher-stakes tests and standardized assessments. Accommodations do not change the content of the test or the academic expectations; they merely provide the needed supports to help the student meet academic expectations.

Student Motivation and the Learning Environment

In this part of our review of Students as Learners, we turn to the key theories, theorists, and terms related to student motivation and to setting up a classroom environment conducive to student learning.

Theorists and Theories to Know

In this section, we review key theorists and theories relevant to student motivation and the learning environment.

Ausubel, David

Theory: Advance organizer

Ausubel suggested a teaching technique called the advance organizer. The advance organizer is introduced before learning begins and is designed to help students link their prior knowledge to the current lesson's content (for example, semantic webs, KWL charts, and concept maps).

Bandura, Albert

Theory: Modeling

Observational learning, or modeling, requires several steps:

1. **Attention:** Attending to the lesson
2. **Retention:** Remembering what was learned
3. **Reproduction:** Trying out the skill or concept
4. **Motivation:** Willingness to learn and ability to self-regulate behavior

Canter, Lee

Theory: Assertive discipline

Teachers clearly communicate expectations and class rules and follow through with expectations. Students have a choice to follow the class rules or face consequences. If a child chooses not to follow a rule, he or she will have to experience the consequences of that action.

Glasser, William

Theories: Choice theory (also known as control theory)

Teachers focus on students' behavior, not students, when resolving classroom conflicts. Teachers who subscribe to choice theory use class meetings to change behavior in the classroom. Students who have a say in the rules, curriculum, and environment of the classroom have greater ownership of their learning. Glasser's approach emphasizes creating a safe space to learn ("our space to learn") and is designed to promote intrinsic motivation to learn and to behave in the classroom.

Kounin, Jacob

Theory: With-it-ness

Teachers must have with-it-ness, or an awareness of what is happening in their classrooms, in order to manage their classrooms well. In addition, teachers must pace their lessons appropriately and create smooth transitions between activities.

Maslow, Abraham

Theory: Hierarchy of needs

Maslow is known for establishing a theory of a hierarchy of needs, in which certain lower needs must be satisfied before higher needs can be met.

1. **Physiological needs:** These very basic needs include air, water, food, sleep, and sex.
2. **Safety needs:** These needs help us establish stability and consistency in a chaotic world, such as a secure home and family. Safety needs sometimes motivate people to be religious, ensuring the promise of safety after they die.
3. **Love and belongingness needs:** This next level of the hierarchy occurs when people need to belong to groups (churches, schools, clubs, gangs, families, and so on). People need to be needed at this level.
4. **Esteem needs:** At this level, self-esteem results from competence or the mastery of a task and the ensuing attention and recognition received from others.
5. **Self-actualization:** People who have achieved the first four levels can maximize their potential. They seek knowledge, peace, oneness with a higher power, self-fulfillment, and so on.

Pavlov, Ivan

Theory: Classical conditioning

Pavlov conducted classical conditioning experiments with dogs in the 1920s. He found that dogs naturally salivate in an *unconditioned response* (one that is naturally occurring) to the *unconditioned stimulus* (one that automatically produces an emotional or physiological response) of food. He showed that dogs also salivate in response to a *conditioned stimulus* (one that creates an emotional or physiological response after learning), and he called that response (salivation) a *conditioned response* (a learned response to something that was previously neutral). Many people credit Pavlov for the experimental basis of behaviorist learning theory.

Skinner, B. F.

Theory: Operant conditioning

Skinner is thought of as the grandfather of behaviorism, because he conducted much of the experimental research that is the basis of behavioral learning theory. His theory of operant conditioning is based on the idea that learning is a function of change in observable behavior. Changes in behavior are the result of a person's response to events (stimuli). When a stimulus-response is reinforced (rewarded), the individual becomes conditioned to respond. This is known as operant conditioning.

Terms to Know

In addition to knowing the key theories and theorists, you will need to know specific terms to identify in the multiple-choice questions and include in your constructed responses. In this section, you will find several common terms from this area of content, along with the definitions of the terms.

Attribution

When one constructs a causal explanation for failure or success.

Classical Conditioning

A process of behavior modification by which a person comes to respond in the desired manner to what was once a neutral stimulus. In classical conditioning, the neutral stimulus has been presented repeatedly along with an *unconditioned stimulus* (a natural, inherent stimulus, such as the smell of food) that eventually elicits the desired response. For example, in the classroom, the teacher creates a positive, supportive classroom environment that eventually conditions a student with anxiety or fears about speaking in front of the class to find this experience enjoyable.

Also see "Operant Conditioning," later in this section.

Cognitive Dissonance

A feeling of mental discomfort in which new information conflicts with beliefs or previously learned information.

Extrinsic Motivation

Motivation that comes from external sources or from outside a person. Stickers, behavior charts, and incentives for learning all are examples of extrinsic motivators for students.

Facilitating Anxiety vs. Debilitating Anxiety

A low level of anxiety, known as facilitating anxiety, actually can enhance student learning and performance on classroom assessments. For example, when a teacher assigns a section of reading for homework and then mentions that there may be a pop quiz on the reading assignment, students may be more apt to complete the reading based on the potential discomfort of taking a quiz. Debilitating anxiety, on the other hand, is high level and detracts from a student's ability to concentrate on the task or even attempt the task out of fear and intense concern.

Intrinsic Motivation

Motivation that comes from within, or from inside a person. Providing students time to reflect on goals and achievements or helping students see what they have learned and how it is important are examples of intrinsic motivators for students.

Learned Helplessness

A tendency for a person to be a passive learner who is dependent on others for guidance and decision making.

Operant Conditioning

Operant conditioning is a form of psychological learning in which the learner modifies his or her own behavior based on the association of the behavior with a stimulus. For example, operant conditioning is at work when a teacher sets up a system of punishments and reinforcements for classroom behaviors. Operant behavior involves interaction with the environment, and the behavior is maintained by its consequences. On the other hand, classical conditioning deals with the conditioning of reflexive behaviors, which are evoked by *antecedent conditions* (those that came before the event). Instructional objectives, contingency contracts, computer-assisted instruction, and mastery learning all have theoretical foundations that are based on operant conditioning.

Also see "Classical Conditioning," earlier in this section.

Punishment

The goal of punishment is to weaken or extinguish an undesired behavior. According to Skinner's operant conditioning theory, presentation punishment involves adding a new stimulus to decrease an undesired behavior; removal punishment involves taking away a desired stimulus to decrease an undesired behavior.

Reinforcement

The process or action of strengthening or reinforcing a behavior. According to Skinner's operant conditioning theory, *positive reinforcement* involves a stimulus to increase a desired response; *negative reinforcement* involves removing a negative stimulus to increase a desired response.

The following chart has helped my students to correctly learn and recall the differences between reinforcement and punishment:

	Positive	Negative
Reinforcement (increases desired behavior)	+ Sticker	– Less homework
	Presentation	Removal
Punishment (decreases undesired behavior)	+ Homework	– No recess

Self-Determination

Self-determination is a paradigm that suggests that humans have a basic need for autonomy when it comes to the courses their lives take.

Chapter 8

Instructional Process

In this chapter, you will study key theorists, theories, and terms related to instruction and assessment content covered on the PLT test for both the multiple-choice questions and the constructed-response questions. This chapter covers at least 35 percent of the content on the PLT test. Carefully study the content in this chapter, as well as the other chapters in Part III of this book. As I mentioned in the Chapter 7, this outline is meant to help you streamline your test-preparation efforts. You should not have to spend your test-preparation time gathering several books and other sources of information. You can use this chapter to determine what you already know and what you need to learn, or to learn about instructional processes. If you need to learn this content for the first time, you then may want to refer back to a current education psychology text or perform an Internet search for a reliable source to give you more complete information about this subject.

Planning Instruction

In this section, we review common aspects of planning a great lesson.

Standards

Standards are specific expectations of what a student must know and be able to do. National, state, and local standards guide curriculum and instruction in the United States. There are two types of standards:

- **Performance standards:** Set the level of performance expectation for student groups (for example, first-graders or 5- to 7-year-olds). Performance standards generally are set at the state and local levels and generally can be found on your state's department of education website or your local school district's website.

- **Content standards:** Provide expectations for the knowledge students must demonstrate. You should be familiar with the content standards for your discipline, which you can find on the websites for the following national specialized professional associations. Many states have adopted the Common Core State Standards in English Language Arts/Literacy and Mathematics to guide curriculum development and student assessment in K–12 schools.

For more specific information on the standards in your content area, go to the following websites:

- **English Language Arts:**
  - Common Core State Standards: www.corestandards.org
  - International Reading Association: www.reading.org
  - National Council of Teachers of English: www.ncte.org
- **Foreign Languages:**
  - American Council on the Teaching of Foreign Languages: www.actfl.org
- **Mathematics:**
  - Common Core State Standards: www.corestandards.org
  - National Council of Teachers of Mathematics: www.nctm.org
- **Science:**
  - National Science Teachers Association: www.nsta.org
- **Social Studies:**
  - National Council for the Social Studies: www.ncss.org

Standards-Based Instruction

Jay McTighe and Grant Wiggens suggest that teachers use a backward design when planning for standards-based instruction. In the past, educators typically sought materials or the content to teach to students, planned the lesson, and then designed an assessment to measure student progress. With backward design, teachers are encouraged to begin with the student's learning needs first, then plan the assessment, and finally plan the rest of the lesson activities and select materials. Educators now know we need to start with the students' needs first, plan assessments next, and then finalize our lesson plan.

As you use backward design to plan instruction, ask yourself the following three questions:

- **What do students need to know and be able to do?** Write objectives to answer this question. Be sure to write lesson objectives that include all levels of Bloom's Taxonomy, not just the knowledge level. You should be familiar with the state and national standards for content and student performance and know how to use them in lesson planning. In addition, you should be familiar with local curriculum guidelines and how a scope and sequence informs your lesson planning.

- **How will you assess what students know and are able to do?** Assessing a lesson's objectives is an important part of backward design. Know how to set criteria for student performance of a lesson's objectives and show how you can measure and evaluate what students know and are able to do. Key assessments include criterion-referenced tests, norm-referenced tests, performance assessments, and rubrics. Chapter 9 of this book is dedicated in its entirety to the topic of assessment.

- **What goes into planning the lesson?** Planning the lesson involves deciding on your teaching methods, ways to engage your students in the lesson content, and how to differentiate instruction so that all students achieve your lesson objectives. In the "Lesson Planning" section, later in this chapter, you'll find specific suggestions for formatting and planning your lesson.

Theory into Practice

I covered many educational psychology terms and theorists in Chapter 7, some of which you see below. On the PLT test, not only will you need to know theories, but you will need to give practical examples of theories in practice.

Cognition

The students you will teach have a variety of ways to think about and learn events. Teachers need to understand how the human memory operates and to help students learn to retrieve information from **short-term and long-term memory.** Students learn more efficiently and effectively when they focus **attention** on the lesson. To help students with memory and attention, teachers can guide students to **rehearse** information, to use **mnemonics** to aid in **recall** or retrieval of information, and to allow students to work with others. Working with other students and adults fosters an opportunity for **distributed cognition**—a process in which two or more people work collaboratively to share ideas and solve problems together, resulting in new cognition that may not have been possible without the other. Other key terms related to cognition with practical examples follow:

- **Schema:** Students' organized sets of facts about a concept or event can be used to help make connections between information in long-term memory (known as schema) and new concepts and ideas. For example, a learner may know a lot about puppies—their eating habits, characteristics, types of play, and need for naps. Teachers can use students' schema about puppies to help students compare and contrast the behaviors and attributes of other living things, such as frogs, coyotes, and cats.

- **Information processing:** Information-processing theorists help us understand that students need to know what they are learning and ways this new information fits with previous information, which is known as **declarative knowledge.** Teachers can elicit declarative knowledge from students by stating lesson objectives, reviewing the practical implications for the lesson content, and reminding students to review what they have learned and to summarize. Another important level of knowledge is **procedural knowledge,** which is the set of steps or procedures on how to do something. For example, when students participate in a science lab, the teacher can aid cognition by establishing clear step-by-step instructions and asking students to recall the procedures and to discuss what they are doing during the lab. The purpose of learning (and the joy of teaching!) is helping students to show what they know and are able to do, not only in the classroom, but also in their everyday worlds. This **transfer** of knowledge is also known as **conditional knowledge** building. Teachers can aid in conditional knowledge construction through guided practice, careful review, and extended practice in new situations.

- **Mapping:** Teachers can use concept mapping and similar graphic organizers to help students see the relationships and interrelationships among concepts and new ideas.

Social-Learning Theory

Let students talk! This is the easiest way to remember the central tenets of social-learning theory. In practice, this means that the teacher needs to allow students to work in pairs and small groups. Following are some specific examples of social-learning theory in practice:

- **Modeling:** Teachers and more capable peers provide important positive models for learners. In the classroom, you might see the teacher sharing his or her thinking while reading a challenging vocabulary word, discussing strategies to figure out the meaning of the word.

- **Reciprocal determinism:** Alfred Bandura posits that people's behavior is controlled by the individual through internal cognitive processes and external events in the environment. In the classroom, you might see reciprocal determinism in action when a child acts out based on his or her dislike of school. The teacher or administrator then responds to the student's acting out by keeping him or her inside during recess, fueling the student's dislike of school further and leading the student to act out more the next day.

- **Vicarious learning:** This type of learning occurs through social interaction and/or observation. Teachers can promote vicarious learning by allowing students to work with more capable peers, mentors, or adults. Students can be vicariously reinforced (in which a learning response increases when another person is reinforced for the response) or vicariously punished (in which the response decreases when another person is punished for that same response).

Constructivism

Individual learners construct or create knowledge through their interactions with the environment and others. When we take a constructivist theoretical perspective on learning, we examine the internal processes of the human learning experience. Following are key theories from constructivism and practical examples:

- **Problem-based learning:** Activities in which students learn new information and skills while working to solve real-world problems. For example, in my fourth-grade classroom my students and I tried to figure out how large dinosaurs were by drawing them to scale on the playground using chalk. We gathered facts online and used graph paper and measurement tools to solve the problem of how to draw the dinosaur to real-life scale.

- **Zone of proximal development:** Lev Vygotsky's notion of zone of proximal development suggests that the teacher or a more capable peer is capable of helping the students learn something just beyond his or her intellectual reach with cognitive support. In the classroom, this might come in the form of a teacher assistant aiding a student learning the 9s multiplication table through teaching patterns to help the student recall the facts.

- **Scaffolding:** Scaffolding is related to the zone of proximal development. In the previous example, the teacher assistant is providing scaffolding to the student learning the multiplication tables.

- **Discovery learning:** Discovery learning fosters inquiry rather than didactic (for example, lecture) methods for learning. Students are encouraged to ask questions and to hypothesize as they deduce the concepts and principles of the lesson experience.

- **Inquiry model:** An inquiry approach to teaching involves students in the process of exploring the natural and/or material world in an effort to help them discover meaning. In social studies, a teacher might have students listen to the music of the Civil War to examine the themes and issues raised in the lyrics. In science, a teacher might have students experiment with a variety of soil types to see which absorbs more water. In mathematics, a teacher might have students use tiles to create tessellations to discover patterns and relationships among the geometric shapes.

Behaviorism

Behaviorism is a theoretical perspective on learning that focuses on what can be observed and measured in learning—people's behaviors (responses) and events in the environment that promote behavior (stimuli). The following terms and practical examples related to behaviorism are important to know on the PLT:

- **Conditioning:** B. F. Skinner describes operant conditioning as a form of learning in which the response increases as a result of reinforcement. In the classroom, conditioning may take the form of praise for a job well done, stickers on a chart for a second-grader, a free homework pass for a middle-schooler, or time to work with peers in the library for a tenth-grader.

- **Intrinsic and extrinsic rewards:** In the previous example, all the rewards are extrinsic rewards—those that are awarded to the student from another. Intrinsic rewards are internal motivators such as joy in learning to play a challenging piano piece.

- **Reinforcement:** Reinforcement can be positive or negative. Examples of positive reinforcement in the classroom include giving a student extra recess time for working hard during reading period and giving students extra credit for correctly answering a challenging question on an exam. You'll note that with positive reinforcement, the reward is *given to* the learner and results in improved learning. Negative reinforcement involves reinforcement by *taking away* something and results in improved learning. Examples include limiting the time you spend on Facebook in order to study for the PLT test or the teacher taking away homework for the night because students worked so hard on a project.

- **Punishment:** Punishment in the classroom is meted out to *decrease* the frequency of the response it follows. There are two types of punishment: removal punishment and presentation punishment. *Removal punishment* involves removing something in order to decrease an undesired behavior; for example, after a student continually talks during the lesson, the teacher keeps him or her in for recess in order to decrease his or her talking in class. *Presentation punishment* involves presenting a new stimulus—one the learner finds unpleasant—to decrease undesired behavior; for example, the teacher assigns additional homework when a student does not do the assignment the night before.

Curriculum

- **Scope:** Scope, as it relates to curriculum, is the material or skill to be taught. For example, during my fourth-grade dinosaur unit, the scope of what I was teaching was measurement—specifically, length and distance, in U.S. standard and metric systems.

- **Sequence:** Sequence, as it relates to curriculum, is the order in which you teach the information. During the dinosaur-measurement unit, first I helped my students become familiar with measurement tools in the classroom, then they completed exercises to build skills, and finally we moved to the more complex (and exciting!) task of drawing the dinosaurs to scale on the playground.

- **Standards of learning:** As you have seen in this chapter, teachers use state and national standards to guide curriculum and lesson development. Standards also are used to design assessment systems. In the state of Virginia, standards of learning is a standardized testing system to measure student academic outcomes.

- **Curriculum frameworks:** Curriculum frameworks list the broad goals of a school district, state, or school, and provide subject-specific outlines of course content, standards, and performance expectations.

- **Curriculum planning:** In order to plan a curriculum, teachers must plan a scope and sequence for a series of units of study, align the curriculum to the district and state standards of learning, and then plan the assessment system to measure students' progress.

- **Emergent curriculum:** An emergent curriculum is based primarily on the interests of children. The teacher works together with family and other community members to set possible direction for a project and then determine the actual curriculum based on student interest. An emergent curriculum is most often used in early-childhood settings, although examples can be found in alternative-model secondary schools that emphasize personalization of student learning and community involvement in education.

Unit Planning

I have discussed curriculum planning, which involves planning instruction for the school year and linking the curricular plan to what knowledge and skills have come before and will come after. Now I will turn to unit planning, a subset of the curriculum, which is a cohesive, interconnected set of lessons usually lasting two to six weeks.

- **Understanding by Design:** State-of-the-art curriculum and unit planning involves a process known as Understanding by Design (UbD), suggested by Jay McTighe and Grant Wiggens. UbD uses the principles of backward design that I have covered previously in this chapter to design a unit of instruction based on what students need to know and be able to do, how to assess student learning, and how to plan a series of lessons.

- **Interdisciplinary-unit instruction:** Interdisciplinary-unit instruction incorporates information from two or more content areas (for example, science, mathematics, physical education, technology, and literacy) to help students see the connections and real-life links across the disciplines. An interdisciplinary unit on the Harlem Renaissance, for example, might include lessons on jazz music and the literary works of Zora Neale Hurston and Langston Hughes, as well as social studies lessons about Greenwich Village, Harlem, and the 1920s and 1930s.

- **Thematic-unit instruction:** Thematic-unit instruction is a way to organize curriculum around large themes. Thematic units are integrated across several content areas, such as reading, social studies, math, and science. Thematic units might include such topics as dinosaurs, friendship, justice, civil rights, or patterns.

Lesson Planning

As I have discussed in the "Curriculum" and "Unit Planning" sections of this chapter, lesson planning is a subset of unit planning. Again, we use backward design to guide our thinking process. Planning a thorough, content-rich, standards-based lesson plan is a hallmark of an effective teacher. There are a variety of templates for lesson planning. In this section, I offer one fail-safe model to use on the PLT test (and in your own classroom!), but you should feel free to use more familiar formats for lesson planning that you may have learned from your teacher-education program or teaching experiences. This template is based on Madeline Hunter's effective teaching model, which emphasizes the following parts of an effective lesson:

- Objectives
- Standards of performance
- Anticipatory set or advance organizer
- Teaching (which includes modeling, student input, directions, and checking for understanding)
- Guided practice and monitoring
- Lesson closure and practice

Use this template to help you remember the key parts of a lesson plan, so that when you are asked to plan a lesson on the PLT test, you will be able to quickly recall all the parts of a lesson. After reviewing this template, read on for further explanation of each part of a well-planned lesson.

Lesson Plan Component	Planning Notes
Grade level of students; topic or title of the lesson	
Instructional objectives	The student will . . . Base objectives on Bloom's Taxonomy of the cognitive, affective, and /or performance domains.
National, state, and/or local standards addressed	Cite standards here.
Materials	List all the materials you'll need for the lesson so you are well prepared. Be sure to choose age-appropriate, quality materials for your students.

Lesson Plan Component	Planning Notes
Learner and environment factors	Include learner factors such as the target grade level for this lesson, as well as any specific learning styles or modalities the lesson addresses. Consider environment factors, including the room arrangement, arrangement of materials, need for student movement, noise-level expectations, and so on.
Opening . . . Develop anticipatory set . . . Make connection to previous lesson . . . Share lesson objectives (in student-friendly terms)	Let your students know what they will be learning and why it is important. As a teacher, it is important to activate, assess, and/or develop prior knowledge during the opening of the lesson.
Middle . . . Model strategy or content to be learned . . . Provide guided practice of strategy or content . . . Monitor student progress	Understand that this is where a lesson varies greatly depending on the instructional method chosen: direct, indirect, independent, experiential, and/or interactive.
Closing . . . Lesson closure . . . Assign independent practice or homework	Summarize, connect to prior knowledge, discuss process or products of the lesson, review key concepts, preview tomorrow's lesson, and so on.
Assessment	Must align carefully with objectives and standards. Develop assessments, which may be informal and/or formal; formative or summative See Chapter 9 for more information on assessment.

Writing Objectives

Teachers must set clear expectations for a lesson and unit of study and ensure that the lesson objectives link to the assessment(s) planned. It is important to help students see what they are learning, why they are learning it, and how this learning connects to other experiences and events. Student ownership of the lesson goals makes a difference in student achievement. Setting goals and objectives for a lesson must be focused, yet not so narrow as to diminish the content's importance. Objectives should have three parts: (1) measurable verb, (2) criteria, and (3) conditions. Here's an example of a measurable objective:

> The student will analyze (1) a short story and a poem and then provide three accurate comparisons (2) and contrasts on a Venn diagram graphic organizer (3).

The objective above is a cognitive objective. You will notice the measurable verb *analyze* is a term from Bloom's Taxonomy in the cognitive domain. Objectives also can be from Bloom's affective or performance/psychomotor domains. Following you will find examples of objectives for each of the Bloom's Taxonomy domains:

- **Affective objective:** The student will actively participate in discussion (1) on the U.S. Civil War after viewing primary documents (2), making two or three key points based on fact (3).
- **Cognitive objective:** The student will summarize (1) two main causes (3) of the Civil War after discussing the third chapter of the textbook (2).
- **Performance/psychomotor objective:** The student will act out (1) a battle from the Civil War (2) demonstrating three accurate facts of the battle (3).

Citing Standards

Once you determine what you want students to know and to be able to do, you should turn to your district/state standards to cite how your objectives align to the standards. For example, the objectives about the Civil War above would lead me to the district and state standards for Social Studies/History as well as the Common Core State Standards for literacy/speaking listening, which are located in the English Language Arts standards. Once you locate the standard that matches the measurable verb and content you are teaching, you can write the number of the standard and element in the section of the lesson plan for citing standards.

Providing Quality Materials for Enrichment and Remediation

A wide range of quality print and nonprint materials should be available to enrich and remediate instruction for all your learners. This means that you will want to have a range of more complex and less complex materials, visuals, audio, magazines, film, books, and more during your unit of study. Instructional technology (for example, computers, CD-ROMs, video, the Internet, downloads, online streaming, and so on) serves as a tool for learning in schools today. Teachers must become proficient in their use of technology to teach and must also help their students skillfully and critically use technology to support learning. Primary source materials or documents are statements or records of law, government, science, mathematics, or history in their original, unaltered form. Public documents such as census records and law reports, as well as private records like personal journals and letters, are examples of primary sources. Teachers use primary sources from libraries, local collections, and the Internet to help their content come alive with real people's everyday lives. Guest speakers or experts you might Skype with online also provide an excellent opportunity for your students to learn. You are responsible for ensuring that the materials—print or nonprint—you choose for your unit of study are accurate, are free from bias or discrimination, and represent a variety of viewpoints or perspectives.

Recognizing Learner and Environment Factors

When a teacher differentiates instruction to meet learner needs, he or she is responding to the wide range of abilities present in the classroom. Carol Ann Tomlinson is a foremost expert in this area. Teachers can differentiate content, learning processes, or products. Content encompasses the concepts, principles, skills, and strategies we want our students to learn. Teachers strive to teach the same core content to all students; to do so successfully, they must differentiate. Learning processes are the methods one uses to present content. Products are the culminating events that demonstrate what the students have learned.

There are a variety of methods to differentiate instruction, including the following:

- **Tiered instruction:** The teacher offers the same core content to each student but provides varying levels of support for students.
- **Curriculum compacting:** The teacher finds the key content that must be learned and reduces the number of examples, activities, or lessons so that a student—usually one who is advanced—can demonstrate the content and move on to another level.
- **Curriculum chunking:** The teacher breaks down a unit's content into smaller units or chunks and provides support and frequent feedback to the student as he or she demonstrates understanding of each chunk of information.
- **Flexible grouping:** Flexible groups are groups that change as the students' learning needs change. For example, students who need to better understand how to make inferences work together until they are proficient, and then the group disbands.

In addition to planning for specific learner differences, the teacher also must consider how to create and maintain a classroom environment that fosters student academic, social, and emotional development. Students must feel safe both physically and emotionally to take risks, to work in groups, and to respond to questions. Teachers must be mindful of those who may be neglected, bullied, involved in gangs, or who are a part of a clique.

Opening of the Lesson

Also known as set induction, creating an **anticipatory set** is an activity at the start of a lesson used to set the stage for learning in order to help motivate students and activate prior knowledge. For example, an English lesson on Harper Lee's novel, *To Kill a Mockingbird,* might begin with primary-source documents of trials set during the civil rights movement.

Middle of the Lesson

The middle of the lesson actively involves students in learning. The teacher decides which type of instructional method(s) will be best to achieve the lesson's objectives. There are five broad categories of instructional methods:

- **Direct instruction:** Direct instruction is an overarching method for teaching students that includes carefully planned lessons presented in small, attainable increments with clearly defined goals and objectives. Direct instruction methods tend to be more teacher centered and include specific instructional strategies, such as demonstration, lecture, mastery learning, review of student performance, and student examination.

  - **Demonstration:** Teacher demonstrations involve explicitly showing students what something is or how to do something. For example, a science teacher might demonstrate the proper use of a Bunsen burner in a lab.

  - **Lecture:** Teachers use the lecture as a means to transmit information. Lectures may be text based, aided by technology, oral essays, or participatory.

  - **Mastery learning:** When a teacher uses a mastery-learning approach, he or she uses a group-based, teacher-centered, instructional approach to provide learning conditions for all students to achieve mastery of assigned information.

- **Indirect instruction:** Indirect instructional methods are primarily student centered and include instructional strategies such as concept mapping, inquiry, discovery learning, case studies, and problem solving.

  - **Discovery learning:** Discovery learning fosters inquiry rather than didactic (for example, lecture) methods for learning. Students are encouraged to ask questions and to hypothesize as they deduce the concepts and principles of the lesson experience.

  - **Inquiry model:** An inquiry approach to teaching involves students in the construction of knowledge through active engagement in questioning and learning.

- **Independent instruction:** Independent instructional methods provide structured opportunities for students to learn at their own paces. Examples of independent instructional strategies include learning contracts, research projects, instructional technology-mediated instruction, learning centers, and distance learning.

  - **Distance learning:** Distance education or distance learning focuses on teaching methods integrated with technology, delivering instruction to students who are at their computers, not in a traditional classroom.

  - **Learning centers:** Learning centers are designed to enable individuals or small groups of students to interact with course content after the teacher has taught the focus lesson or while the teacher is leading small-group sessions. The success of learning centers in the classroom depends on several factors: the teacher's planning, management, and supervision, as well as the student's ability to work independently and with others. Purposes of learning centers vary. They may include providing an alternative to seat work, rewarding students, providing enrichment or remediation, fostering collaboration, and accommodating individual learning styles.

    Common learning centers in an elementary classroom are blocks, computers, writing, reading, math games, listening, and creative play. Though they're used less frequently at the middle-school and high-school levels, learning centers at these levels include writing, conferencing, independent reading, and computers.

- **Experiential and virtual instruction:** This instructional approach ties information to an "anchor" and also may be known as anchored instruction. In other words, the student uses concrete applications of the concept being taught (the anchor) to connect what he or she is learning to a concrete experience. For example, students learning about the civil rights movement might simulate walking over the Edmund Pettus Bridge at a local river bridge. Doing so teaches students through hands-on and experiential learning and provides a concrete experience for the students to build on. The teacher (in this real-life example, my colleague Mrs. Wildman) can then anchor the students to this experience as they read and discuss the civil rights movement during their social studies lessons. Experiential learning also can occur virtually, or using computer-simulation experiences. For example, frog dissections can now be conducted using virtual frog-dissection software! Experiential learning also can occur through field trips, which are excursions off the main campus of a school that provide students with an opportunity to gain deeper, real-life, hands-on knowledge about a concept of study. Field trips commonly are used after the culmination of a unit, but field trips used at the beginning of a unit can build students' background knowledge and provide an anchor for future lessons.

Teachers use **simulations** to help students become immersed in the content being studied. For example, in an interdisciplinary unit of study on the westward movement in the United States, students are grouped into wagons and wagon trains and provided with realistic scenarios to consider during each day of the simulation. Computer and video technology offers teachers many opportunities for simulations.

- **Interactive instruction:** Interactive instructional methods involve exactly what the title suggests—lots of student interaction! Methods include cooperative learning, reciprocal teaching, think/pair/share, and more.

  - **Cooperative learning:** Cooperative-learning activities require students to work together to solve a problem or achieve a goal. Key features of cooperative learning activities include the following:

  - **Positive interdependence:** Students must work together to successfully accomplish a task.

  - **Positive interaction:** Student interaction is designed to promote face-to-face or individual interaction and relationships.

  - **Individual and group accountability:** Students must contribute to the group's success and complete their portion of the task to receive a successful assessment.

  - **Interpersonal skills:** Students must be taught and learn to use teamwork and positive social skills when working with others.

  - **Group processing:** Teachers must provide an opportunity for feedback, not only on the group's product but also on the group's process.

  Examples of cooperative learning structures for lessons include the following:

  - **Student Teams Achievement Divisions (STAD):** Students are assigned to heterogeneously grouped teams of four or five members who collaborate on worksheets designed to provide extended practice on instruction given by the teacher.

  - **Jigsaw:** Instructional materials are divided and then studied by individuals or pairs of students. After students become "experts" on their sections of information, they share the information with the group.

  - **Numbered heads together:** Students are heterogeneously grouped into a "home team." Then each student is assigned a number so that he or she can join all the students with the same number to become an "expert" on assigned materials. For example, all the students who were assigned the number five read about and discuss music during the Harlem Renaissance. Once each of the numbered groups has had time to learn the assigned materials, the students return to their home team and teach their peers the content they have learned.

  - **Think-pair-share:** The teacher poses a problem or situation and asks students to think individually. The teacher then suggests that each student pair with a peer and share his or her thinking on this problem or situation. Sometimes students then share their ideas as a whole group; other times, the students share only in pairs.

  - **Reciprocal teaching:** The teacher and the student engage in a discussion of the text. Both the student and the teacher question and respond to the text in an effort to improve the student's comprehension of the material.

Closing of the Lesson

The closing of the lesson provides students with the opportunity to summarize and synthesize what has been learned thus far. The teacher wants to act as a facilitator of student thinking at this phase of the lesson-planning process. For example, the teacher might ask students to respond to a quick-write prompt or to share the key points of today's lesson. The emphasis in the closing should be on student talk and/or thinking, not teacher talk. Students are able to use previously learned material in a new situation or context. Teachers can promote students' ability to transfer learning experiences to new situations by developing "conditional knowledge" or helping students know when and how they might use the learned information in a new setting. Transfer of learning often is supported in the closing of the lesson and during extended practice opportunities.

The closing is also the place where the teacher assigns opportunities for students to practice the lesson objectives. Homework provides an opportunity for extended practice of a lesson. Homework should vary from grade level to grade level; require minimal, if any, parental involvement; and merit teacher feedback. Research on homework best practice shows that homework should not be an afterthought; instead, it should be an integral part of instruction to help students acquire the content presented.

Assessment

The assessment section of the lesson-plan template is last but certainly not least during this time of educational accountability. As you will recall from an earlier section on backwards design to lesson planning, your assessment plan should be your second consideration after you establish your objectives. Be sure that your assessment carefully aligns to your objective(s). Your assessment plan can be either formative or summative. Formative assessments check for student understanding to inform the next moments or days of instruction. Summative assessments are designed to measure student achievement at the close of the instructional cycle. Assessments may also be informal or formal. Informal assessments include observations, checking for student understanding, and conferencing with students. Formal assessments, on the other hand, measure student achievement by such means as quizzes, tests, or performances. Chapter 9 is dedicated to assessment.

Strategies and Instructional Activities for Encouraging Complex Cognitive Processes

Critical Thinking

Critical thinking is rationally deciding what to believe or what to do. When a person rationally decides something, he or she evaluates information to see if it makes sense, whether it is coherent, and whether the argument is well founded on evidence.

Graphic Organizers and Nonlinguistic Representations

Knowledge is stored in two forms:

- Nonlinguistic (visual, kinesthetic, and whole body)
- Linguistic (reading or hearing)

Students should have many opportunities to use both forms of storing knowledge to represent their learning and an opportunity to use all senses when learning. Nonlinguistic representations have been found to stimulate and increase brain activity. Teachers can foster nonlinguistic representations by using words and symbols to convey relationships and by using physical models and physical movement to represent new information. Visual-representation software (programs that provide tools for making graphic organizers) offers students a way to express their understanding of content in a nonlinguistic form.

Graphic organizers are visuals that show relationships between concepts, terms, facts, or ideas in a learning activity. Other terms related to graphic organizers that you may encounter are visual, visual structures, concept maps, cognitive organizers, advance organizers, and concept diagrams. There are several types of graphic organizers.

Cause-and-Effect Maps

Visuals, such as this cause-and-effect map, help students identify causes and effects in narrative or expository texts.

Cause and Effect

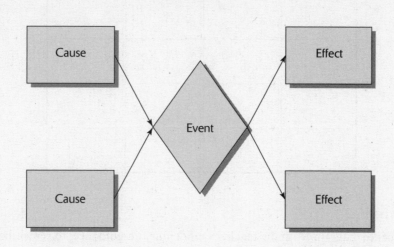

Continuums

A continuum graphic organizer can be used to help students learn key vocabulary or concepts. For example, the teacher can label the sample continuum *Feelings* and ask students to generate a list of words that represent feelings along a positive-to-negative continuum. The teacher or students chart the terms on a graphic organizer, which provides an opportunity for students to activate and develop prior knowledge of the feeling words that will be discussed in an upcoming health lesson on interpersonal relationships.

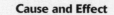

Continuum

Cycle Maps

A cycle map is beneficial when a teacher wants students to understand the cyclical nature of a text. For example, the graphic organizer shown here can be used to chart events at the beginning, middle, and end of a butterfly's life cycle.

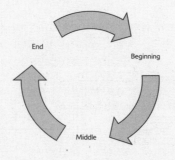

Matrixes

A matrix graphic organizer can be used for a variety of purposes to help students recall information. For example, a teacher might list categories along the first row and ask students to provide examples from the lesson for each category.

Matrix

[a 4x4 grid matrix]

Sequence Diagrams

Students can use a sequence diagram, with the teacher's modeling and guidance, to remember the sequence of events in a factual or fictional text.

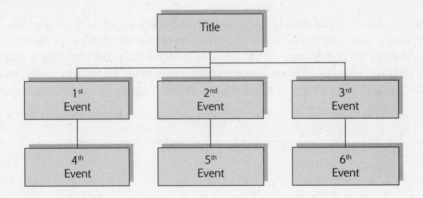

Story Maps

Story maps are used with narrative texts to help students identify and recall key story elements, such as characters, setting, plot, and conclusion.

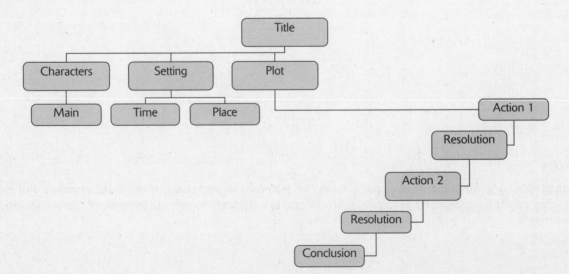

Metacognition

Metacognition simply means thinking about one's own thinking. It involves both self-monitoring and self-regulation. In the classroom, students who are demonstrating metacognitive proficiency are able to set goals, manage time, organize information, monitor their own learning progress, reflect on their learning process, and adjust their learning environment to create a productive space to work.

Problem- or Project-Based Learning

Includes an in-depth investigation of a real-world, authentic topic or problem that is meaningful to students. The students work in small groups or pairs to solve a problem or learn more about the topic. The teacher facilitates student projects and supports students' inquiries and discoveries.

Transfer

Students are able to use previously learned material in a new situation or context. Teachers can promote students' ability to transfer learning experiences to new situations by developing "conditional knowledge" or helping students know when and how they might use the learned information in a new setting. Transfer of learning often is supported in the closing of the lesson and during extended practice opportunities.

Grouping Practices

Teachers must offer a wide variety of grouping practices to meet the needs of all learners. Types of groups include the following:

- **Partner check or pair/share:** Individual students complete work and then pair with an assigned student to check work and discuss content.
- **Small-group investigation:** Students are assigned a topic and prepare a report or summary to share with the whole class.
- **Whole-group instruction:** Students work as a class to read, discuss, or solve a problem. This method is desirable when teacher modeling or direct instruction is necessary. Teachers should use whole-group methods only for short amounts of time because this grouping structure can allow some students to become less active or passive learners.
- **Independent study sessions or units:** Students are given a chance to work at their own pace under the teacher's leadership or guidance. Independent study units can be particularly beneficial for students who need course material modified to be more challenging or simplified.

Teachers must also know different grouping techniques and strategies, such as:

- Cooperative learning (see previous section in this chapter)
- Heterogeneous grouping (mixed-ability groups)
- Homogenous grouping (similar ability groups)
- Collaborative learning (students working together)
- Multiage group
- Grouping by gender or interest

Reflection Process in Teaching

Donald Schön suggests that effective teachers use a reflection process that involves reflection *in* action and reflection *on* action.

Reflection in Action

Prior to teaching and during the lesson, the teacher thinks ahead, analyzes the classroom situation, experiences the lesson, and then critically responds to his or her instruction. It is during this reflection-in-action process that the teacher uses teachable moments that may not have been planned prior to the lesson. Teachable moments are opportunities that occur during the lesson when the learning of a particular or idea becomes easiest and apparent. Examples of teachable moments include the following:

- After a student question, the teacher links a previous experience to the question and adds a new lesson on the topic.
- After a holiday or a personal student experience, the teacher spends time teaching students about this period of history.

During the lesson, the teacher also monitors student progress through direct observation, questioning, conferencing, and examining student work. If possible, the teacher adjusts the lesson as he or she notes the need to do so. This is the essence of what Schön means by reflection in action.

Reflection on Action

During this phase of the reflection process, the teacher looks back on the instructional process. He or she thinks through the previous lesson to consider what worked effectively and what could have been revised to improve all students' achievement. The teacher might do this reflective thinking while driving home, in a discussion with colleagues, or in writing as part of a professional journal entry or personal log. The essence of reflection on action is that the teacher looks back at strengths and areas of concern and determines future instructional opportunities.

Questioning Techniques and Considerations

Room Arrangement

To promote active discussion, your room arrangement must facilitate face-to-face communication. Horseshoe table arrangements, semicircles, or clusters of tables are more effective than arrangements where students' backs are to one another, such as rows.

Getting the Discussion Started

Methods to start a discussion include opening with a shared experience, using a concrete experience (such as showing an object that symbolizes a key concept), reading aloud a passage of the text, showing a film clip, or playing a music clip. Students also can complete a quick-write (a free recall writing) based on the experience or the reading assignment. It is also helpful to set out the parameters of the discussion, such as guidelines for turn taking and for ending the discussion.

Factual Recall

Questions on the knowledge level of Bloom's Taxonomy require factual recall. For example, *who, what, when, why,* and *how* questions. Other ways to promote factual recall include flash cards, games that require memory and immediate recall, and computer drill programs. Approaches to improving memory may include the following:

- **Mnemonic devices:** A learning technique to help you remember information; for example, the acronym HOMES helps you remember the names of the U.S. Great Lakes (Huron, Ontario, Michigan, Erie, and Superior).
- **Mental imagery:** Suggesting students form pictures in their minds.
- **Patterns of organization:** Presenting material to students in a logical and organized manner and helping students see the pattern to the content.
- **Recitation:** Having students read and repeat important content out loud.

Higher-Level Thinking

Higher-level thinking can be promoted in a variety of ways in the classroom. Questions based on Bloom's Taxonomy at the evaluation, synthesis, and analysis levels promote higher-level thinking. Higher-level thinkers ask pertinent questions, make inferences, assess arguments, and are able to suspend judgment until all facts are gathered and considered. Teachers must be mindful to promote higher-level thinking in the classroom and not just factual recall. Open-ended questions require higher-level thinking and probe for student understanding. Open-ended questions have no right or wrong answers.

Probing for Student Understanding

When following up on a student's initial response, teachers offer an opportunity to help the student think more deeply. Teachers can ask probing questions, ask other students to respond to the student's initial response, or ask higher-level questions. In addition, following up on a student's response shows the student that the teacher recognizes, appreciates, and values the student's ideas. Teachers might probe for student understanding by saying the following:

- How do you know?
- Can you tell me more?
- Please explain your thinking.
- Convince us of your strategy or argument.
- Why did you make this conclusion?

Student Question Generating

Good questions make great hypotheses. When students ask good questions, they are demonstrating a higher level of understanding of concepts. Teaching students to generate good questions is important to their higher-level thinking. Best practices for teaching students to generate questions include the following:

- Probing for understanding
- Modeling higher-level questioning
- Highlighting patterns and connections
- Providing a framework for the questioning
- Providing scaffolding of instruction and watching for misconceptions (correcting, as needed)

All Pupil Response

There are several techniques teachers can use to ensure that more than one student responds to a teacher's inquiry. For example, you can give each of your students a set of letters to practice spelling the words you are teaching in a word study lesson.

Wait Time

Wait time is a purposeful pause of time that a teacher uses to give a student and the remainder of the class a chance to think and more deeply formulate a response. Research studies have shown that teachers usually wait less than one second between asking a question and moving to a response. Be sure to give students time to think. Effective discussion leaders use wait time and refrain from interrupting the thinking process with a prompt or another question.

Helpful Roles in a Discussion

You can teach your students several roles they can enact during a discussion, such as the following:

- **Summarizer:** This person listens to the discussion carefully and summarizes either one person's point or the entire discussion.
- **Note taker or illustrator:** This role requires active listening and good note taking or drawing skills. The notes can be read at the close of the discussion or to open the discussion another day. A visual representation of the discussion can be shared to further the understanding of the group.
- **Quotable quotes:** In this role, the student finds a meaningful line or passage from the text and reads it to the group to trigger deeper understanding in the discussion.
- **Gatekeeper:** This person watches the time for the overall discussion, as well as the equitable chances for people to speak.
- **Question generator:** This person asks probing questions or asks for clarification.
- **Facilitator:** The facilitator manages the overall discussion to keep students actively moving toward deeper understanding.
- **Evaluator:** The evaluator offers a critical, constructive view of the discussion's process and content.

Teachers use questioning strategies to help students make meaning of their content. Many teachers use Bloom's Taxonomy to guide their questioning of students at a variety of levels. Bloom's Taxonomy also is helpful when writing the measurable verbs in lesson objectives. A common structure for classroom questioning is IRE—Initiate, Respond, and Evaluate. In this pattern of discourse, the teacher begins the discussion with a question, the student(s) respond, and the teacher evaluates the quality of the student response. Sample question categories along Bloom's Taxonomy include the following:

- **Knowledge:** Remember; recognize; recall who, what, where. . . .
- **Comprehension:** Interpret, retell, organize, and select facts.
- **Application:** Subdivide information and show how it can be put back together (How is *this* an example of *that?*).
- **Analysis:** What are the features of . . . ? How does this compare with . . . ?
- **Synthesis:** Create a unique product that combines ideas from the lesson (What would you infer from . . . ?).
- **Evaluation:** Make a value decision about an issue in the lesson (What criteria would you use to assess . . . ?).

Using Cues, Questions, and Advance Organizers

Cues, questions, and advance organizers help prepare students' minds for instruction. Advance organizers are structures (either visual or verbal) that provide a general idea of the new information to be learned, building knowledge of the key concepts to be learned in the lesson. David Ausubel introduced advance organizers in the 1960s and suggested that new information is more easily acquired when it can be linked to previously learned experiences or knowledge. Researchers have found that learning increases when teachers focus on what is most important, not on what students might think is the most interesting.

Stimulating Discussion and Responses in the Classroom

Discussion is a key instructional technique in which students actively engage in discourse about course content. Discussions can be teacher led or peer led. Peer-led discussion structures include literature circles and cooperative-learning activities. Teacher-led discussion structures include lectures, recitations, reciprocal teaching, and Socratic seminars.

Planning for Discussions

Teachers should be mindful of the following points when preparing for classroom discussions:

- Determine goals of the discussion.
- Assess prior knowledge and experiences of the students.
- Assess and build your background knowledge on the topic.
- Provide a supportive environment for discussion.
- Offer your viewpoint, when necessary, to build knowledge or correct misinformation.
- Allow for alternative viewpoints—to agree to disagree.
- Plan for meaningful connections between the discussion, other course content, and real-life experience.

Discussion Methods

Whole Class

The entire group is taught in whole-class discussion. Teachers often use whole-class discussion for lectures, demonstrations, explanations, questioning, recitations (oral practice), and work on a set of problems, or use of the same materials, such as a science text or a piece of literature. Whole-class discussions are helpful when the information to be covered requires a common understanding for all, but it should not be the only or primary method of discussion because differentiated instruction cannot occur in this configuration. Also, students have fewer opportunities for active participation during whole-class discussions, which can lead to disruptive classroom behaviors.

Small Group

Effective small groups are made up of between four and six students. Small groups can be comprised of heterogeneous (different level or style) learners or homogenous (similar) learners. Common types of small groups include the following:

- **Ability groups:** Ability groups are groups of students who have been judged to be performing on a similar academic level in a particular content area.
- **Peer tutors:** Peer tutoring involves peers teaching peers. Teachers can set up peer tutors within the same classroom or partner with another classroom or grade level of students.
- **Cooperative-learning groups:** Cooperative-learning groups are discussed earlier in this chapter.

Literature Circles

Literature circles are small groups of students who read and discuss the same materials together. The teacher talks to all the students about their responsibilities, key roles, and necessary new content, and then they break into small groups, each group working independently to discuss and understand the text. Common literature-circle roles include facilitator, connector, summarizer, vocabulary master, and illustrator. Literature circles offer students an opportunity to actively participate in discussions and to take responsibility for learning.

Panels and Debates

A panel is a formal discussion structure in which four to eight participants discuss a topic while the rest of the class listens. After the panel discussions, the class is able to question the panel members and discuss the topic further.

A debate is another formal discussion structure made up of a set of speeches by students from two opposing views. Debate groups present their views, followed by rebuttals of the opposing side's views.

Reports

Students can prepare reports to present and discuss with the class or a wider audience. In doing so, students can employ a variety of creative formats. For example, students might use PowerPoint presentations or artwork to present report information to the school community in an effort to inform others about a topic of interest.

Reader Response

Readers can respond to text in two main ways:

- **With an efferent stance:** When students discuss the text with an efferent stance, they make sense of the content, the meaning of the text, or the factual points of the text.
- **With an aesthetic stance:** When students discuss the text with an aesthetic stance, they connect personal experiences to the text, discussing thoughts and feelings about the text.

Reader response is grounded in the theory that readers bring prior knowledge and experiences to reading and attempt to make meaning from text. The following formula provides a visual representation of a current view of making meaning with texts:

$$Reader + Text = Meaning$$

A teacher with this view of student response strives to question students in order to help them come to their own interpretations of the text, not necessarily the teacher's or the author's view. Reader response is a way of communicating with students about their interpretation of texts.

Communication Techniques

Teachers need to deeply understand how people learn and how we use a variety of verbal and nonverbal cues to communicate. This section will provide you with key aspects in effective communication techniques in the classroom and school community.

Environmental Factors to Promote Communication

First, let's consider ways to establish a classroom environment that fosters a caring, productive, and safe place for all students to learn.

Promoting Respect and Caring

Effective communication is fostered in an environment that promotes caring and respect. The teacher continually acts as a role model for effective communication and plays a key role in setting up a classroom conducive to open discourse. Teachers who are empathetic, patient, resourceful, and consistent provide an exemplary model of the kinds of behaviors that promote good communication. Active listening, valuing differences, highlighting student strengths, and turn taking help promote caring and respect between teacher and student, as well as among students.

Teachers should be mindful to use appropriate humor to diminish tension if it builds in the classroom, but they should be cautious in their use of sarcasm, especially when it is at the expense of a student. "Saving face" is very important in many cultures, and it is especially important to students in their teenage years. Use of sarcasm can diminish trust and respect in a classroom.

Students also must have responsibilities in the classroom, which helps the student develop a sense of shared ownership in the work of school. One of the key responsibilities students can experience is the requirement that they care for others, themselves, and school property.

Goal Setting

Early in the school year, the teacher can help students to articulate long-term and short-term learning goals. Parents also can provide direction and support for a student's goal setting. Once goals have been established, the teacher can show respect and support for each student's goals and share student successes with the class. This practice fosters a sense of teamwork and camaraderie among students, and it helps the students to see individual goals and differences as strengths.

Effective Class Management

Whichever style you choose for your classroom management, the following suggestions will help your classroom become a place where students can learn and communicate openly:

- Move around the classroom and maintain eye contact with your students.
- Pace and structure your lessons.
- Establish a quiet signal or routine.
- Maintain an interruption-free place to work.
- Offer positive reinforcement for each student's efforts.
- Allow students to interact and talk with one another during collaborative work times. Of course, there are times when quiet or independent work is necessary, but this should not be the majority of the class period or day.

In addition, it is important for teachers to establish daily routines and schedules and to establish classroom rules and consequences. Teachers also must use effective communication skills when working with colleagues and the students' caregivers. It is important for the teacher to maintain two-way communication with parents and guardians, keep accurate records, provide timely feedback, respond to student behavior, and offer objective descriptions of student behavior while maintaining student confidentiality.

Problem Solving

In a classroom environment that promotes problem solving, students see challenges as problems to be solved rather than negative or frustrating events. Students who are problem solvers consider their goals, the current situation, and the means to achieve the goal. Teachers play an important role in problem-solving discussions by asking probing questions and encouraging students to articulate their goals and situations and then consider possible ways of achieving these goals. Also, teachers can model their thinking process in a variety of situations throughout the school day.

There are two main ways teachers aid students in resolving problems or conflicts in the classroom:

- **Conflict-resolution techniques:** Conflict resolution helps students who have had a conflict to work together to arrive at a mutually beneficial solution. The goal is for students to resolve conflicts peacefully and cooperatively without using the traditional school discipline plans or structures.
- **Behavior-modification techniques:** Behavior-modification techniques are used to change observed behavior. The steps include:
  1. Identifying the problem behavior
  2. Planning a method for changing the behavior
  3. Offering positive reinforcement when the student's behavior is positive
  4. Using positive reinforcement consistently to shape and change the problem behavior

Curbing School Violence

If students do not feel safe, they will struggle to do well in school. School violence not only involves guns, knives, drugs, and gangs, but also includes bullying, harassment, intolerance, and insults. One way schools are working to curb violence is to create a more personalized school environment. Smaller class sizes, advisories, and schools within a school are models for creating a personalized environment. Research shows that when children feel a strong sense of belonging in school, they engage in fewer violent acts and do not allow their peers to engage in violence. Two-way communication between home and school also can diminish school violence.

Risk Taking

In order for students to take risks—to ask a "silly" question or to offer an incorrect response—the teacher must ensure that the classroom environment promotes risk taking. Such an environment does not allow sarcasm, interruption, ridicule, or harassment. The teacher can reframe "incorrect" responses as positive steps toward achieving deeper understanding and achieving a learning goal.

Stimulating Curiosity

There are many ways a teacher can stimulate student curiosity to promote student discussion and engagement, including music, thought-provoking questions, mystery, film clips, and so on. One example is the "Mission Impossible" opening of a lesson conducted by one of my student teachers in an urban high-school English classroom. Prior to the arrival of his students, Mr. Wynkoop set up their desks in a circle and put one desk in the center of the classroom. On the center desk, he placed a cassette tape player. As the students arrived, Mr. Wynkoop encouraged the students to play the tape and learn what they would do in English class today. The tape began with the theme from *Mission Impossible,* which segued to Mr. Wynkoop's mysterious voice telling the students that they were about to begin a mission that would be impossible to complete without the teamwork of the class. His narration directed the students to an envelope under the center desk. A letter inside the envelope provided further directions for the mission—to read a new piece of literature collaboratively. Clearly, Mr. Wynkoop stimulated the students' and my curiosity, which promoted lots of student discussion to open the lesson effectively!

Positive Interdependence

Positive interdependence is built when students must work well together to successfully complete a task. The previous example of Mr. Wynkoop's *Mission Impossible* also built positive interdependence. Once the students opened the envelope in the center of the classroom, they learned that they would be working in groups of four and that each group had tasks assigned to help the whole class achieve their "mission." Within each group, individual students had responsibility for a part of the assignment. For example, one student had to define three key vocabulary words; another had to learn more about the author. The students were able to help each other achieve the task and had to work together responsibly and effectively. Each student had to make a contribution, and each received an individual grade for his or her contribution.

Techniques to Foster Verbal and Nonverbal Communication

Following are several ways you can promote effective verbal and nonverbal communication in your classroom.

I Messages

When communicating with students, parents, or colleagues in difficult situations, you may want to use I messages to convey a sense of openness to resolve the conflict collaboratively and nonaggressively. Examples of I messages include the following:

- "I feel upset when I hear you say that you do not care about your friend's feelings."
- "I know that you care about your son's progress in seventh grade. Let's work together to think of ways to help support him with his homework completion."

Setting Clear Expectations

Clear expectations can be conveyed in several important ways. First, the teacher can tell the students what they are going to learn in a lesson and why it is important. At the close of the lesson, the teacher can help students see when they can and cannot use this new information in new contexts. Clear expectations for student performance and behavior can be set in mutually agreed-upon rules and criteria for excellence in student work. Setting up routines, procedures, and schedules help students become more responsible for their own learning and provide necessary structure to the school day. Teachers can provide clear expectations about units of study, goals, and standards the unit addresses for students, parents, and administrators.

Providing Clear Directions

Beginning teachers must take time to plan for clear directions. Clear and focused directions require no more than three student actions in one statement: state the type and quality of performance expected, describe each step of the task, and provide visual as well as oral representation of more complex directions. Beginning teachers often plan a narrative script ahead of time and demonstrate or model a task before asking students to perform the activity on their own.

Breaking Down Complex Tasks

Breaking down more complex tasks, such as long-term projects or group projects, is important for students, especially those with learning differences and attention difficulties. The teacher should provide clear directions, as stated in the previous section of this chapter, and should offer frequent "check-ins" to encourage students when they are making progress and to reteach students when they are having difficulties.

Signaling Transitions

Having a classroom routine and a posted schedule implicitly signals transitions from one activity to the next, but teachers often need to explicitly signal transitions for the wide variety of learners in the classroom. The elementary teacher often uses a clapping pattern, a song, or a bell to signal five minutes of work time left or time's up. The secondary teacher often lets the students know more verbally when transitions will occur, although I have worked with several teachers who use music or timers to signal transitions in the upper grades. For example, students work for a set amount of time, and then when time is up they share their work.

Explicit Teaching

Barak Rosenshine (1987) suggests 10 basic principles for the development of an explicit teaching session:

1. Create a short statement of lesson purpose.
2. Provide a short review of previous, prerequisite learning.
3. Present new material in small steps, with student practice.
4. Provide clear, detailed explanations and instructions.
5. Provide active practice for all students.
6. Ask effective questions, check for student understanding, and encourage all pupil response.
7. Guide students during practice.
8. Offer feedback and corrections.
9. Provide practice for independent work and monitor students.
10. Continue practice until students are ready to use new information confidently and independently.

These 10 principles will help you with your effective communication with students, as well as planning for effective instruction and assessment.

Highlighting Key Information

Effective communicators highlight the key points to remember. You can literally highlight key points on the chalkboard, overhead projector, SMART Board interactive whiteboards, or PowerPoint presentations. Other ways to "highlight" important information include opening and closing a lesson with the key points to remember, preparing study guides for students, and signaling students when they have learned something important.

Gesturing

Nonverbal communication, such as gesturing, also plays an important role in effective classroom communication. Positive gestures include nodding, giving the thumbs-up sign, and smiling. Gestures also may communicate negative messages, so teachers must be mindful of their nonverbal messages, such as turning away from a student to attend to something else, pointing, or tapping a foot.

Teachers often videotape lessons to reflect on lesson strengths and areas to improve. Video can help teachers see the gestures they use and student reactions. Many of us have gestures that are part of a habit of communication (using my hands to gesture when I talk is one of mine), so video or peer observations can help teachers know which communications are perceived positively and which are perceived in a less desirable way.

Making Eye Contact

Some students believe their teachers really do have eyes in the backs of their heads! This, of course, is not a prerequisite to good teaching, but keeping your eyes on your students, making eye communication, and fully attending to your students' communication all are signs of a teacher who communicates effectively. One should be mindful that not all students will be comfortable making eye contact with the teacher, though. This could be for cultural reasons, or it could be because of a timid personality or difficulties with social skills.

Displaying With-it-ness

Jacob Kounin describes teacher with-it-ness as an ability to know what is going on in the classroom at all times. For example, the teacher must be able to attend to a group and also be aware of the actions of the remainder of the class. One lesson beginning teachers learn early is not to keep their backs to the class for too long a period of time!

Respecting Personal Space

Teachers can communicate respect for students by understanding their students' need for personal space. Some children need lots of personal space, while others do not seem to know where their space ends and a classmate's begins. For example, a first-grader may need redirection or structure when she wants to always sit next to the teacher or to brush her friend's hair. One fourth-grade student I observed appeared to cringe when the student teacher knelt at a reasonable distance beside him to explain something. I later learned from the classroom teacher that this student was diagnosed with a mild level of autism and that the student needed an exceptional amount of space when working with others. In addition, a simple gesture such as patting a student on the back can be misunderstood or upsetting to the student. It is important to know and respect your students' needs for personal space. Of course, you will also want to teach your students to respect each other's needs for personal space, as well as your own.

Paying Attention to Noise Level

Too much noise and too little noise can hamper classroom communication. Teachers must determine the "just right" noise level they can tolerate and clearly communicate with students when they are approaching too much noise. Nonverbal cues, such as red, yellow, and green index cards can signal when students can freely talk, when they are at a warning noise level, and when they must stop talking. Conversely, teachers must not require so little noise in the classroom that students have little to no opportunity to talk with one another. Borrowing from James Britton's quote, "Talk is the sea upon which all else floats." Classroom communication clearly requires a certain amount of noise.

Communicating in a Culturally and Linguistically Diverse Classroom

The demographics of our communities are rapidly shifting. This rapid change suggests that the enrollment of schoolchildren from linguistically and culturally different populations (from the so-called "mainstream" U.S. culture) is expected to increase. To improve the achievement of all children, teachers must be responsive, sensitive, and informed about the variety of cultures in the United States—particularly in their school communities. By linguistic diversity, I refer to the many students whose first language is not English, as well as the variants of English that are spoken in American schools. By cultural diversity, I refer to Sonya Nieto's (1999) definition of culture, which describes cultural diversity as "a multidimensional constellation of ever-changing values, traditions, relationships, and worldview that binds a people together." People can come together by a combination of factors, such as shared history, geographic location, language, social class, and religion. Researchers have found that teachers' expectations, when communicated both verbally and nonverbally, influence children's behavior and performance. Therefore, teachers must treat all students as competent and expect high standard work from all children. To do so, teachers must know not only their content, but also their students.

Dawn Abt-Perkins and Lois Matz Rosen (2000) suggest five important knowledge bases for teachers of culturally and linguistically diverse students:

- **Self knowledge:** Teachers must first understand the influence of their own cultures before they can meet the diverse cultural and linguistic needs of their own students. Teachers must critique their own values to ensure that these values are not inadvertently creating barriers to teaching all children.

- **Cultural knowledge:** A teacher with cultural knowledge shows an understanding of the importance of culture and how culture affects student views of the world. Teachers can meet the diverse needs of their students by knowing their students' families, languages, literacy practices, communities, and values.

- **Linguistic knowledge:** Teachers must understand the patterns of communication and dialects of the students they teach. Even though Standard American English (SAE) is the language of instruction in a majority of public schools, it is not always the language in the classroom. Lisa Delpit (1993) suggests that teachers must acknowledge and validate a student's home language. Teachers can foster a student's classroom communication by building on the student's home language and linguistic strengths.

- **Culturally informed teaching knowledge:** Teachers who have culturally informed teaching knowledge create a collaborative and culturally sensitive classroom environment. Teachers must learn to support the learning needs of each individual student, be sensitive to and respectful of a student's culture, and see the students' differences as "funds of knowledge" (Moll, 1992).

- **Knowledge of multicultural materials and methods:** Multicultural literature and texts that present balanced global views of historical events offer powerful ways for teachers to show respect for their students' cultures, as well as promote cross-cultural understanding.

Communication is a key aspect of culture. Differences between cultures can be perceived as threatening, so a teacher must be mindful of these differences in the classroom. The best way to learn about another's language and culture is, quite simply, to experience that language and culture. I am reluctant to share specific patterns of cultural and linguistic communication in this book because many misconceptions and stereotypes exist. I will leave this to anthropologists, linguists, sociologists, and you, the future classroom teacher. Nonetheless, I strongly suggest that, as a role model for your students, you learn as much as possible about the diverse languages and cultures in your community.

Next, we'll examine four general elements of communication that will help you to consider your own cultural and linguistic communication style and compare and contrast your style to that of your students:

- **Degree of directness:** First, we'll consider the level of directness in communication. On the most direct side of a communication continuum, people say what they mean and mean what they say. There is little subtlety, and it's important to tell it like it is. A person with a direct communication style believes honesty is the best policy and that the truth is more important than sparing a person's feelings.

On the other end of this communication continuum, people with an indirect communication style imply or suggest what they are saying. You must be a good interpreter of the person's meaning and use inference to gather the person's true message. Those with an indirect communication style believe that, if the truth hurts, it should be tempered.

- **The role of context:** The second pattern involves context—a continuum of low-context to high-context communication. Context means the amount of instinctive understanding a person is expected to bring to the communication setting.

  Low-context communication cultures tend to be heterogeneous and individualist. In this culture, little is believed to be known, so there is a high emphasis on verbal communication.

  High-context communication cultures tend to be homogeneous and collectivist (emphasis is placed on the group, not the individual). In a high-context culture, much is already known by the members, so the spoken word is not the primary means of communicating. Nonverbal cues and the communication setting are central in the communication process.

- **The importance of "saving face":** Another important communication continuum to consider is where the importance of "saving face" falls in a culture. By saving face, I refer to an act that avoids the loss of a person's dignity or prestige. In a culture where saving face is highly valued, people tend to maintain harmony, avoid confrontation, and have a difficult time saying no. The overall goal in such a culture is harmony. Often, what one says and what one feels are not the same.

  In a culture where saving face is less important, a person's dignity is less important. Facts and getting something done efficiently are more highly valued. Criticism and feedback are straightforward, and it is fine to confront people or to say no.

- **The task and the person:** The last pattern of communication we'll consider is the importance of the task compared to the importance of the person. In a culture where the task is foremost, the task is separated from the person. People do business first and socialize or engage in a bit of small talk. Building relationships is not central to getting the job done well.

  In a culture where the person is foremost, the goal is to build relationships first. The task and the person cannot be separated. The people in this culture often begin with small talk and then move to business. Personal relationships are central to getting the job done well.

Other Areas of Diversity in Classrooms Today and Communication Considerations

In addition to being knowledgeable and appreciative of cultural and linguistic diversity in your classroom, teachers also must be understanding and aware of other areas of diversity in classrooms today to foster positive communication among all learners.

Socioeconomic Background

Socioeconomic status (SES) and school achievement are highly correlated. Teachers must consider similar aspects of understanding differences in SES cultural and linguistic diversity as they do for students from cultural and linguistically diverse backgrounds. You may experience teaching students from a much higher SES or much lower SES than your own. The key here is to have high expectations for all your students and to communicate these expectations positively and supportively.

Social Styles

Are you the type of person who loves a big gathering with lots of friends, or would you prefer a smaller get-together with a close friend or a few couples? Your students also have social styles that impact their learning in the group setting of your classroom; therefore, students need opportunities to work in the whole group, small groups, and individually in the course of the school day, in the case of younger learners, and in the course of the school week, in the case of older students.

Learning Styles

As discussed in Chapter 7, people have a variety of ways of making sense of what they are learning, such as visual, auditory, kinesthetic, or tactile learning styles. Teachers strive to communicate with their students in a way that is most beneficial to each student's learning style. For example, after I explained a three-step task to my juniors, I wrote a brief, bulleted list of the directions on the chalkboard and then asked students to visualize each step and ask questions, as needed.

Scholastic Abilities and Challenges

You may teach students who have been identified as possessing giftedness, a learning disability, a musical or athletic talent, a physical handicap, an attention deficit, a bipolar disorder, Tourette's syndrome, or an addiction to alcohol. Each of these students brings abilities to the classroom that you, the teacher, can identify and capitalize on when teaching your lesson. Each student brings abilities and challenges; therefore, a teacher must assume responsibility for teaching each student in his or her classroom and must persevere to find the right instructional strategies for each child. Sometimes, you will need to confer with colleagues who have more experience or expertise with students possessing scholastic abilities and challenges.

Lifestyles

There are many configurations to our students' families, all of which require us, as teachers, to suspend judgment and to keep an open mind, even when a child's family structure is very different from the teacher's perception of a "good" family. Children live in the homes of happy and healthy single parents, grandparents, foster parents, stepparents, same-sex parents, married parents, and more. Of course, not all children live in families that are happy and healthy. As a teacher, it is your responsibility to strive to teach all your students well.

In addition, some children live in several homes in the course of a school year or do not live in a permanent home at all. Although working with the diverse lifestyles of our students' families can be a challenge, teachers are responsible for professionally communicating with all children and for communicating with students' caregivers no matter their living situation. Again, focusing on student strengths and valuing what their caregivers can teach us about their children are important strategies for teachers. Support personnel, mentors, and colleagues—such as social workers, psychologists, school nurses, and principals—can provide professional expertise and experience as you strive to teach all children well.

Chapter 9

Assessment Strategies

Along with planning a great lesson using backward design, which you learned about in Chapter 8, you will need to assess what your students have learned in order to plan future instruction and to inform others of your students' progress. In this chapter, I review assessment types, key aspects of educational measurement, and response to intervention.

Assessment Types

There are several ways to assess student learning. Here is a helpful list of the many types of assessments and the primary purpose of each:

- **Ability tests** are standardized tests used to evaluate an individual's performance in a specific area (for example, cognitive or psychomotor).

- **Achievement tests** are written for a variety of subjects and levels designed to measure a student's knowledge or proficiency in something that has been learned or taught. Examples of achievement tests include the Stanford Achievement Tests (SAT), the Metropolitan Achievement Test (MAT), and the California Achievement Test (CAT).

- **Analytical rubrics** are designed to provide specific information about each aspect of a task in order to share specific strengths and weaknesses of a student.

- **Anecdotal records** are the written notes teachers maintain based on their observations of individual children. Teachers use a variety of methods to organize anecdotal records, such as file folders, mailing labels, index cards, and Post-it notes.

- **Aptitude tests** are standardized (or norm-referenced) tests that are designed to measure a student's ability to develop or acquire skills and knowledge.

- **Authentic assessments** measure student understanding of the learning process and product, rather than just the product. For example, student understanding of patterns can be assessed by using teddy-bear counters. Students actually create patterns using the counters, identify the patterns, and explain how they know this pattern to the teacher, who actively observes the student at work. In authentic assessments, students develop the responses rather than select from predetermined options. Clear criteria of success are established, which relate closely to classroom learning opportunities.

- **Criterion-referenced tests** determine how well a student performs on an explicit objective relative to a predetermined performance level, such as grade-level expectations or mastery. Criterion-referenced tests do not help teachers compare student results to those of other test takers. An example of a criterion-referenced test is a teacher-made or publisher-made exam at the end of a social studies text chapter.

- **Diagnostic evaluations** are usually standardized or norm referenced and are given before instruction begins to help teachers understand students' learning needs. These tests help teachers learn about students' areas of difficulties but not the cause of those difficulties.

- **Essay questions** require students to make connections between new and previously learned content, apply information to new situations, and demonstrate that they have learned the new information.

- **Formative evaluations** provide information about learning in progress and offer the teacher and the student an opportunity to monitor and regulate learning.

- **Journals** can be used as an authentic assessment of a student's understanding of key concepts or his or her ability to communicate ideas in writing. Generally, journals are used as places to draft, and the teacher assesses the process, not the product, informally. In other words, a teacher rarely corrects spelling and grammar in a journal entry; rather, the teacher reads the journal entry to understand the student's thought process on a topic of study.

- **Norm-referenced tests** are also known as standardized tests. These tests are used to determine a student's performance in relation to the performance of a group of peers who have taken the same test. Norm-referenced tests most often are used by school personnel to make decisions about curriculum and school performance levels.

- **Observation of students** is arguably the most important assessment tool in your teaching toolkit. Also known as *kidwatching,* a term suggested by Ken Goodman in the 1960s, observing student interactions and learning behaviors is important to any classroom assessment plan. Teachers can take notes on their observations, called anecdotal records, or reflect on student observations after a lesson. It is important for teachers to observe students in other settings besides the classroom environment to gain a deeper understanding of a student's performance in school.

- **Performance assessments** require a student to perform a task or generate his or her own response during the assessment. For example, a performance assessment for a composition class would require a student to write something rather than answer multiple-choice questions or match test question items.

- A **portfolio** is a carefully selected collection of student products, and sometimes teacher observations, collected over time, that reflect a student's progress in a content area. Well-prepared student portfolios include student decision making in the portfolio contents, demonstration of instructional outcomes, multiple measures of student performance, and multiple products created over time.

- **Responses** can take many forms across the content areas. Students can respond orally, in writing, or through the visual and performance arts. Responses can be used as authentic assessments and often are assessed by using a set of criteria and a scoring rubric.

- **Rubrics** are scoring guides used in assessments. Rubrics can be subject specific, task specific, or generic.

- **Self-evaluation** is a not-to-be-forgotten assessment. Students' monitoring and regulation of learning is important in the transfer of learning to new experiences. A student self-evaluation can provide "a window into the student's mind" that can let a teacher know how the student sees his or her progress and how the teacher might improve instruction for that student. Self-evaluations can be free-form in a discussion or in writing or can be more structured tasks, such as a self-evaluation in the form of a Likert scale. Teachers should be mindful to ask for student evaluation on the course content, as well as the student's learning process.

- **Standards-based assessments** measure student progress toward meeting goals based on local, state, and/or national goals. Standards-based assessments can be based on content or performance standards and can be criterion referenced or norm referenced.

- **Summative evaluations** provide information about learning to be used to make judgments about a student's achievement and the teacher's instruction.

Educational Measurement

Following are the important aspects of educational measurement that may be on the PLT test and will definitely impact your teaching once you begin your career. You will want to be able to understand this information thoroughly so that you can interpret assessment results and report them to students, parents/caregivers, and other school personnel.

- **Age-equivalent scoring:** This type of scoring allows us to compare student performance to typical students in that same age group.

- **Analytical scoring:** Analytical scoring is typically used to assess constructed-response test questions (essays, short-answer) and includes detailed descriptions of the criteria. For example, a teacher might ask for two reasons why the United States engaged in the Civil War. The teacher would construct an analytical scoring guide that includes all the possible correct responses to the prompt before reading the student responses. If a student included two of the causes listed on the analytical scoring guide, then the student would earn full credit. Analytical scoring guides are particularly useful when a teacher is new to an assessment or when a teacher has many items to score.

- **Grade-level equivalent scores:** Grade-level equivalents demonstrate the grade and month of the school year to which a student score can be compared. For example, a score of 5.1 would indicate that a student is performing at a fifth-grade, first-month level.

- **Holistic scoring:** Holistic scoring is typically used for constructed-response questions (essays, journals, and short answer). It uses general descriptions of the criteria for success on each question. Holistic scoring can be more efficient than analytical scoring if the teacher has fewer test items to score.

- **Mean, median, and mode:** The *mean* is the average of a set of scores. The *median* is the midpoint of a set of numbers. The *mode* is the most common number in a set of numbers.

- **Percentile rank:** Percentile ranks show the percentage of students in a group (either a national or a local norm) whose scores fall above or below the given student's scores. The score range is between 1 and 99. If a student scored in the 50th percentile, 50 percent of the scores in the norm group fell below on this same test.

- **Quartiles:** When you divide a normal distribution of scores into four equal parts, you can describe student data as it falls into one of the three quartiles—the first quartile or lower quartile (the bottom 25 percent), the second quartile or the media (the middle 50 percent), and the third quartile or upper quartile (the top 25 percent).

  - Q1 = The first quartile cuts off the lowest 25 percent of the data set = 25th percentile (lower quartile).

  - Q2 = The second quartile cuts the data set in half = 50th percentile (median).

  - Q3 = The third quartile cuts off the highest 25 percent or the lowest 75 percent of the data set = 75th percentile (upper quartile).

  Quartiles enable school personnel to see the distribution of student scores and can help define student achievement patterns over time.

- **Raw score:** A student's raw score is equivalent to the number of questions he or she answered correctly on an assessment. Raw scores are helpful in determining the number of items actually answered correctly or incorrectly.

- **Reliability:** Reliability is the extent to which an assessment is consistent with its measures.

- **Samples:** A sample is a smaller number of participants drawn from a total population. Sometimes it is not feasible for researchers to collect or analyze all the scores of a given population; therefore, a sample of scores is selected.

- **Scaled scores:** Scaled scores are based on a mathematical transformation of a raw score. Scaled scores can be helpful when determining averages and to study change over time.

- **Standard deviation:** Standard deviation is a measure of variability that indicates the typical distance between a set of scores of a distribution and the mean, or average, score. For example, students' motivation level was rated on a scale of 1 to 4, with 4 being the highest and 1 being the lowest. For one class set of scores, the average score was 2.5, and the distribution of scores was uneven with scores primarily at the 1 or 4 level. The standard deviation was determined to be 2, meaning that the amount of variability between scores on the distribution was two points. If the classroom teacher had used only the average student score on the motivation measure (a 2.5), he or she might have determined that students' motivation was moderate. Standard deviation becomes very helpful in this situation because it helps the teacher see that overall student motivation is very high or very low, not moderate at all for this class (distribution of scores).

- **Standard error of measurement:** The standard error of measurement is the standard deviation of test scores you would have obtained from a single student who took the same test multiple times.

- **Stanines:** Stanines (derived from *sta*ndard *nine*) are based on a nine-point standard scale with a mean of 5 and a standard deviation of 2. Rarely do classroom teachers (with the exception of math teachers) actually use the formula to calculate a stanine, but all teachers will have to read score reports that often contain stanine scores. Stanines enable school personnel to see the distribution of scores for any grade level or group of students and may help schools see patterns of change in student achievement over time.

- **Validity:** A test is found to be valid if it measures what it was designed to measure.

Response to Intervention

In this last section of Chapter 9, we will take a look at Response to Intervention (RTI), an assessment-driven, student-centered process that schools use to help students who are struggling academically or behaviorally. RTI is important to know because it aims to close achievement gaps for students and provides a practical application of the techniques and concepts studied previously in this chapter.

There are typically three levels of intensity in an RTI process:

- **Tier 1:** Screening assessments are administered to determine which students are at-risk for learning difficulties. Diagnostic assessments also may be administered for all students or only for those who are showing lower levels of achievement. For students at risk, the classroom teacher designs and monitors an intervention, usually lasting no more than six to eight weeks, and then assesses the student again to see if the intervention was successful in closing achievement gaps. Student progress is monitored carefully. If the student has not made satisfactory progress after the intervention, the teacher moves the student to the Tier 2 level support.

- **Tier 2:** This level of support provides targeted interventions, monitored closely over intervals of time usually longer in duration than Tier 1, usually taught in collaboration with the classroom teacher and a specialist. If the intervention is successful, teachers and specialists use data to inform future instructional programming for the child and monitor the student's progress regularly. If the student is not successful at the Tier 2 level of support, then Tier 3 supports are warranted.

- **Tier 3:** This level of support continues using data to inform student instruction and intervention planning, but it adds additional intensive and individualized support, often with the advice of a special educator or team of educators. If a child is not successful with the Tier 3 level of intervention, the student is likely to be referred for a full or individual evaluation as required by the Individuals with Disabilities Education Act (IDEA).

Professional Development, Leadership, and Community

In this section, we will review the last of the four categories of content on the PLT test: Professional Development, Leadership, and Community. This content is found on both the multiple-choice questions and the constructed-response questions. Although there tend to be fewer questions from this category (15 percent of the test), this content is important to review. My pre-service teachers report that they appreciate this outline review, which includes information about teachers as reflective practitioners, the rights of teachers and students, key historical information about U.S. schools, and other legal aspects of teaching in the United States.

Professional Development Practices and Resources

Professional Associations

Each content area has a national professional association, and many professional associations have local chapters. By joining a professional association you show your willingness to become a lifelong learner and good colleague. Inevitably, you will benefit from the many publications, website resources, conferences, and people you will interact with while a member of the association.

Following is a list of major professional associations, but remember that more are available to you:

- **English Language Arts:**
  - International Reading Association: www.reading.org
  - National Council of Teachers of English: www.ncte.org
- **Foreign Languages:**
  - American Council on the Teaching of Foreign Language: www.actfl.org
- **Mathematics:**
  - National Council of Teachers of Mathematics: www.nctm.org
- **Reading:**
  - International Reading Association: www.reading.org
- **Science:**
  - National Science Teachers Association: www.nsta.org
- **Social Studies:**
  - National Council for the Social Studies: www.ncss.org

Colleagues

Your colleagues, both new and experienced, are valuable resources in your teaching toolkit. Teaching with excellence is a complex and demanding task. By networking with colleagues, you develop a mutually beneficial relationship to ease the demands of teaching, as well as model the type of cooperative behavior you expect of your students. Colleagues often form learning communities, a group of teachers interested in improving their instruction who embark typically on a year-long or semester-long inquiry and sharing experience. Study groups are similar to learning communities but are usually topic specific, are shorter in duration, and do not emphasize the learning and teaching environment the way that learning communities do. Finally, experienced colleagues often serve as mentors, either formally or informally. Many schools have mentoring programs in which a beginning teacher meets regularly with an experienced teacher to discuss whatever the new teacher may have questions about and to learn from the experience of the mentor.

Conferences

Reflective practitioners are lifelong learners. Attending conferences is one great way to learn more about teaching. There are many conference opportunities, both locally and nationally, of which you should take advantage. Besides the important information you will gain, conferences offer an opportunity to network with colleagues outside your school building. They also provide time to reflect upon your teaching practice.

Professional Reading

When you join a national professional association, you usually will receive a professional journal or newsletter as a membership benefit. Professional journals and newsletters are available in many libraries, perhaps even the one at your school. Professional magazines are available by subscription. Many professional literature resources can be accessed online. Professional literature provides the opportunity for you to stay current in your field and to read about the best, research-based practices. Teachers often learn from their own independent research, either informally through professional reading of blogs, research articles, and books, or more formally through action research as part of a graduate program.

Professional Development

Professional development, or in-service education, is an opportunity for you to learn and grow as an educator. You may attend a small discussion group, a large conference, or an individual session with a coach. You could also register for a college course. Internships are another professional development opportunity for teachers. In an internship, the classroom teacher is freed from several teaching responsibilities so that he or she can shadow a colleague, such as a specialist or an administrator, to learn about this position in action. Whatever the format, professional development provides a chance for you to reflect, refine your teaching skills, and add to your teaching knowledge base.

Evidenced-Based Practice

There is an abundance of resources teachers can access to determine which instructional methods and approaches are the most effective, evidence-based practices. For example, reciprocal teaching (an instructional method covered in Chapter 8) has a carefully researched and well-established record of student achievement. As a teaching professional, you will need to know how to access the research—through online libraries or at your university/ college library, professional subscriptions to peer-reviewed journal articles, and listservs of teaching researchers and professionals, such as the International Reading Association and the Literacy Researchers Association.

Teachers also need to understand how to interpret student assessment data and derive conclusions from the data. In Chapter 9, I cover the Response to Intervention (RTI) process, which is one way teachers use assessment data to inform instruction. Finally, teachers must be knowledgeable about the research and trends in the profession in order to use evidence to form professional opinions, positions, and decisions. In other words, basing professional decisions on personal experience is not enough; teachers must use their experiences as well as the research-based evidence to inform their practice.

Role of the Reflective Practitioner

As discussed in Chapter 8, teachers must constantly reflect on their teaching *in action* and *on action,* as Donald Schön suggests. Following are ways in which teachers act as reflective practitioners:

- **By writing in a reflective journal:** Teachers can write in a personal journal daily or weekly.
- **By participating in self-assessment and peer assessment:** Assessment is a process in which the teacher reexamines his or her teaching, either alone or with the assistance of a colleague.

- **By conducting incident analysis:** In a concerns-based reflection model, as suggested by Fred Korthagen, the teacher deeply thinks about one particular teaching or learning event that concerns her. She looks back to her thoughts, feelings, and the event from multiple perspectives, trying to reveal what is the central issue in this situation.

- **By preparing a portfolio:** A teaching portfolio often contains evidence of teaching effectiveness and professional development, such as lesson plans, recommendation letters, student artifacts, photos, and reflections.

- **By allowing for peer observation:** Inviting a peer into your classroom to observe can be a fulfilling and eye-opening experience. Prior to the observation, you should ask your colleague to observe specific aspects of your instruction or specific students you are trying to reach more effectively. During the peer observation, your colleague sits unobtrusively in the classroom, taking nonjudgmental field notes on what is happening during your lesson. After the lesson, you and your colleague find time to meet privately to discuss your lesson and to share ideas.

- **By drawing on a critical friend:** In the previous example, the peer observing in your classroom may be your critical friend. A critical friend is a colleague who provides you with nonjudgmental, constructive feedback, which is not part of a formal evaluation, but a part of your ongoing reflection and professional development.

Promoting Partnerships

Respectful Communication

Listening, frequent and positive communication, and understanding all contribute to respectful communication with caregivers. Too often, school personnel contact families only when there is a problem. Special consideration must be given to families whose primary language is not English or who have other issues (for example, financial, physical, and emotional) that make communicating with teachers a challenge. Teachers must be aware of the ways culture affects communication. Some families may prefer face-to-face communication, home visits, or parent conferences. Others may prefer phone calls, e-mails, or notes.

Shared Decision Making

It is very important to give caregivers a voice in their child's education. Family members can serve on action research teams, multidisciplinary teams, or ad hoc committees. During parent-teacher conferences, teachers can ask parents for their suggestions, ask what their goals are for their child, and ask about ways the family has met success when working with the child.

School as Resource

Parent resource centers are places where caregivers can go to gather information, network with school personnel or other parents, and work with school personnel on issues related to education. Some schools choose to extend the school library hours to offer this service to the child's family. Many schools offer childcare, homework clubs, or enrichment activities prior to and after school hours. Some schools offer adult-education classes, such as adult literacy, computer, or exercise classes.

Teacher as Resource

There are many ways a teacher can serve as a resource to students' parents and other community members. School newsletters, bulletin boards, interactive homework assignments, and reading lists are just a few examples of ways a teacher can provide resources to a caregiver. The teacher also can offer expertise to the community by leading a club, serving on a search committee, or leading a book drive to benefit a charity.

Collaboration with Educational Partners

Teachers must develop strong, positive relationships with a variety of educational partners in order to meet the needs of all students. As the expression goes, "It takes a village to raise a child." These partners may include the following:

- **Guidance counselors:** Professionals with an advanced degree whose primary role involves facilitating communication between student, home, and school, particularly when a student is struggling academically, socially, or emotionally. Guidance counselors also meet with students individually to support students with goal setting, transition from high school to career or college, and personal issues.

- **Individualized Education Plan (IEP) team members:** A variety of professionals, such as teachers, social workers, school psychologists, behavioral specialists, reading specialists, speech/language specialists, occupational therapists, nurses, administrators, and parents. In the secondary-school grades, students also may serve on their own IEP team.

- **Library media specialists:** Professionals with advanced degrees who provide individual and group instruction or assistance to students and teachers seeking more information on a topic. Library media specialists are experts in locating print and nonprint resources.

- **Paraprofessionals:** Educational support professionals who typically assist individuals or small groups of students or the classroom teacher. In some schools, these professionals are also known as teacher assistants.

- **Reading specialists:** Professionals with an advanced degree in reading or literacy that provide individual, small-group, or whole-group instruction to improve students' reading achievement. Reading specialists also may serve as a literacy coach, one who provides model lessons, offers resources to teachers, and assists with student testing and data analysis.

- **Special education teachers:** Professionals with an advanced degree who facilitate and provide direct instruction to students with learning differences.

- **Speech, physical, and occupational therapists:** Professionals with advanced degrees who provide direct instruction individually or in small groups to students who have speech/language, physical, or functional needs.

- **Teachers of gifted-and-talented students:** Professionals with expertise in understanding how students with exceptional academic knowledge and skills think. They may provide direct support to individuals or small groups of students and also serve as resources to classroom teachers.

Strategies for Collaboration and Teaming

As you can see, classroom teachers must work with a variety of educational professionals on a day-to-day basis. Meeting the needs of your students and working well with adult colleagues takes expertise and knowledge of how to maximize one another's role in the educational process. Following is a list of strategies to assist you in developing a collaborative, collegial relationship with other school professionals:

- **Determine roles and strengths.** Get to know your colleague before you jump in and begin working together. This step is extremely important. Have a conversation about each other's strengths, as well as how you see each of your individual roles in this partnership.

- **Develop an action plan.** Work together to develop an action plan that includes your weekly schedule, when you'll plan together, and how you can share information. Then analyze the results together.

- **Identify purpose of collaboration.** Establish goals for your students together. How will you both know you are successfully meeting students' needs? This important step keeps the focus on the students' needs, which is what teaching is all about!

- **Identify stakeholders.** Work together to determine other stakeholders who can assist in your action plan. Will the principal, parent(s), or school counselor also be a part of your plan?

- **Seek support.** Acknowledge that you don't know everything—no teacher does! Reflective teaching professionals seek more information and support from a variety of sources.

- **Support effective communication.** As discussed at length in Chapter 8, recognize the need for teachers to foster effective communication not only with students but also with other education professionals. When student goals are not being met or when communication begins to break down, the teaching professional must strive to bridge communication gaps effectively to achieve goals.

The School and Society

Public schools in the United States play a key role in society. Public schools represent the greater public interest by promoting democratic principles, teaching common values, and educating about the diverse cultures of global society. Schools also offer parents and citizens a variety of ways to have a voice in the direction of public education. Parents and citizens alike have an interest in the ability of our nation's students to acquire the knowledge, skills, and dispositions to lead productive, healthy, responsible, and successful lives. The ways students are educated today will affect the quality of American life for years to come. U.S. citizens living in a free and democratic nation must value and practice a common set of principles, such as equality and freedom for all, equal opportunity, self-governance, civic responsibility, respect for the laws of the nation, and social mobility. Decisions about content standards, performance standards, curriculum, and texts, as well as lessons in content areas and activities in school governance, provide opportunities for students and citizens to practice working effectively in a democratic society. Public education offers an opportunity for students and citizens to learn about the diverse members of our global society and to practice tolerance, respect, and understanding for people of different cultures and backgrounds.

Teachers must become reflective practitioners in order to be most effective. Reflective practice is grounded in John Dewey's progressive education movement. Dewey emphasized the need for teachers' reflective action to facilitate the knowledge of their students. Reflective practitioners display such characteristics as:

- Not being afraid to say they do not know or understand something
- Demonstrating a desire to be caring educators
- Showing a willingness to collaborate and to discuss experiences
- Having an ability to critically analyze their practices
- Viewing teaching and student behaviors through a reflective lens
- Demonstrating rational, careful thought to improve practices
- Possessing an awareness of one's culture, values, and beliefs
- Viewing diversity as a positive, enriching aspect of teaching
- Showing persistence
- Possessing effective interpersonal communication skills
- Valuing the importance of empowering learners

Advocacy for Learners

Teachers must advocate for the educational needs of all learners. Ways in which teachers advocate for learners include, but are not limited to, the following:

- Attending professional development training
- Staying abreast of the latest education findings and practices
- Actively participating in meetings about their students
- Fostering open communication with caregivers, colleagues, and other personnel who work with their students
- Modifying instructional practice to meet unique learning needs

Teachers must understand the awesome responsibility placed upon one in the teaching profession. Your local school district may have a stated code of ethics for teachers. In addition, professional associations like the

National Education Association (NEA) provide guidance on ethical standards for teachers. Teachers must demonstrate, for example, the highest commitment to students and to the teaching profession through actions such as the following:

- Nurturing each student's academic, social, emotional, physical, and civic growth
- Creating and sustaining a positive, challenging, and safe school environment
- Committing to lifelong learning for all, including the teacher's own learning
- Collaborating with colleagues, students' caregivers, and other professionals
- Advancing the intellectual foundation of the school community and education profession
- Following U.S. laws, including those that pertain specifically to schools, such as:
  - Discrimination against students, teachers, parents, or others based on race, sex, ethnicity, or religion
  - Prayer in public schools
  - Using books that have been removed from the school library or curriculum by a decision of the school board
  - Withholding school records from parents or guardians

Due Process

Due process is a constitutional, fundamental guarantee that proceedings will be fair and stakeholders will be given notice and an opportunity to take part in any proceedings. For example, if a student was suspended from school, parents and the student have a right to discuss this administrative decision and the opportunity to raise their concerns with a higher authority if they had evidence of possible legal rights infringement.

Equal Access

Students have legal rights to equal access to a quality education. For example, admission policies and procedures must account for all students fairly and equitably.

First Amendment Rights

These rights include respecting the establishment of religion, free exercise of religion, freedom of speech, freedom of the press, the right to peaceably assemble, and the right to make a complaint to the government without fear of reprisals. In schools, we may experience challenges to First Amendment rights, such as concern about viewpoints expressed in the student newspaper or students peaceably walking out of class to protest a school rule they believe is unfair.

Intellectual Freedom

Intellectual freedom is the right to freedom and expression of thought. In schools, this issue may arise when parents or guardians feel an assigned reading book or a film is not appropriate for their children. This may result in banning a book or censorship of information, an issue often addressed by school library media specialists, administrators, and school committee members.

Liability

Liability issues in schools usually are based on a claim of negligence. For example, a coach may be held liable for a student's injury if proper safety procedures were not followed.

Licensing and Tenure

In the United States, teachers must obtain a teaching license in their area(s) of certification from the state department of education. Tenure in the education field refers to an employment status teachers earn after fulfilling school district requirements. Tenure is a recognition of faculty competence and helps to foster a school environment that values academic freedom and professional responsibility.

Privacy and Confidentiality

Education professionals have a responsibility to maintain students' rights to privacy and hold students' personal matters confidential and discuss issues only among those professionals who need to know this information. For example, student academic files and report cards are personal, private records that may be shared only with the student and his or her legal parents/caregivers. Privacy and confidentiality are matters a school counselor often is trained to address, so teachers can turn to these professionals when they need advice on student matters.

Reporting Child Abuse or Neglect

This aspect of the teaching profession was definitively the most difficult experience I had as a teacher. At some point in your career, you are likely to work with a student who is being abused or neglected. You have a legal responsibility and, I believe, a moral responsibility to act in that child's best interest and to report your observations to the appropriate agency or professionals. In Rhode Island, the law is clear. Any citizen—teacher, parent in the carpool, neighbor, congregation member—who observes signs of child abuse or neglect must call a toll-free number to report their concerns. On the PLT test, you will want to state that you would report your concerns to the child protective services agency in your state as required by law and also would discuss your concerns confidentially with the school counselor, social worker, and/or administrator as appropriate. The important point here is that you have a legal responsibility to report your concerns to child protection services or the police, with or without the support of other school personnel, and have the professional responsibility also to report your concerns to school personnel.

Teachers' Rights

You may be asked questions about the rights of teachers in the United States. It is important for you to know that teachers have several rights, guided by school and civic law, including the following:

- Teachers have the right to withhold information unrelated to employment, such as age, marital status, sexual orientation, and so on.
- Pregnant teachers cannot be required to take maternity leave.
- Teachers cannot be fired for behavior that does not interfere with teaching effectiveness. Although teachers have a right to a personal life and behaviors associated with a personal life beyond school, the teacher may be fired for personal behavior that impacts teaching effectiveness both during the school day and beyond.
- Teachers can be sued and may be found liable for negligence. For example, if a teacher could have reasonably foreseen a situation, or if the teacher acted differently from the way in which a reasonable teacher placed in the same situation would have acted, the teacher may be found liable.
- Teachers have freedom of speech, as well as all other freedoms guaranteed in the U.S. Constitution.
- Although corporal punishment is not unconstitutional, it may be illegal and can only be administered according to the laws of the state.
- Teachers have a right to freely associate on and off school hours with whomever they choose, such as any political party, religious group, or community group, even those not seen favorably by the school committee or local administration.
- Teachers can be suspended or dismissed for not doing their jobs, but such administrative actions must include due process.

Students' Rights

Several court cases have helped to form the basis of students' rights in American schools today. In the *Tinker v. Des Moines Independent Community School District* case of 1969, the court established that students do not lose their constitutional rights of freedom of speech or expression in school. In the *Goss v. Lopez* case of 1971, the court established that students facing suspension must be afforded a hearing and notice before being denied their right to an education. This became known as due process.

Students' rights are more frequently infringed in the areas of search and seizure, freedom of speech and expression (for example, censorship, school dress codes, and privacy invasion), zero tolerance, and corporal punishment. Students have a limited freedom of press and a limited freedom of speech in schools. For example, student newspapers supported by the school system may be edited by school personnel. School periodicals supported solely by student groups may not be censored or edited by school officials. A student's freedom of speech may be withheld if it causes a major disruption in the school. A student may not use speech considered vulgar or offensive. School records must be made available to students and their parents upon request. Handicapped students between the ages of 3 and 21 have a right to a free and appropriate public education. This education must take place in the least restrictive environment.

Students and Teachers' Rights

School violence, bullying, and cyber-bullying have become serious issues for teachers and students. School violence is pervasive and there are a variety of ways to respond to and deter school violence. The Internet has created increased difficulties for school personnel and those who are bullied. Teachers must use professional judgment and expertise when allowing students to use the Internet during school hours.

The Larger Community: Educational Law

Americans with Disabilities Act (ADA), Title II

The Americans with Disabilities Act is a federal law that prohibits discrimination on the basis of a person's disability for all services, programs, and activities provided or made available by local and state governments. The ADA is not dependent on the receipt of federal funds.

Copyright

The American Library Association provides school personnel with helpful guidance on what may or may not be photocopied or presented for educational purposes. Known as fair use, one may show a video or DVD that is the original or has been rented from a video vendor as long as it is for curriculum purposes, for example. As far as photocopying, there is no one simple, easy answer. For example, teachers can make multiple copies of a chapter or an article for educational purposes as long as the work is relatively brief, spontaneously created, and cited, and as long as the copyright notice is displayed. These copies may not be used more than once and may not be made if they were created to avoid the purchase of a textbook or other copyrighted materials. For more information, visit the ALA website at www.ala.org.

The Family Education Rights and Privacy Act (FERPA), 1974

This law guarantees that parents can access their children's records and also prohibits release of school records without parental permission or student permission once the student is 18 years old.

Individuals with Disabilities Act (IDEA), 1990

The Individuals with Disabilities Act is a federal statute made up of several grant programs targeted at helping the states to educate students with disabilities. The IDEA specifically lists types of disabilities that render a child entitled to special education.

Individualized Education Plan (IEP)

An Individualized Education Plan (IEP) is a written education plan for a student with disabilities developed by a team of professionals (teachers, special educators, and school psychologists) and the child's parents or caregivers. An IEP is based on a multidisciplinary team (MDT) evaluation of the child, describing how the child is presently doing, what the child's learning needs are, and what services the child will need. Each IEP is reviewed and updated yearly. IEPs are required under Public Law 94-142, the Individuals with Disabilities Education Act (IDEA).

Lau v. Nichols, 1974

Federally funded schools must provide their non-English-speaking student with either English instruction or instruction in their native language.

Section 504 of the Vocational Rehabilitation Act, 1973

Section 504 is a civil rights law. Enacted in 1973, the law forbids organizations and employers from preventing individuals with disabilities an equal opportunity to receive program benefits and services.

The Education of All Handicapped Children Act—Public Law 94-142

Public Law 94-142 was passed into legislation during the Ford Administration in 1975. This law was created to ensure a free and appropriate education is provided to handicapped children and adults ages 3 through 21. The term *least restrictive environment* originated with this law; it states that handicapped persons must be educated, to the maximum extent possible, with their regular education peers. Special-education programs and meetings to determine special-education eligibility and placement are regulated by the original Public Law 94-142 and more recent iterations of the law. One important aspect of the law requires a school to provide written permission from the parent or guardian before conducting any evaluation of a child.

Massachusetts Laws of Education 1642 and 1647

The Law of 1642 established that parents (or "masters") were responsible for instilling the principles of religion and the capital laws of the Commonwealth of Massachusetts. All children and servants were required to demonstrate competency in reading and writing as outlined by the government. Not all children attended formal schools; therefore, it was the responsibility of parents to teach children basic literacy skills so they could abide by the governing laws of the land.

The Law of 1647 was established to combat parental negligence in educating the child or servant according to the Law of 1642. This law required that towns of 50 families or more hire a schoolmaster who could teach the children to read and write. Education became more of a social responsibility with the enactment of the Massachusetts Law of 1647.

Land Ordinance of 1785

By 1785, the separation of church and state were evident in American education. The Land Ordinance of 1785 helped to establish a way to fund public education. The sixteenth section in each township was reserved for the maintenance of public schools.

Northwest Ordinance of 1787

The Northwest Ordinance of 1787 provided land in the Great Lakes and Ohio Valley regions for settlement. One part of the ordinance stated that religion, morality, and knowledge are necessary for a strong government. The federal government began to create a public school system offered to all children.

Plessy v. Ferguson, 1896

After the Civil War ended, many Southern states were driven to limit the rights of former slaves. A group of New Orleans black businessmen decided to test the laws limiting their rights to use the railroads freely, laws supported in the South but not by the railroad owners. A man named Homer Plessy volunteered to break the law by taking a seat in a "white-car only." Plessy was arrested, and at his trial he argued that the laws violated his civil rights. Judge Ferguson found Plessy guilty and charged him a $25 fine. The Supreme Court reviewed the case of *Plessy v. Ferguson* and found the law of separate railroad cars constitutional. The Supreme Court ruled that "separate but equal facilities" was allowable by law. In 1896, Brown wrote the majority opinion; Associate Justice John Marshall Harlan was the lone dissenting vote. Brown wrote that a state law providing separate but equal facilities for black and white passengers does not infringe upon the Thirteenth Amendment or Fourteenth Amendment of the U.S. Constitution. The "separate but equal" view prevailed in the United States until the Supreme Court ruled that separate is "inherently unequal" in *Brown v. Board of Education.*

Oregon School Case of 1925

This case is also known as *Pierce v. Society of Sisters.* The Oregon school system participated in a decision to "Americanize" schools by requiring all children ages 8 to 16 to attend public schools. Exceptions were offered in a few instances, such as for those with physical handicaps and those who had completed the eighth grade successfully. The Society of Sisters of the Holy Names of Jesus and Mary and a group of educators from a nearby private military school disputed the constitutionality of this Oregon state law. In 1925, the court ruled that the state of Oregon could not require all students to attend public schools, because this violates a student's Fourteenth Amendment right of "personal liberty." Students can be required to attend public or private schools.

Brown v. Board of Education, 1954

On May 17, 1954, the Supreme Court announced its decision in the *Brown v. Board of Education* case that "separate educational facilities are inherently unequal," thereby changing the face of U.S. education forever. The decision effectively denied the legal basis for segregation in Kansas and 20 other states with segregated classrooms. *Brown v. Board of Education* was an important first step toward providing equal rights for all children in U.S. schools. For many years, several schools in the South continued to challenge "separate is unequal." In 1957, nine black students from Little Rock, Arkansas, nonviolently and bravely decided to challenge their right to attend the all-white Rock Central High. The students were met with racial slurs, and rocks and bottles were thrown at them. Federal soldiers had to escort the children through the doors of the school. The courageous students who advanced the civil rights movement became known as "The Little Rock Nine."

Separation of Church and State, 1947

The separation of church and state is part of a clause in the First Amendment to the U.S. Constitution. In short, public schools, in their role as a government-funded organization, must remain neutral toward religion. Teachers and students are affected by this constitutional right in a variety of ways, including the following:

- There will be no religious instruction in schools.
- There will be no ceremonial prayers in schools.
- There will be no invocations or benedictions by clergy at ceremonies.

- There will be no reading from the Bible unless the purpose is entirely secular (no religious basis).

- There may be religious objections to public school practices, such as reciting the Pledge of Allegiance and saluting the U.S. flag.

- School personnel and school boards must be mindful of curriculum that may be considered offensive to teachers' or students' religious beliefs.

History of U.S. Education

Colonial Period (1600–1776)

The Puritan Influence

The Puritans were a group of people who worked toward religious, moral, and societal reforms. They grew unhappy with the Church of England, escaped persecution from church leaders and the king of England, and fled to America. Free schooling was offered to all children, and the Puritans formed the first formal American school in 1635, called the Roxbury Latin School. In 1638, the first printing press was used. The Puritans were the first to write books for children. Schools during this time were strongly influenced by religion. In 1642, a law was passed stating that all children should learn to read. It was the Puritans' belief that an inability to read was Satan working to keep people from reading the Bible.

Latin Grammar School

The Roxbury Latin School was the first Latin Grammar School, established in 1635. Originally, these schools were designed for the sons of upper social classes who were destined to become leaders in the church, state, or judicial system. Girls were not considered for these schools. The schools taught reading, writing, and arithmetic. Besides preparing the boys for leadership positions, the more practical purpose of the Latin Grammar School was to prepare the boys for the entrance examination for Harvard College. These schools can be compared to the American Secondary Schools, which prepare today's students for higher education.

Establishment of Harvard College

Harvard College was established in 1636 by vote of the Great and General Court of the Massachusetts Bay Colony. The initial mission of the college was to ensure that the leaders of the church, state government, and judicial system were well prepared and learned. During these early years, Harvard offered a classic academic course of study, not only based on the English university model, but also consistent with the Puritans' philosophy of education.

Hornbooks

Hornbooks were used by children for several centuries starting in the mid-fifteenth century in Europe. A hornbook consisted of a wooden paddle, parchment with the lesson, and a cover for the lesson made of a piece of transparent horn. Lessons included such things as the alphabet, the Lord's Prayer, vowels, and consonant patterns.

New England Primer

The Primer was a textbook used by students. First printed in 1690, over 5 million copies of the book were sold. The New England Primer combined alphabet study with Bible verses.

Early National Period (1776–1840)

Benjamin Franklin (1706–1790)

Among his many contributions, Benjamin Franklin advanced formal education in America. He established a plan for the English-language grammar school in Philadelphia in 1749. The school would teach English, rather than Latin, and enact a curriculum focused on scientific and practical skills. The English grammar schools would educate a wider range of students who could make contributions to politics, government, society, as well as a variety of occupations and professions. Franklin's plan, which was never instituted, called for schools to be equipped with laboratories, books, maps, and globes so that students could connect practical knowledge with the world around them. The English grammar schools did not succeed, but Franklin's proposal led the way to the future American education institutions, which offered a comprehensive curriculum designed for the growing needs of the growing nation.

Thomas Jefferson (1743–1826)

The third U.S. president, Thomas Jefferson, worked for several years after his presidency to create the University of Virginia at Charlottesville, which was established in 1825. His vision for the school was to introduce American students to new ideas about government and equality. He understood that different students had different educational needs, so he allowed for electives in the curriculum. Jefferson conceived of every aspect of the university—surveying the site, planning for the buildings, supervising the construction, and establishing the curriculum.

Noah Webster (1758–1843)

Noah Webster established the first uniquely American dictionary, published in 1828 and called the *American Dictionary of the English Language.* His dictionary was adopted by Congress in 1831 and was considered the national standard for English in the United States. Webster also influenced American education by opposing the British texts used in schools and suggesting the need for American textbooks that included our language and experiences. He also established a grammar book, a reader, and *The American Spelling Book.*

Yale Report of 1828

This report demonstrated the strength of the conservative view of education—the need for a classical curriculum—which was centered at Yale University. The following issues at the time were causing controversy in higher education:

- Church control vs. state control of higher education
- The value of a college education vs. a university education
- The importance of the classical curriculum vs. the curriculum that allows for electives

Common School Period (1840–1880)

Common School

The common school was a school that would be available to all people, a part of the birthright of every American child, and founded on the principle of "social harmony." The common school movement contained elements of oppression and emancipation. Common schools attempted to respond to the needs of expanding capitalist industries and the realities of growing cities, such as the training of immigrants, so that these individuals could become productive workers. The common school movement also provided educational opportunity for children who had previously been excluded.

Horace Mann (1796–1859)

Horace Mann believed that a "common school" would be the great equalizer. Horace Mann is considered the father of American education, and, as Secretary of Education in 1839, he presided over the establishment of the first normal school in the United States. Normal schools were established for the primary purpose of training teachers.

Henry Barnard (1811–1900)

Henry Barnard was a great education reformer of the nineteenth century. He was a lifelong advocate for common schools—a design for a universal system of public education. Barnard also strongly believed in the importance of educating women. Barnard created the first board of education in Connecticut and became the first secretary of education in that state in 1838. Barnard faced resistance of his progressive ideas for education from the conservative political forces, parochial schools, and some parents. The conservative political forces were concerned that common schools would mean that children were less available to work and that taxes would be higher. Parochial schools felt that public education threatened their religious values. Some parents were concerned with the concept of a universal education, fearing that schools would become charitable organizations, more concerned with equality in education than excellence for their children.

Normal School

The first normal school in the United States was established in 1839 in Lexington, Massachusetts, for the purpose of training teachers. This first normal school is today known as Framingham State College. The normal schools were developed to support the growing need for teachers in the common schools.

McGuffey Readers

The first McGuffey Readers were published in 1836. These texts had a great influence on public education in the United States. The books had graded, or "leveled," readers, which upheld the values, beliefs, and way of life for Americans during this time. The first editions sold 7 million copies; by 1879, more than 60 million had been sold. There were several readers—The Eclectic First and Second Readers (1836), the Third and Fourth Readers (1837), the Fifth Reader (1844), the Sixth Reader (1857), and the Eclectic Spelling Book (1846). The readers passed through several publishers and were revised in 1879 by Van Nostrand Reinhold to include a collection of eight revised editions.

Compulsory Education

The Massachusetts Compulsory Attendance Act of 1852 required compulsory school attendance for children between the ages of 8 and 14 for at least three months of the calendar year; it also mandated that at least six weeks of each child's school attendance be consecutive. The penalty for not sending a child to school was a maximum fine of $20. The compulsory attendance law was revised in 1873, with the age limit lowered to 12 and the required length of attendance increased to 20 weeks each calendar year. By 1918, a compulsory education attendance law had been enacted in all U.S. states.

Morrill Act of 1862

Also known as the Land Grant College Act, the Morrill Act of 1862 established institutions in each state to provide an education in agriculture, home economics, mechanical arts, and other practical professions. The goal was to assure that education would be available to people in all social classes.

National Education Association (NEA)

The National Education Association (NEA) began in 1857 as the National Teachers Association and was founded by 43 educators in Philadelphia. The NEA is currently the largest educational association in the world. It was founded to advance the teaching profession, increase interest in teaching, and promote the cause of public education in the United States. The NEA allowed women to become members in 1866.

Establishment of Kindergartens

In 1837, the first kindergarten in the world was established by Friedrich Froebel, who became known as the father of kindergarten. In the United States, early kindergarten programs were established in 1856 in Wisconsin and in 1873 in Boston. Kindergartens were created first to support children living in poverty and those with special needs. The curriculum emphasized the importance of play. In 1872, kindergartens won the support of the NEA.

Progressive Period (1880–1920)

Impact of Business and Industry on American Education

Our present American education system was heavily influenced by the Industrial Revolution. During this period in history, the United States had to prepare people trained in agriculture to work in factories. The importance of mass production influenced the design of schools during this time, and vestiges of this system still influence American secondary schools today. The "mass production" mentality created a school system that was efficient and produced measurable gains. Successful graduates were ready to meet the increasing demands of industry and business. In the Southern black schools at the turn of the century, the goal was to ensure that African Americans remained agricultural and domestic workers. The General Education Board (GEB) established three key programs: State Supervisors for Negro Rural Schools, County Supervising Teachers, and County Training Schools. The discriminatory practices of these programs continued at least until *Brown v. Board of Education,* but vestiges of these discriminatory educational policies are still seen in U.S. schools today (for example, in inadequate funding for poor, urban schools, which educate a majority of minority students).

The Superintendent

Horace Mann was an education reformer concerned with school policy and leadership. He suggested that a senior teacher provide leadership in the school. To free the teacher for administrative duties, teacher aides and advanced students taught groups of the senior teacher's students. This practice became known as monitorial education, and it did not prove practical in many parts of the United States, but it did serve as a model for future schools. The term *superintendent of schools* came from the Industrial Revolution terminology of the times, with similar leaders in superintendent of railroads, superintendent of the factory, and so on. The first training program for administrators began at Teachers College at Columbia University at the turn of the century.

The Principal

As with the role of the superintendent, the role of the principal is rooted in Horace Mann's concept of the principal teacher and dates back to the turn of the century. The principal served as a middle manager and acted as teacher, as well as many other roles in the community, such as town clerk, store clerk, and church secretary. The role of principal started in the secondary schools and eventually spread into the primary schools.

Division of Schools into Grades

As noted in this text's section on the Colonial period of education, American education was founded to prepare the elite for leadership positions and for Harvard College. As a result of the Land Ordinance of 1785 and the Northwest Ordinance of 1787, towns had to set aside land for the building and operation of schools. This provided the context for the one-room schoolhouse. In these schools, one teacher usually taught between 30 and 40 students from all ages and ability levels. As more and more children began to attend schools, the one-room schoolhouse design no longer met the needs of the children and their teachers. More buildings were erected and school buildings became larger, creating the need for effective ways to group the children. At first, most schools grouped their students by age, with children ages 6 through 8 in one room and children ages 9 through 14 in another. If a child moved beyond the upper-level room, he or she would either attend college or join the workforce. Over time, the U.S. education system established a 12-grade-level system with an initial kindergarten year.

The Cardinal Principles of Secondary Education

There were seven cardinal principles of secondary education issued in a report by the Commission on the Reorganization of Secondary Education in 1918:

- Health (secondary schools should promote good health habits)
- Command of fundamental processes (writing, reading, oral and written expression, and mathematics)
- Worthy home membership (schools should promote good relationships)
- Vocation (know the variety of career options)
- Civic education (develop awareness and concern for one's community)
- Worthy use of leisure (advance skills to enrich a student's mind, body, spirit, and personality during leisure time)
- Ethical behavior (instilling personal responsibility and initiative)

NEA Committee of Ten

In 1882, the NEA appointed a committee, known as the Committee of Ten, which wrote a report calling for changes to liberalize the American high school. This report recommended the standardization of curricula for American high schools and elementary schools. The committee recommended eight years of elementary education, four years of secondary education, and the following four curriculum strands:

- Classical
- Latin-scientific
- Modern language
- English

American Federation of Teachers

The American Federation of Teachers (AFT) was formed in 1916. The AFT is a teachers' union associated with the American Federation of Labor and Congress of Industrial Organization (AFL-CIO). AFT's motto is "Democracy in Education and Education for Democracy."

Manual Training Movement

The manual training movement in American education provided the foundation for the vocational education programs in schools today. A manual training education offered wood and metal working, and it was seen as an enhancement to the traditional high school curriculum.

Modern Period (1920–Present)

John Dewey (1859–1952)

John Dewey made contributions to many areas during his life's work—philosophy, politics, social thought, psychology, and education. He is considered a foremost voice of American education philosophy. His philosophy of education is known as progressive education. Dewey's core beliefs included the following:

- There is a close connection between education and social action in a democracy.
- Students should be taught to become problem solvers.
- Students should participate in decisions about what they learn.

Dewey wrote several influential texts on educational philosophy, including *Experience and Education* and *The School and Society.* Dewey founded the American Association of University Professors in 1915 upon the principle of "academic freedom."

Adult Education

Although U.S. adult education's roots can be traced back over the last 200-plus years to events like Benjamin Franklin's establishment of the public library and his first adult-education organization, adult-education programs made several advances during the modern period. The Smith-Lever Act of 1914 helped to create cooperative extensions through the Land Grant University (Morrill Acts of 1860 and 1892), which offered adult education in agriculture, rural energy, and home economics. In the 1960s, the efforts of President Kennedy and President Johnson led to the Economic Opportunity Act of 1964, which created the first Adult Basic Education program grant program.

Testing Movement

Lewis Terman (1877–1956) introduced the Stanford-Binet intelligence test in 1916. Terman next provided consulting services to the U.S. military and initiated a testing program to sort and categorize recruits in an effort to match each soldier with the most appropriate military occupation. He also created the Stanford Achievement Test and coined the term *intelligence quotient,* or IQ. Terman used a scientific approach to determine and classify student ability; this was received with overwhelming support from the Progressive educators of the early 1900s. This method of scientifically proving immigrants and minorities scored lower than whites on these tests seemingly "proved" the prevalent discriminatory views that these people were mentally inferior.

Sputnik

U.S. education dramatically changed after October 4, 1957, when the Soviet Union successfully launched the world's first satellite. The *Sputnik* launch led to the creation of the National Aeronautics and Space Act (NASA), as well as American outcry for advanced coursework in mathematics and science in our schools.

ESEA

The Elementary and Secondary Education Act (ESEA) of 1965 was a federal program enacted to respond to the inequity in schools for the educationally disadvantaged. ESEA was related to President Johnson's "War on Poverty," which created a wide range of programs, including early childhood and others targeted for the education of economically disadvantaged children. ESEA has evolved over the years and has introduced programs such as Title I, Chapter I, Reading Excellence, Reading First, and No Child Left Behind.

A Nation at Risk

A Nation at Risk was an important report written by the National Commission on Excellence in Education in 1983. The report provided evidence that American education, particularly secondary schools, was falling behind that of other countries. The connection between the United States economic health and education was emphasized. The report called for the creation of teaching, teacher education, and education standards, and it suggested that current education majors and those in the teaching force were not all highly academically qualified to teach, particularly in the content areas.

Goals 2000: The National Education Goals

Goals 2000: The National Education Goals were established during the Clinton Administration and continued in the George W. Bush Administration as "America 2000." Under the plan, key goals include that by the year 2000:

- All students will start school ready to learn.
- High school graduation rates will meet or exceed 90 percent.
- Students will leave grades 4, 8, and 12 having demonstrated competency in challenging curricula in English, mathematics, foreign language, civics, history, geography, economics, and art.
- Teachers will have access to high-quality professional development.
- Students in the United States will be first in the world in science and mathematics achievement.
- Every adult in the United States will be literate and possess the skills and knowledge necessary to be a good U.S. citizen and to compete in the global economy.
- Schools will be free of drugs and violence.
- Schools will promote partnerships to increase parental involvement in education.

No Child Left Behind of 2001 (NCLB)—P.L. 107-110

No Child Left Behind (NCLB) is an historic, bipartisan education reform effort spearheaded by President George W. Bush. The No Child Left Behind Act of 2001 reauthorized ESEA, the main federal law affecting education from kindergarten through high school. NCLB is based on four principles:

- Accountability for results
- More choices for parents
- Greater local control and flexibility
- An emphasis on doing what works based on scientific research

Race to the Top Fund-Recovery Act of 2011

Race to the Top is a $4.35-billion competitive grants program to reward states that create the conditions for education improvement, innovation, and reform. This act was part of the American Recovery and Reinvestment Act of 2009, which was created during the Obama Administration.

PART IV

FULL-LENGTH PRACTICE TESTS

Chapter 11

PLT Early Childhood Practice Test

This full-length PLT Early Childhood practice test (0621) is designed to give you an overall sense of the test's format and to help you determine the content areas you need to focus on in your studies. You may want to practice your pacing while taking this full-length practice test. You will have a total of two hours to complete the entire PLT test, which consists of 70 multiple-choice questions and 4 constructed-response questions.

After you complete the full-length practice test, score your answers and use the explanations to self-diagnose content areas to study in Part III of this guide. You also may want to complete the other practice tests in Chapters 12, 13, and 14 to aid you in determining which content areas to study. Even though these additional practice tests are written for other PLT test grade levels, the question topics (Students as Learners; Instructional Process; Assessment; and Professional Development, Leadership, and Community) remain the same.

CUT HERE

(Remove this answer sheet and use it to mark your answers to the multiple-choice questions.)

Answer Sheet

1 Ⓐ Ⓑ Ⓒ Ⓓ	41 Ⓐ Ⓑ Ⓒ Ⓓ
2 Ⓐ Ⓑ Ⓒ Ⓓ	42 Ⓐ Ⓑ Ⓒ Ⓓ
3 Ⓐ Ⓑ Ⓒ Ⓓ	43 Ⓐ Ⓑ Ⓒ Ⓓ
4 Ⓐ Ⓑ Ⓒ Ⓓ	44 Ⓐ Ⓑ Ⓒ Ⓓ
5 Ⓐ Ⓑ Ⓒ Ⓓ	45 Ⓐ Ⓑ Ⓒ Ⓓ
6 Ⓐ Ⓑ Ⓒ Ⓓ	46 Ⓐ Ⓑ Ⓒ Ⓓ
7 Ⓐ Ⓑ Ⓒ Ⓓ	47 Ⓐ Ⓑ Ⓒ Ⓓ
8 Ⓐ Ⓑ Ⓒ Ⓓ	48 Ⓐ Ⓑ Ⓒ Ⓓ
9 Ⓐ Ⓑ Ⓒ Ⓓ	49 Ⓐ Ⓑ Ⓒ Ⓓ
10 Ⓐ Ⓑ Ⓒ Ⓓ	50 Ⓐ Ⓑ Ⓒ Ⓓ
11 Ⓐ Ⓑ Ⓒ Ⓓ	51 Ⓐ Ⓑ Ⓒ Ⓓ
12 Ⓐ Ⓑ Ⓒ Ⓓ	52 Ⓐ Ⓑ Ⓒ Ⓓ
13 Ⓐ Ⓑ Ⓒ Ⓓ	53 Ⓐ Ⓑ Ⓒ Ⓓ
14 Ⓐ Ⓑ Ⓒ Ⓓ	54 Ⓐ Ⓑ Ⓒ Ⓓ
15 Ⓐ Ⓑ Ⓒ Ⓓ	55 Ⓐ Ⓑ Ⓒ Ⓓ
16 Ⓐ Ⓑ Ⓒ Ⓓ	56 Ⓐ Ⓑ Ⓒ Ⓓ
17 Ⓐ Ⓑ Ⓒ Ⓓ	57 Ⓐ Ⓑ Ⓒ Ⓓ
18 Ⓐ Ⓑ Ⓒ Ⓓ	58 Ⓐ Ⓑ Ⓒ Ⓓ
19 Ⓐ Ⓑ Ⓒ Ⓓ	59 Ⓐ Ⓑ Ⓒ Ⓓ
20 Ⓐ Ⓑ Ⓒ Ⓓ	60 Ⓐ Ⓑ Ⓒ Ⓓ
21 Ⓐ Ⓑ Ⓒ Ⓓ	61 Ⓐ Ⓑ Ⓒ Ⓓ
22 Ⓐ Ⓑ Ⓒ Ⓓ	62 Ⓐ Ⓑ Ⓒ Ⓓ
23 Ⓐ Ⓑ Ⓒ Ⓓ	63 Ⓐ Ⓑ Ⓒ Ⓓ
24 Ⓐ Ⓑ Ⓒ Ⓓ	64 Ⓐ Ⓑ Ⓒ Ⓓ
25 Ⓐ Ⓑ Ⓒ Ⓓ	65 Ⓐ Ⓑ Ⓒ Ⓓ
26 Ⓐ Ⓑ Ⓒ Ⓓ	66 Ⓐ Ⓑ Ⓒ Ⓓ
27 Ⓐ Ⓑ Ⓒ Ⓓ	67 Ⓐ Ⓑ Ⓒ Ⓓ
28 Ⓐ Ⓑ Ⓒ Ⓓ	68 Ⓐ Ⓑ Ⓒ Ⓓ
29 Ⓐ Ⓑ Ⓒ Ⓓ	69 Ⓐ Ⓑ Ⓒ Ⓓ
30 Ⓐ Ⓑ Ⓒ Ⓓ	70 Ⓐ Ⓑ Ⓒ Ⓓ
31 Ⓐ Ⓑ Ⓒ Ⓓ	
32 Ⓐ Ⓑ Ⓒ Ⓓ	
33 Ⓐ Ⓑ Ⓒ Ⓓ	
34 Ⓐ Ⓑ Ⓒ Ⓓ	
35 Ⓐ Ⓑ Ⓒ Ⓓ	
36 Ⓐ Ⓑ Ⓒ Ⓓ	
37 Ⓐ Ⓑ Ⓒ Ⓓ	
38 Ⓐ Ⓑ Ⓒ Ⓓ	
39 Ⓐ Ⓑ Ⓒ Ⓓ	
40 Ⓐ Ⓑ Ⓒ Ⓓ	

CUT HERE

Time: 2 hours

70 multiple-choice questions and 4 constructed-response questions

Multiple-Choice Questions

Directions: For each multiple-choice question, select the best answer and mark the corresponding letter space on your answer sheet.

1. Miss Rachel, a first-grade teacher, rarely teaches her students as a whole group; instead, she works individually with students. She carefully observes the students in their environment and plans lessons around each individual student's needs and interests. One could best describe Miss Rachel's teaching style as

   A. direct instruction.
   B. Montessori.
   C. Hunter.
   D. advance organizer.

2. Zach is a 5-year-old boy who used to love to play alone with his action figures in the sandbox but now often asks to play with his friend Harry. The boys enjoy figuring out how to build castles in the sandbox and like to experiment with a variety of tools to make the best castles. According to Jean Piaget, one can best describe Zach's level of development as which of the following?

   A. Preconditional
   B. Post-operational
   C. Sensorimotor
   D. Preoperational

Questions 3–4 are based on the following passage.

   Pete is a student with a learning disability who has had many unsuccessful school experiences, especially in the area of mathematics. He appears unmotivated and disengaged in his second-grade classroom. Pete often avoids the task by asking to use the bathroom or by playing in the blocks area.

3. Based on the information provided, the best explanation for Pete's apparent lack of motivation is

   A. psychomotor development.
   B. low socioeconomic status.
   C. learned helplessness.
   D. multiple intelligence.

4. A student who has an IQ range between 50 and 75, is able to learn skills up to the sixth-grade level, and is able to become fairly self-sufficient most likely has

   A. developmentally appropriate delays.
   B. formal operational thinking.
   C. functional or mild mental retardation.
   D. auditory discrimination.

5. An activity that is found to stimulate brain activity and that requires students to use visual, kinesthetic, or whole body movement is known as

   A. nonlinguistic representation.
   B. verbal representation.
   C. linguistic representation. *(reading or hearing)*
   D. musical representation.

6. As part of a science unit on plants, Miss Webb brought her first-graders to a greenhouse at the local university. The children then returned to the classroom for hands-on learning experiences about plants. Miss Webb can explain the value of this field trip to her principal by saying she is using which instructional approach?

   A. Anchored instruction
   B. Tiered instruction
   C. Cooperative learning
   D. Advance organizers

7. Mr. Moore is a kindergarten teacher who uses the following centers in his early childhood classroom:

   ▪ Art easel
   ▪ Sand and water table
   ▪ Dress up
   ▪ Community (a center with changing themes such as post office, library, and grocery store)

   One can say that Mr. Moore values which aspect of early childhood education in his choice of center activities?

   A. Reading
   B. Playing
   C. Writing
   D. Rote memory

8. Mrs. Foster plans her first-grade curriculum based on her students' interests. She works with the children's families and other community partners to enrich her lessons and to establish learning goals for her students. Miss Foster's approach to curriculum is called which of the following?

   A. Cognitive
   B. Behavioral
   C. Standards based
   D. Emergent

9. Teachers who are lifelong learners and professionals need to attend _____ to stay current in their teaching areas.

   A. binding arbitration
   B. professional journals
   C. reflective practitioners
   D. professional development

10. Teachers who foster open communication with parents or caregivers, colleagues, and administrators show their ability to

    A. withhold school records.
    B. advocate for all learners.
    C. stay current in the latest research.
    D. exercise freedom of speech.

11. Which of the following is NOT a teacher's right?

    A. Sharing information unrelated to school employment, such as age and marital status
    B. Being fired for behavior that does not interfere with teaching effectiveness
    C. Being permitted to take maternity leave
    D. Using books that have been removed from the school library by decision of the school committee

12. Which of the following books was used during the Colonial period to support lessons on the alphabet, the Lord's Prayer, vowel and consonant patterns, and reading?

    A. Dick and Jane series
    B. *Webster's Dictionary*
    C. The hornbook
    D. McGuffey Readers

13. Mrs. LaPlante believes that her students should be problem solvers and active decision makers in education. She also believes that students should be presented with real-life problem situations and that a project-based approach to learning is best. Mrs. LaPlante's teaching philosophy is most influenced by

    A. Gilligan.
    B. Erikson.
    C. Dewey.
    D. Smith.

14. Ricky has a difficult time following basic rules in his second-grade classroom. His parents report that he has similar difficulty at home and cannot be trusted alone with his baby brother or the family pets. He has shown unusual anger toward his baby brother and has become violent when playing with the family cat. Ricky may need further evaluation by a professional for what type of disorder?

    A. Autism-spectrum disorder
    B. Behavior disorder
    C. Multiple-disciplinary disorder
    D. Mental-retardation disorder

Questions 15–16 are based on the following passage.

Dee is a new student in Mrs. Baris's first-grade class. Mrs. Baris learns from Dee's school records that she has recently moved to the United States from Vietnam and that her family speaks Vietnamese in their home. Dee has been nearly silent in the classroom this first month of school, and Mrs. Baris would like to get to know Dee's literacy and educational needs better. Mrs. Baris has three other students who speak both Vietnamese and English in her classroom this year.

15. Which of the following best describes Dee's current language/literacy status?

A. Alliterate
B. Primary Language Not English (PLNE)
C. Beginning reader
D. Developmentally delayed

16. Mrs. Baris can better understand and teach her students by understanding the following three levels of Vietnamese culture: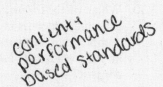

A. Concrete, formal, religious
B. Concrete, operational, formal
C. Concrete, sequential, symbolic
D. Concrete, behavioral, symbolic

17. Which of the following are specific expectations of what a student must know and be able to do?

A. Goals
B. Benchmarks
C. Standards
D. Frameworks

content + performance based standards

18. Mr. Addison often closes his lessons with time for students to discuss how their work went, what areas students need help in, and what they learned. Mr. Addison most likely values which type of assessment for his students?

A. Standardized testing
B. Self-evaluation
C. Portfolios
D. Analytical scoring

19. Miss Burton is a new teacher at East Elementary School. She has been asked by district administrators to give an end-of-the-school-year test to her second-graders. This math test has been created by a district assessment committee and requires short-answer responses that can be time-consuming and difficult to score. The district assessment committee has created a scoring guide to support the second-grade teachers and to ensure valid and reliable assessment. What type of scoring guide has the committee created?

A. Analytical
B. Equivalent
C. Holistic
D. Raw

20. Miss Burton's school district also has started to assess their students' achievements each fall using a standardized test. Student scores are reported to the teacher by _____ to show where a student falls compared to those students who took the test nationally.

A. raw score
B. rubric rank
C. mean
D. percentile rank

21. In *Goss v. Lopes* (1971), the court established that students facing school suspension must be afforded a hearing and notice before being denied their right to an education. This became known as _____ process.

A. suspension
B. detention
C. IEP
D. due

22. Which of the following laws was passed into legislation in 1975 to ensure that a free and appropriate education is provided to handicapped children and adults ages 3 through 21?

A. P.L. IDEA
B. No Child Left Behind
C. P.L. 94-142
D. Elementary and Secondary Education Act

23. In 1837, to support children from poverty and those with special needs, Freidrich Froebel established which of the following? *father of Kindergarten*

    A. Multi-aged classrooms
    B. Kindergartens
    C. Normal schools
    D. Common schools

24. Common schools, established from the 1840s to 1880s in the United States, were designed to be available to all people and were founded on the principle of social harmony. A supporter of the common school, _____ is known as the father of American education.

    A. Horace Mann
    B. Henry Barnard
    C. Thomas Jefferson
    D. Benjamin Franklin

25. Based on Jones's time-on-task studies, which of the following is the most likely classroom management problem you will face as a beginning teacher?

    A. Talking
    B. Tardiness
    C. Goofing off
    D. School violence

26. Which of the following is an important learner factor to be aware of before teaching a lesson?

    A. Anticipatory set
    B. Attention difficulties
    C. Bloom's taxonomy
    D. Classroom setup (tables, individual desks, size) *(environmental factors)*

Questions 27–28 are based on the following passage.

Mrs. Dougherty's school district has just implemented yearly grade-level testing for all children in grades 1 through 8. These tests are standardized and are nationally normed to provide district administrators with data to inform curriculum decisions. Mrs. Dougherty is concerned about five of her students' ability to take these tests because they are nonreaders and receive special education or Reading Recovery support.

27. Which one of the following questions would you advise Mrs. Dougherty to ask her administration?

    A. Do my first-graders need to take these tests?
    B. What is the purpose of a first-grader taking a norm-referenced test?
    C. What testing accommodations are available to my students?
    D. What other tests are available?

28. In addition to testing accommodations, students with documented learning differences also may be eligible for

    A. short breaks.
    B. criterion-referenced assessments.
    C. testing in the resource room.
    D. alternative assessments.

29. A test such as the SDRT4 offers teachers a _____ of a student; this provides the teacher with information about the student's areas of strength and weakness, which can be used to inform instructional planning for that child.

    A. criterion evaluation
    B. hearing evaluation
    C. diagnostic evaluation
    D. placement evaluation

30. Which of the following cooperative-learning grouping practices involves individual students completing their work and then teaming with another student to assess their work and discuss content?

    A. Group investigation
    B. Partner check
    C. Whole-group instruction
    D. STAD

31. Mr. Manning prepares his second-grade students for a lesson on animal habitats by taking the children on a walking field trip through the woods near the schoolyard. He engages the children in discussion about all the places woodland animals might live. When Mr. Manning and his students return to the classroom, he asks the children to contribute to a chart all about woodland animal habitats. Which of the following best describes Mr. Manning's rationale for the walking field trip?

    A. Creating an anticipatory set for the lesson *(prior knowledge)*
    B. Creating the mood for the lesson
    C. Monitoring student achievement in science
    D. Providing an authentic culminating assessment of his science objectives

32. Mrs. Horton tells her students that there is *A RAT* in the word *separate* to help her students remember how to spell this challenging word. What principle of learning is she using to help her students improve their spelling?

    A. Phonics
    B. Inquiry
    C. Play
    D. Mnemonics

33. Prout School offers its primary grade students and their families several services during and after school hours, such as a parent resource library, homework clubs, enrichment activities, and adult-education programs in the evening. Which of the following best describes the principles of teaching that this school values?

    A. Parents as shared decision makers
    B. Schools as a resource
    C. No Child Left Behind
    D. Teacher as a resource

34. Miss Nelson sends a weekly newsletter to her students' families and invites families into her classroom to assist her while she's teaching. She has received feedback from the families of children who have been promoted from her classroom that working in the classroom helped the parents become better teachers of their children in the home. Miss Nelson most likely values which principle of teaching and learning?

    A. National Education Association (NEA)
    B. Parent Teacher Associations (PTAs)
    C. Respectful communication
    D. Teacher as a resource

35. During the Progressive period in the history of U.S. education, most schools moved from being organized as one-room schoolhouses to

    A. groups of children by age, ages 6–10 and 11–16.
    B. groups of children by grade, K–12.
    C. groups of children by age, ages 6–8 and 9–14.
    D. groups of children by grade, 1–6, 7–8, and 9–12.

36. This professional association for teachers began in 1857 in Philadelphia. It was founded to advance the teaching profession, stimulate interest in teaching, and promote public education in the United States.

    A. National Education Association
    B. National Reading Association
    C. American Federation of Teachers
    D. United Education Association of Teachers

37. Kinesthetic, visual, and auditory are all

    A. learning modalities.
    B. learning centers.
    C. brain-based learning.
    D. multiple intelligences.

38. A student who is not learning to his or her potential in one or more areas, such as reading, writing, or mathematics, may be found to have a _____ by a multidisciplinary team or physician.

    A. behavioral objective
    B. short attention span
    C. learning disability
    D. personal literacy plan

Questions 39–40 are based on the following passage.

Brandon and his twin sister, Mary, are kindergarten students in Mrs. Rose's classroom. Mrs. Rose has noticed learning and developmental differences for each child. Mary often clings to her mother at drop-off time and once in the classroom doesn't engage with the other children. She prefers to sit off to the side of the class and observe others or to sit right next to the teacher. Brandon, on the other hand, cooperates well with his peers, is active in all sorts of play activities (especially imaginative games), and gives his mom a cheerful goodbye and kiss at drop-off time.

39. Erikson would describe Brandon as a child who has healthily developed through childhood's psychosocial crisis called   *independence*
    A. learning initiative vs. guilt.
    B. industry vs. inferiority.
    C. knowledge vs. cooperation.
    D. trust vs. mistrust.

40. Mary, on the other hand, is having difficulty with a stage of development for children ages two to six. The theorist Erikson might suggest that she needs to have social interactions to help her experience which of the following stages?
    A. Elementary- and middle-grades stage: competency vs. inferiority
    B. Early childhood stage: initiative vs. guilt
    C. Toddler stage: autonomy vs. doubt
    D. Preschool stage: individuality vs. cooperation

41. Mrs. Bergman often shares stories of previous first-grader's successes, or she highlights an individual student when he or she shows effort toward a learning goal. For example, yesterday Mrs. Bergman asked the class to listen to Julie explain how she solved her math problem. Julie needed to try several different ways to solve the problem before she was successful. After Julie shared her story, Mrs. Bergman let the class know that she appreciates Julie's hard work and she can see that Julie has learned a lot today. Mrs. Bergman then wrote a quick note to Julie's parents that emphasized how important Julie's efforts were to her success today. Which of the following principles of instruction are guiding Mrs. Bergman's practice in this situation?
    A. Reinforcing and providing recognition
    B. Numbered heads together
    C. Homework and practice
    D. Identifying strengths and weaknesses

42. Mr. Christie, a kindergarten teacher at East Elementary School, has just begun a unit on the author Eric Carle. Besides introducing his students to this popular and prolific children's author, Mr. Christie's goals include teaching the students about science using books such as *A House for a Hermit Crab* and *The Very Hungry Caterpillar.* He also hopes to teach the students a social-emotional goal about how small things can lead to great success using additional Carle texts, such as *The Mountain That Loved a Bird, The Honeybee and the Robber,* and *The Very Busy Spider.* Which of the following is the best way to describe Mr. Christie's unit plans?
    A. Interdisciplinary study
    B. Thematic unit
    C. Literature unit
    D. Inquiry based

43. During a study of patterns, Mr. Forte's second-grade students participated in the following activities:

   - Exploration of patterns in the classroom and around the school
   - Examination of patterns in children's literature texts *El Caminando* (*Taking a Walk*) and *A Pair of Socks*
   - Hands-on study of patterns using teddy-bear counters and pattern blocks

   The children worked in small groups to learn more about patterns and the teacher facilitated student projects by providing resources, guidance, and ideas for further study. Which of the following best describes the principles of teaching and learning used in this lesson?

   A. Basal-text unit plan
   B. Mathematics instruction
   C. Simulation learning
   D. Project-based learning

44. Miss Britton, a first-grade teacher at Curtis School, makes a point of taking notes on her students' interactions with each other and their achievements during learning-center time and independent-work time. She writes what she observes, and later she adds her notes in an ongoing notebook for each student. This helps Miss Britton to reflect on her students' progress and to plan for her lessons in the future. Which of the following best describes this authentic assessment practice?

   A. Anecdotal records
   B. Portfolio assessment
   C. Personal assessment plan
   D. Aptitude records

45. During the Colonial period of U.S. education, this type of school was originally designed for the sons of upper social classes who were destined to be leaders of the church, state, or judicial system. Girls were not considered for these schools. Besides preparing the students for leadership positions, the practical purpose of these schools was to prepare the boys for the entrance examination for Harvard College.

   A. Hornbook school
   B. Latin grammar school
   C. Early elementary school
   D. Common school

46. This school employee position first was suggested by Horace Mann and is derived from Industrial Revolution terminology.

   A. Teacher
   B. Teacher assistant
   C. Business manager
   D. Superintendent

47. Teachers must demonstrate the highest commitment to students and the teaching profession by creating and sustaining a positive, challenging, and safe school environment. This statement is an example of a teacher's

   A. mission.
   B. code of ethics.
   C. vision.
   D. action plan.

48. During a job interview for a first-grade position at Coventry Oaks School, Mr. Mathews showed his willingness to collaborate with colleagues, discuss teaching practices, and critically analyze his own practice. The school principal, Mrs. Daisy, assessed that Mr. Mathews showed which of the following teaching characteristics?

   A. Reflective practitioner
   B. Instructional practitioner
   C. Advocate for learners
   D. Instructional leader

49. In order to shape her students' learning response, Mrs. Indie awards stickers and prize pencils. Which theoretical perspective is Mrs. Indie using?

   A. Sociocultural theoretical perspective
   B. Behaviorist theoretical perspective
   C. Constructivist theoretical perspective
   D. Information-processing theoretical perspective

50. Mr. Fudela believes in the value of talk in his classroom, so that students can learn not only from him, but also from the many experiences and perspectives of peers. Which best describes the theoretical perspective Mr. Fudela is using?

   A. Sociocultural theoretical perspective
   B. Behaviorist theoretical perspective
   C. Constructivist theoretical perspective
   D. Information-processing theoretical perspective

51. Miss Taylor knows that her students learn best when she tells students what they will be learning, known as developing declarative knowledge. This helps students place knowledge in their working memory, which hopefully then moves to long-term memory after instruction. Which best describes the theoretical perspective Miss Taylor is using?

    A. Sociolcultural theoretical perspective
    B. Behaviorist theoretical perspective
    C. Constructivist theoretical perspective
    D. Information-processing theoretical perspective

52. Mr. O'Malley concerns himself with the internal aspects of how his students learn. For example, he knows that students construct knowledge, not absorb it, so he provides many hands-on experiences using artifacts from his world travels. Which best describes the theoretical perspective Mr. O'Malley is using?

    A. Sociocultural theoretical perspective
    B. Behaviorist theoretical perspective
    C. Constructivist theoretical perspective
    D. Information-processing theoretical perspective

53. Mrs. Dougherty teaches her students about animal habitats by immersing them in reading, writing, and inquiry about animals during the month of January. She helps each student gather information about his or her chosen animal's habitat by accessing a website designed for early learners. Which of the following best describes Mrs. Dougherty's instructional process?

    A. Understanding by Design
    B. Thematic-unit instruction
    C. Interdisciplinary lesson plan
    D. Backward design

54. Instructional objectives should have which of the following three components?

    A. Measurable verb, assessment plan, standards
    B. Conditions, criterion, measurable verb
    C. Materials, measurable verb, environmental factors
    D. Standards, measurable verb, conditions

55. Miss Moffitt, a first-grade classroom teacher, is assigned to work with Mrs. Peck, a paraprofessional who is supposed to work with a child with autism in Miss Moffitt's classroom. Mrs. Peck is often late to class and then chats with other students in the classroom, hardly paying attention to the student she is assigned to. Which of the following is the most effective communication technique for Miss Moffitt to use to make initial attempts to resolve this instructional dilemma?

    A. Writing a disciplinary report
    B. Speaking with other teachers who work with Mrs. Peck
    C. Utilizing nonviolent principles
    D. Sending "I messages"

56. Miss Cathy has a train whistle she uses to let students know that it is almost time to go to lunch, recess, or home. Miss Cathy is using which instructional process?

    A. Transition signal
    B. Elaboration
    C. Modeling
    D. Positive reinforcement

57. The students in Mr. Adamy's second-grade class gather information about plants, and then each student creates a poster or PowerPoint presentation to teach classmates about his or her chosen plant. Mr. Adamy and the class then provide feedback to student presenters about how much they learned about plants during the sharing session. Which of the following best describes the type of assessment Mr. Adamy is using?

    A. Standards-based assessment
    B. Evidence-based assessment
    C. Authentic assessment
    D. Direct assessment

58. Listening, frequent and positive communication, as well as understanding when communicating with children's parents or caregivers are all hallmarks of which type of communication teaching professionals should use?

    A. Reciprocal communication
    B. Parent/teacher communication
    C. Respectful communication
    D. Multicultural communication

59. Mr. Pope is teaching a drawing lesson in which students must trace and then reproduce a picture of a pilgrim. Which of the following best describes the domain for Mr. Pope's lesson objective?

    A. Cognitive domain
    B. Psychomotor domain
    C. Psychological domain
    D. Affective domain

60. Jared is a first-born kindergartner who is afraid to leave his mother at the classroom door each morning. Miss Connor helped Jared overcome this fearful situation by creating a positive environment and experience each morning as he and his mother approached the classroom door. The approach Miss Connor used is best known as which of the following?

    A. Classical conditioning
    B. Modeling
    C. Contingency contract
    D. Community of learners

61. Dave and Nishita often enjoy working together during writing class. Dave has creative story ideas and is very expressive verbally. Nishita has a superior vocabulary and strong writing skills. Which of the following best describes the reason behind Dave and Nishita's successful learning?

    A. Distributed cognition
    B. Sense of community
    C. Self-efficacy
    D. Primary reinforcer

62. Mr. Holmes has set up a homework tracking chart for his second-graders. When students complete homework, they place a sticker on the chart. After students earn 10 stickers, they have the opportunity to choose a prize from the teacher's treasure chest. Which of the following best describes the theory Mr. Holmes is using to motivate homework completion?

    A. Zone of proximal development
    B. Operant conditioning
    C. Social information processing
    D. Positive psychology

63. Jean Piaget defined _____ as the mental representation of an associated set of perceptions, ideas, and/or actions.

    A. assimilation
    B. accommodation
    C. script
    D. schema

64. Mrs. Niebala explains how she approaches reading difficult words by sharing her thought processes with her first-graders. Which of the following best describes the instructional process Mrs. Niebala is utilizing?

    A. Rote learning
    B. Reciprocal causation
    C. Modeling
    D. Mastery learning

65. Mrs. Geibler assigns additional homework when students do not do the assignment the night before. As used in Mrs. Geibler's classroom, _____ involves presenting a new stimulus—one hopefully the learner finds unpleasant—to decrease undesired behavior.

    A. positive reinforcement
     B. presentation punishment
    C. removal punishment
    D. reciprocal reinforcement

66. This type of curriculum is based primarily on the interests of children. The teacher works together with family and other community members to set possible direction for a project and then determine the actual curriculum based on student interest.

    A. Enacted curriculum
    B. Scope-and-sequence curriculum
    C. Emergent curriculum
    D. Thematic curriculum

67. Social-cognitive theory can best be described as learning

    A. based on cultural and linguistic experiences.
     B. through the observation of others.
    C. based on stimuli and responses.
    D. socially appropriate knowledge and skills.

68. The information-processing theoretical perspective on learning can best be characterized as being concerned with

    A. how people create or construct knowledge.
    B. why the human mind does not operate like a computer.
    C. how cultural constructs are shared between one person and another.
    D. what happens inside the learner's mind.

69. Which of the following are you LEAST likely to see in a student-centered lesson?

    A. Discovery learning
    B. Cooperative learning
    C. Direct instruction
    D. An experiment

70. Which of the following best exemplifies a signal in a lesson transition?

    A. Stating "1-2-3, eyes on me"
    B. Giving a student a warning for talking out of turn
    C. Opening the lesson with a motivating activity
    D. Telling the students to continue reading and writing

Constructed-Response Questions

Directions: The following questions require you to write short answers, or "constructed responses." You are not expected to cite specific theories or texts in your answers; however, your knowledge of specific principles of learning and teaching will be evaluated. Be sure to answer all parts of the question. Write your answers in the space provided.

Instructional Scenario I

Scenario: Miss Cindy

Miss Cindy is a beginning kindergarten teacher at South School. Her principal, Mrs. Galligan, is planning a formal observation as required by the school district's teacher contract. Miss Cindy is planning to be observed during an integrated language arts block in which she'll use poems from the book *Chicken Soup with Rice* by Maurice Sendak. Miss Cindy is required to submit a lesson plan to Mrs. Galligan in advance of the observation. Her lesson plan is provided here as Document 1.

Document 1

Objectives

- The student will identify the letter and the sound /o/ in the poem "October."
- The student will repeat the poem after the teacher.
- The student will point to words in the poem.
- The student will be able to discuss the poem "October"—specifically the fall season, Halloween, and the months before and after October.
- NAEYC Standard: 4b Teaching and Learning: Using Developmentally Effective Approaches

Resources

- *Chicken Soup with Rice* by Maurice Sendak (big book format)
- CD of "October" poem sung by Carole King
- "October" poem on chart paper
- Pointer
- Letter Person *O*—Ollie the Ghost
- Oaktag *O* shapes prepared by teacher
- Precut magazine pictures of fall images and objects with the /o/ sound

Motivation

Play the song version of the "October" poem in *Chicken Soup with Rice*. Encourage the children to sing along the second and any other times the song is played. Discuss October, Halloween, and the fall images in the song/poem.

Procedures

1. Play and sing the song.
2. Read big book.
3. Teach sounds of /o/.
4. Read "October" poem.
5. Identify letter *O*, sounds of /o/, and words with *O* in the poem.

Warm-Up

Sing along to *Chicken Soup with Rice* CD sung by Carole King.

Preview

Read aloud the big book version of *Chicken Soup with Rice*, paying careful attention to the months of the year, the illustrations, and the four seasons. Have a general discussion about the book to help students make personal connections and to check for understanding. Discuss which months come before and after October.

Teach

Introduce Letter Person "Ollie the Ghost," who will help us to read the "October" poem from *Chicken Soup with Rice*. Discuss the sounds *O* makes and ask children to make the sounds and hear the sounds.

Read the "October" poem on the chart. The teacher points to each word as she reads. Reread and encourage children to echo read or sing read. Continue discussion about October, fall season, and months before and after October.

Assessment

Ask the children to find *O*s in the "October" poem by coming up to the chart and using the pointer. Ask children which words have an *O*.

Independent Work

On a cutout of a large *O* prepared by the teacher, each student will draw or cut out pictures of objects from October, Halloween, or with the sound of *O*. The teacher or her assistant will talk with students in small groups about their *O* independent work to reinforce the sounds of long and short *O* and to be sure each student can correctly identify the sound, as well as know the names of the months before and after October.

Miss Cindy and Mrs. Galligan meet to discuss the lesson plan and to discuss particular areas she would like Mrs. Galligan to observe. Miss Cindy asks Mrs. Galligan to provide specific feedback on assessment of student performance on the objectives.

The next day, Miss Cindy teaches the lesson with great success in some parts and areas of concern in others. Document 2 is an excerpt from Mrs. Galligan's observation feedback to Miss Cindy.

Document 2

Miss Cindy asked me to observe her lesson on October from Maurice Sendak's *Chicken Soup with Rice*, with particular emphasis on her assessment of each student's achievement of the lesson objectives. The lesson opening appeared to be motivating to all students. The children sang the song and learned the melody and most of the words to the "October" poem quickly. This provided appropriate support for students to listen to the printed poem "October" and for all students to identify the letter *O* in the poem. Several students appeared to have difficulty identifying the sound of the letter *O*. In addition, several students could not differentiate between a letter and a word when working with the chart after reading the poem.

1. Suggest TWO ways Miss Cindy could strengthen the assessment for this lesson plan. Be certain to base your suggestions on your careful reading of the instructional scenario, as well as principles of assessment.

2. Identify TWO strengths of Miss Cindy's lesson plan and discuss the principles of student learning behind her good instructional practice. Be sure to cite the specific theories or standards that support this practice and base your response on principles of the instructional process and students as learners.

Instructional Scenario II

Scenario: Annie

Annie is a first-grader who brings many strengths to her learning at school. She has numerous interests, such as animals (especially her cat, Raja, and dog, Jasmine), crafts, dance, and mathematics. Annie likes to count things, to make collections, and to know how much money things cost. She stands out as a leader among her peers, most often providing positive leadership in the classroom, but from time to time she can lead others to silly, talkative behavior. Annie is exuberant in her approach to life—she loves learning, field trips, science experiments, and listening to the teacher read aloud. She does not prefer to read to herself and often avoids this in the classroom. She has many friends, both boys and girls, and is able to work with a wide variety of students because of her excellent social and communication skills. Annie is a kinesthetic learner who is achieving at a second-grade level or higher, especially in the areas of mathematics and science.

At a recent parent/teacher conference, Annie's teacher, Miss Lisa, shared Annie's progress with her parents and suggested ways that they can help Annie at home. Two ideas Miss Lisa suggested were the following:

- Setting up a behavior plan for "positive leadership" in which the teacher and the parent communicate via a home/school communication notebook
- Establishing a home reading program to help Annie practice her school reading

3. Identify ONE of Annie's strengths and suggest TWO instructional activities that would meet Annie's learning style and needs. Be sure to state why these activities are best for learners like Annie. Be sure to base your response on principles of students as learners and instructional processes.

4. Suggest TWO effective classroom-management techniques that will support Miss Lisa's instructional goals and Annie's learning style. Be sure to base your response on principles of communication techniques and instruction.

Answers and Explanations

Multiple-Choice Questions

Answer Key

Question	Answer	Content Category	Where to Get More Help
1	B	Students as Learners	Chapter 7
2	D	Students as Learners	Chapter 7
3	C	Students as Learners	Chapter 7
4	C	Students as Learners	Chapter 7
5	A	Instructional Process	Chapter 8
6	A	Instructional Process	Chapter 8
7	B	Instructional Process	Chapter 8
8	D	Instructional Process	Chapter 8
9	D	Professional Development, Leadership, and Community	Chapter 10
10	B	Professional Development, Leadership, and Community	Chapter 10
11	D	Professional Development, Leadership, and Community	Chapter 10
12	C	Professional Development, Leadership, and Community	Chapter 10
13	C	Students as Learners	Chapter 7
14	B	Students as Learners	Chapter 7
15	B	Students as Learners	Chapter 7
16	D	Students as Learners	Chapter 7
17	C	Instructional Process	Chapter 8
18	B	Assessment	Chapter 9
19	A	Assessment	Chapter 9
20	D	Assessment	Chapter 9
21	D	Professional Development, Leadership, and Community	Chapter 10
22	C	Professional Development, Leadership, and Community	Chapter 10
23	B	Professional Development, Leadership, and Community	Chapter 10
24	A	Professional Development, Leadership, and Community	Chapter 10
25	A	Students as Learners	Chapter 7
26	B	Students as Learners	Chapter 7
27	C	Assessment	Chapter 9
28	D	Assessment	Chapter 9
29	C	Assessment	Chapter 9
30	B	Instructional Process	Chapter 8
31	A	Instructional Process	Chapter 8
32	D	Instructional Process	Chapter 8
33	B	Professional Development, Leadership, and Community	Chapter 10
34	D	Professional Development, Leadership, and Community	Chapter 10
35	C	Professional Development, Leadership, and Community	Chapter 10

Question	Answer	Content Category	Where to Get More Help
36	A	Professional Development, Leadership, and Community	Chapter 10
37	A	Students as Learners	Chapter 7
38	C	Students as Learners	Chapter 7
39	A	Students as Learners	Chapter 7
40	C	Students as Learners	Chapter 7
41	A	Instructional Process	Chapter 8
42	A	Instructional Process	Chapter 8
43	D	Instructional Process	Chapter 8
44	A	Assessment	Chapter 9
45	B	Professional Development, Leadership, and Community	Chapter 10
46	D	Professional Development, Leadership, and Community	Chapter 10
47	B	Professional Development, Leadership, and Community	Chapter 10
48	A	Professional Development, Leadership, and Community	Chapter 10
49	B	Students as Learners	Chapter 7
50	A	Students as Learners	Chapter 7
51	D	Students as Learners	Chapter 7
52	C	Students as Learners	Chapter 7
53	B	Instructional Process	Chapter 8
54	B	Instructional Process	Chapter 8
55	D	Instructional Process	Chapter 8
56	A	Instructional Process	Chapter 8
57	C	Assessment	Chapter 9
58	C	Professional Development, Leadership, and Community	Chapter 10
59	B	Students as Learners	Chapter 7
60	A	Students as Learners	Chapter 7
61	A	Students as Learners	Chapter 7
62	B	Students as Learners	Chapter 7
63	D	Instructional Process	Chapter 8
64	C	Instructional Process	Chapter 8
65	B	Instructional Process	Chapter 8
66	C	Instructional Process	Chapter 8
67	B	Students as Learners	Chapter 7
68	D	Students as Learners	Chapter 7
69	C	Instructional Process	Chapter 8
70	A	Instructional Process	Chapter 8

Answer Explanations

1. **B** Maria Montessori's method was developed in the early 1900s. This method is widely used with preschool children, but it is used by many teachers of older children, as well. There are no textbooks, and students rarely work on the same thing at the same time. Students learn directly from their environment or from other students. Students gather in large groups from time to time at the beginning of class or for special events. The teacher scientifically observes students and uses these observations to inform instruction. Choice B, direct instruction, does not involve working individually with students. Choice C, the Hunter method, is a way of lesson planning and delivering instruction, rather than learning from the environment or from other students, as Miss Rachel does. Choice D, advance organizer, is a specific instructional method in which the teacher provides a visual activity prior to instruction.

2. **D** Piaget's preoperational stage is distinguished by children typically ages 2 to 7 whose language and behavior become less egocentric and more social. Children at this stage become problem solvers and enjoy social interaction with peers and caregivers. At this stage, the child makes progress in understanding logical concepts, but understanding is still quite concrete and limited. Choices A and B are distracters based on similar terms in Piaget's stages. Choice C, sensorimotor stage, is a Piagetian stage that begins at birth and typically ends by age 2.

3. **C** Studies of learning-disabled students have shown that some children show a learned helplessness after repeated school failures and lack of success.

4. **C** Children with functional or mild mental retardation have an IQ between 50 and 75, usually are able to learn information generally up to a sixth-grade level, and often possess the life skills to live independently as an adult with social and community supports.

5. **A** Activities that involve nonlinguistic representations help students to store knowledge using visual, kinesthetic, or whole-body movement. Teachers are encouraged to include both linguistic (involving reading or hearing) and nonlinguistic representations for students to make meaning from the lesson.

6. **A** Anchored instruction involves a concrete learning activity for students to tie information to. The teacher uses the "anchor" to help students make connections and learn important concepts.

7. **B** Based on the centers listed, one can infer that Mr. Moore believes that play is child's work. These centers provide opportunities for students to learn both academic and social lessons through play.

8. **D** An emergent curriculum is most typically found in early-childhood classrooms, but it can be noted in high grade levels that emphasize personalization of learning and community involvement. This approach to curriculum places the student at the center of planning, and it values family and community involvement in education.

9. **D** Professional development provides teachers with the opportunity to learn. Professional development can take place in many forms—small groups after school, large-group in-service, college coursework, or one-on-one work with a school coach.

10. **B** Early-childhood professionals understand the importance of advocating for all learners. In order to be effective at advocacy for children, teachers must effectively communicate and collaborate with parents/caregivers, colleagues, administrators, and other stakeholders.

11. **D** Teachers have several rights that are guided by school and civic law. A teacher does not have the right to use a text that has been removed from the school library by a vote of a group, such as the school committee. If a book is objectionable to an individual, but it has not been banned by the school committee, the teacher may choose to use such a text, but he or she may want to discuss this issue and the text with the school librarian and the principal.

12. **C** The hornbook was used by children for several centuries starting in the mid-fifteenth century in Europe. It continued to be used in U.S. schools during the Colonial period (1600–1776). Hornbooks were made of a wooden paddle, parchment with the lesson, and a cover for the lesson, which was made of transparent horn. The McGuffey Readers, the distracter in this question, were used during the Common School period (1840–1880) of U.S. education.

13. **C** Dewey is considered the father of progressive education. He promoted individuality, project-based learning, and school as a social institution. Dewey believed that real-life problem solving was a valuable experience for learners.

14. **B** Children with behavior disorders show some of the following behaviors: violating rules, aggression toward people and/or animals, destruction of property, deceitfulness, and other inappropriate behaviors typical of a child.

15. **B** Based on the passage, Dee's language/literacy status is best described as PLNE. Mrs. Baris can support Dee by building on her culture, supporting Dee's language/literacy proficiency in her primary language (Vietnamese), and offering opportunities for Dee to work in small groups. It is common for PLNE students to remain near silent in the classroom for several months until they gain proficiency in English.

16. **D** Hidalgo's three levels of culture are as follows: concrete, behavioral, and symbolic. Mrs. Baris can understand the concrete level of Dee's culture by learning more about the foods, music, games, and clothing in Vietnam. At the behavioral level of culture, Mrs. Baris must strive to understand the gender roles, nonverbal communication, and family structure of Dee's home. At the symbolic level of culture, Mrs. Baris must learn more about Dee's family's value structures, customs, and beliefs.

17. **C** National, state, and local standards guide expectations of what a student must know and be able to do. There are two types of standards: content based and performance based.

18. **B** Self-evaluation is an important assessment strategy in which students monitor and regulate their learning. Self-evaluation can be in free-form discussion, as Mr. Addison does in this scenario, or in written form. Choice C, portfolios, is the distracter here. Although Mr. Addison may use portfolios, this choice is too broad and not the best answer choice based on the information provided in the question.

19. **A** Analytical scoring guides typically are used to assess essays and short-answer responses, which can be difficult to score with reliability and validity. Analytical scoring guides are particularly helpful when a teacher is new to the assessment and when there are many items for the teacher to score.

20. **D** Percentile ranks show the percentage of students in a group (either a national or a local norm) whose scores fall above or below the norm group scores. For example, if a student scored in the fiftieth percentile rank, this would mean that 50 percent of the scores in the norm group fell below this student's score on this same test.

21. **D** Due process is the procedure that must be followed before a student's rights to an education are denied or before a student's education programming is changed, specifically in the area of special-education services.

22. **C** Public Law 94-142 was passed into law during the Ford Administration in 1975. This law was established to ensure that a free and appropriate education is provided to handicapped children and adults ages 3 through 21.

23. **B** Froebel established the first kindergarten in 1837, and he became known as the father of kindergarten. Kindergarten curriculum emphasized the importance of play and was recognized by the National Education Association (NEA) in 1872.

24. **A** Horace Mann was known as the father of American education and supported the common school concept of education. Mann also served as secretary of education in 1839 and established the first normal school in the United States.

25. **A** Frederic Jones studied time-on-task and found that one-half of all instructional time was lost because students were talking (80 percent) or goofing off (20 percent). Teachers can improve this problem by carefully planning for and managing independent practice time. Three strategies to improve time-on-task include: using teacher body language (such as the "look" or walking nearby the student), implementing incentive systems, and providing timely individual help for students.

26. **B** Learner factors are key when lesson planning. These may include, but are not limited to, students with attention difficulties, learning differences, giftedness, learning modalities, gross and fine motor skills, and multiple intelligences.

27. **C** Although Mrs. Dougherty may have concerns about the rationale for testing first-graders and would prefer her students take other assessments (choices A, B, and D), she would not be wise to raise them now that the assessments have been selected. In the future, she might raise these questions as a committee member or when the decisions about testing are being made. The most important question at this point is to find out what, if any, accommodations are available to her students, such as shorter sessions, having a scribe (someone to write student responses), or having more time for testing.

28. **D** An alternative assessment that has been agreed upon by a multidisciplinary team, including the child's parents, may be available to students with documented disabilities. Choices A and C are testing accommodations; therefore, neither of these can be the correct choice because the question stem asks for a response "in addition to testing accommodations." Choice B, a criterion-referenced assessment, would not be plausible as this type of test does not provide comparisons with other groups.

29. **C** Diagnostic evaluations offer teachers a view of each student's strengths and weaknesses based on grade-level expectations. This type of evaluation is meant to provide immediate feedback to teachers and parents to better inform each student's instructional program.

30. **B** Partner check is a cooperative-learning grouping strategy in which students work individually to complete their work and then partner with a peer to check the assigned work and review the content. Choices A (group investigation) and C are cooperative-learning grouping approaches. Choice D, STAD, is a distracter based on another cooperative-learning approach.

31. **A** When a teacher creates an anticipatory set for a lesson, as Mr. Manning is doing with this walking field trip, he or she activates or develops prior knowledge of the lesson's concepts. This practice gives students an opportunity to organize information in their minds, as well as to add new information to existing schema. Choice B, creating a mood for the lesson, is a plausible choice, but not the best response according to principles of teaching and learning. Choices C (monitoring student achievement in science) and D (providing an authentic culminating assessment of his science objectives) are not "prior to instruction" options as the questions requires.

32. **D** Mnemonics is an instructional strategy often used to help students remember challenging bits of information. Common examples of mnemonics include "*i* before *e* except after *c*" in spelling and "Every Good Boy Does Fine" (EGBDF) to help a student remember the notes on a treble clef in a music class.

33. **B** The opportunities provided at Prout School show that this school sees itself as a resource to its school community. Although the teachers may be a resource at this school (Choice D), this is not the best response because several of the activities listed could be facilitated by other individuals who are not teachers.

34. **D** In this situation, Miss Nelson sees herself as a resource to families as well as to her students (Choice D). Although Miss Nelson most likely must use respectful communication with families (Choice C), this is not the best answer choice.

35. **C** When more and more children began to attend school, the one-room schoolhouse design no longer met the needs of the children and teachers. At first, most schools grouped children by age: ages 6 to 8 in one room and ages 9 to 14 in another. After a child moved beyond the upper-level room, he or she either attended college or joined the workforce.

36. **A** The National Education Association (NEA) was started in 1857 as the National Teachers Association. The NEA is currently the largest educational association in the world. The other plausible response, Choice C, the American Federation of Teachers, was formed in 1916 and has as its motto, "Democracy in Education and Education for Democracy."

37. **A** Learning modalities, also known as learning styles, are important to consider when planning lessons. Students have strengths in at least one of the modalities—tactile (touching), kinesthetic (doing, movement), visual (seeing), and auditory (hearing).

38. **C** Learning disabilities are determined by a multidisciplinary team—a team of educators, administrators, specialists, and the child's parents—or by a physician. There are three main areas of learning disability: reading, writing, or mathematics. Some common characteristics of students with learning disabilities

include, but are not limited to, the following: dislikes being touched, limited vocabulary, impulsivity, short attention span, poor coordination, and distractibility.

39. **A** Erikson's eight stages of human development are based on a crisis or conflict that the person resolves during that period of their lives. Brandon is healthily mastering the early childhood conflict of initiative vs. guilt (Choice A), which can be seen in his ability to cooperate with peers, not being overly reliant on adults, and use of a healthy imagination in his play. Erikson's stages and conflicts are as follows:

Stage	Age Range	Crisis or Conflict	Key Event
Stage 1: Infancy	0 to 1	Trust vs. mistrust	Feeding
Stage 2: Toddler	1 to 2	Autonomy vs. doubt	Toilet training
Stage 3: Early childhood	2 to 6	Initiative vs. guilt	Independence
Stage 4: Elementary and middle	6 to 12	Competence vs. inferiority	School
Stage 5: Adolescence	12 to 18	Identity vs. role confusion	Sense of identity
Stage 6: Young adulthood	18 to 40	Intimacy vs. isolation	Intimate relationships
Stage 7: Middle adulthood	40 to 65	Generativity vs. stagnation	Support next generation
Stage 8: Late adulthood	65 to death	Integrity vs. despair	Reflection and acceptance

40. **C** The question asks for the previous stage to the early childhood stage (ages 2 to 6), which would be Choice C, toddler stage. Erikson's theory suggests that Rose needs social experiences in this stage to help her become more confident, less guilty, and more independent before she can tackle the key conflict of the early childhood stage, initiative vs. guilt.

41. **A** Mrs. Bergman is reinforcing and providing recognition to her students because she believes there is a relationship between a student's attitudes and beliefs and his or her achievement. Choice B, numbered heads together, is a cooperative-learning structure in which students are assigned the same number to work together to become experts on a segment of content. Choice C, homework and practice, is an "essential nine" research-based instructional strategy, but it is not the best choice for this situation. Choice D is too narrow for the scenario presented; Mrs. Bergman is identifying strengths here, not weaknesses.

42. **A** Mr. Christie's unit plans are best described as interdisciplinary because they involve reading, literature study, science goals, and health goals. You may have been tempted to choose thematic unit (Choice B), but a thematic unit has one overall theme, which this unit has within one component, but not across the entire unit of study. Choice C, literature unit, is tempting, but this is not the best way to describe Mr. Christie's unit plans. Choice D, inquiry based, is similarly incorrect to Choice B. There may be an inquiry-based science component to Mr. Christie's unit plans, but this is not the case across the entire unit of study.

43. **D** Project-based learning, like the unit Mr. Forte is teaching on patterns, involves in-depth investigation of a real-world, authentic topic or problem that is meaningful to students. The students work in small groups or pairs to solve a problem or to learn more about the topic. The teacher serves as facilitator and supports the students' projects and discoveries. Choice A is a distracter since basal texts are typically used in reading instruction, if used at all. Choice B, mathematics instruction, is too narrow of a response. Choice C is incorrect because simulations involve reenactment of a situation using computer-assisted instruction or in a group activity.

44. **A** Anecdotal records are an authentic assessment used by teachers to record each student's progress and plan next best lessons for the student. Choice B, portfolio assessment, is too broad, but it is plausible in this teaching situation. Choices C (personal assessment plan) and D (aptitude records) are similar to other assessment practices, but they are not actually principles of assessment.

45. **B** Latin grammar schools were established in 1635 to prepare boys for leadership positions in the church, state, and judiciary establishments. The practical purpose for these schools was to prepare the boys for the Harvard College entrance examinations. Choice A, hornbook school, is a nonsense response based on the hornbook used by children as a learning tool during this time period. Choice C, early elementary school, appears to be a logical response, but schools during this time period were not called elementary schools.

Choice D, common school, was a type of school initiated during the Common School period (1840–1880), not the Colonial period (1600–1776). The common school had a very different philosophy of education than the Latin grammar school described in the multiple-choice question.

46. **D** The superintendent of schools role was suggested by Horace Mann, an education reformer concerned with school policy and leadership. The terms *superintendent* and *principal* are derived from Industrial Revolution terminology similar to superintendent of railroads, factory superintendent, and so on.

47. **B** Teachers must understand the awesome responsibility placed upon them in the teaching profession. Professional associations and local school districts provide guidance on ethical standards for teachers. Choice B, code of ethics, is the credited response. Teachers are responsible for creating and sustaining a positive, challenging, and safe school environment. Choices A (mission), C (vision), and D (action plan) are terms related to strategic planning, typically at the school level.

48. **A** A reflective practitioner possesses many reflective characteristics such as those presented in this multiple-choice question: collaboration, willingness to discuss experiences, and ability to critically analyze practice. Choice B, instructional practitioner, is a fictitious term. Choices C (advocate for learners) and D (instructional leader) are plausible responses but neither is the best response.

49. **B** Behaviorists view learning as a process of accessing and changing associations between stimuli and responses. We see behaviorist theory in action in approaches to classroom management and establishing positive contexts for learning. B. F. Skinner, Edward Thorndike, and Ivan Pavlov are key contributors to our understanding of how people learn from a behaviorist perspective.

50. **A** Sociocultural theorists posit that the combination of social, cultural, and historical contexts in which a learner exists has great influence on the person's knowledge construction and the ways teachers must organize instruction. A key theorist to study is Lev Vygotsky and his theory on the zone of proximal development.

51. **D** Informational processing theorists focus more on what happens inside the learner's mind, considering the processes of learning, memory, and performance. Some theorists believe that the human mind works a lot like a computer processor; therefore, they contributed terms such as *storage, retrieval, working memory,* and *long-term memory*. There are no key theorists whose names you'll need to know on the PLT, but you should be able to define and provide examples for several terms that involve what happens inside a learner's mind.

52. **C** Constructivist theorists suggest that people construct or create knowledge (as opposed to absorb knowledge) based on their experiences and interactions. Some theorists focus on *individual constructivism* (how one person makes meaning) and others focus on *social constructivism* (how working together people gain knowledge).

53. **B** Thematic unit instruction is a way to organize curriculum around large themes. Thematic units are integrated across several content areas, such as reading, social studies, math, and science. Thematic units might include such topics as dinosaurs, friendship, plants, or patterns. Choices A (Understanding by Design) and D (backward design) are too broad; they are overarching approaches to lesson and unit planning. Choice C, interdisciplinary lesson plan, involves helping students see the connections across two or more content areas; the teacher's aim in this scenario is to animal habitats, not to help students see connections across the disciplines of reading and writing.

54. **B** Objectives should have three parts: measurable verb, criteria, and conditions.

55. **D** When communicating with students, parents, or colleagues in difficult situations, a person may want to use "I messages" to convey a sense of openness to resolve the conflict collaboratively and nonaggressively. Examples of "I messages" include: "I feel upset when I hear you say that you do not care about your friend's feelings," or "I know that you care about your son's progress in seventh grade. Let's work together to think of ways to help support him with his homework completion." Choice A (writing a disciplinary report) may be premature and certainly will not aid in improving communication. Choice B (speaking with other teachers who work with Mrs. Peck) is unprofessional communication; therefore it is incorrect. Choice C (utilizing nonviolent principles) is a distracter.

56. **A** Using a train whistle to signal that it is almost time for lunch, recess, or home is known as a transition signal. Having a classroom routine and a posted schedule implicitly signals transitions from one activity to the next, but teachers often need to explicitly signal transitions for the wide variety of learners in the classroom. The elementary teacher often uses a clapping pattern, a song, or a bell to signal five minutes of work time left or time's up.

57. **C** Mr. Adamy is using authentic assessment in his classroom. Authentic assessments measure student understanding of the learning process and product, rather than just the product. For example, student understanding of patterns can be assessed by using teddy-bear counters. Students actually create patterns using the counters, identify the patterns, and explain how they know this pattern to the teacher, who actively observes the student at work. In authentic assessments, students develop the responses rather than select from predetermined options. Clear criteria of success are established, which relate closely to classroom learning opportunities. Choice A (standards-based assessment) is not the credited choices because which, if any, standards are being addressed is not spelled out. Choices B (evidence-based assessment) and D (direct assessment) are distracters.

58. **C** Respectful communication involves listening, frequent and positive communication, as well as understanding. Choices A (reciprocal communication) and D (multicultural communication) are distracters. Choice B (parent/teacher communication) is too narrow of a choice.

59. **B** Mr. Pope is asking his students to perform a task; therefore, his objective targets Bloom's psychomotor or performance domain, which involves manual or physical skills one uses, which are divided into seven subdivisions: perception, set, guided responses, mechanism, complex overt responses, adaptation, and origination. Choices A (cognitive domain) and D (affective domain) are the other two domains of Bloom's Taxonomy, but they do not focus on teaching students to trace and reproduce information visually. Choice C (psychological domain) is a distracter.

60. **A** Miss Connor is using classical conditioning with her student. Classical conditioning is a process of behavior modification by which a person comes to respond in the desired manner to what was once a neutral stimulus. In classical conditioning, the neutral stimulus has been repeatedly presented along with an unconditioned stimulus (a natural, not taught stimulus, such as the smell of food) that eventually elicits the desired response. For example, in the classroom, the teacher creates a positive, supportive classroom environment that eventually conditions a student with anxiety or fears, like Jared, to find his school experience enjoyable. Choice B, modeling, involves providing a student or teacher role model to help Jared see how to act appropriately. Choice C, contingency contract, is a behavior modification approach in which the teacher sets up a plan with Jared and provides feedback and consequences based on his behavior. Choice D, community of learners, is too broad.

61. **A** The scenario describes two students working together who are able to complete a task successfully based on the strengths each student bring to bear, which is known as distributed cognition. Choice B, sense of community, is a distracter. Choice C, self-efficacy, involves one person's sense of his or her ability to complete a task. Choice D, primary reinforcer, is a consequence that satisfies a biologically built-in need, such as food, water, or warmth.

62. **B** Mr. Holmes is using operant-conditioning principles to motivate his students to complete homework. Operant conditioning is a form of psychological learning in which the learner modifies his or her own behavior based on the association of the behavior with a stimulus. For example, operant conditioning is at work when Mr. Holmes sets up a system of punishments and reinforcements for homework completion. Choice A, zone of proximal development, involves a cognitive process in which the teacher seeks to find the "just right" next concept or skill to teach a student. Choices C (social information processing) and D (positive psychology) are distracters.

63. **D** Piaget defined schemas as students' organized sets of facts about a concept or event that can be used to help make connections with information in long-term memory with new concepts and ideas. Choices A (assimilation) and B (accommodation) are other learning theories of Piaget's. Choice C, script, is term often confused with schema; a script involves a predictable sequence of events related to a particular activity.

64. **C** Mrs. Niebala is serving as an important positive model for her learners, sharing her thinking process to model for students how do approach a challenge term when reading. Choice A, rote learning, involves helping students memorize. Choice B, reciprocal causation, is a distracter. Choice D, mastery learning, involves teaching students one topic thoroughly before moving to the next topic; this choice is too broad.

65. **B** Mrs. Geibler is using presentation punishment, which involves presenting a new stimulus—one the learner finds unpleasant, such as assigning more homework—to decrease undesired behavior (that is, the students not completing homework the night before).

66. **C** An emergent curriculum is based primarily on the interests of children. As stated in the question stem, an emergent curriculum is developed when the teacher works together with family and other community members to set possible direction for a project and then determine the actual curriculum based on student interest. An emergent curriculum is used most often in early-childhood settings. Choice A, enacted curriculum, is too broad. Choice B, scope-and-sequence curriculum, relates to curriculum development and is also too broad. There is not evidence in this question that leads you to know if this is a thematic curriculum (Choice D).

67. **B** The social-cognitive theoretical perspective on learning is focused on how people learn through observation of others. Choice B (through the observation of others) relates to a behaviorist theoretical perspective. Choices A (based on cultural and linguistic experiences) and D (socially appropriate knowledge and skills) are distracters.

68. **D** The information-processing theoretical perspective on learning is focused more on what happens inside the learner's mind, such as how the mind stores and retrieves information. Choice A (how people create or construct knowledge) is related to the constructivist theoretical perspective. Choices B (why the human mind does not operate like a computer) and C (how cultural constructs are shared between one person and another) are distracters.

69. **C** Student- or learner-centered instructional approaches actively involve the student in hands-on activities filled with more spontaneous student talking and observing, such as cooperative learning (Choice B), discovery learning (Choice A), and an experiment (Choice D). Direct instruction, the credited response, is a teacher-centered approach in which the teacher leads students through a careful series of activities that involve modeling and guided practice.

70. **A** Stating a familiar chant, such as "1-2-3, eyes on me" provides students with a signal or notice that the teacher is about to give directions about the lesson transition. Choice B (giving a student a warning for talking out of turn) is a signal that an individual student is not following directions, not a signal for the lesson transition. Choice C (opening the lesson with a motivating activity) is a positive way to open a lesson and does not include a signal. Choice D (telling the students to continue reading and writing) includes a signal but does not involve a lesson transition.

Constructed-Response Questions

Instructional Scenario I

1. **Suggested content:** Miss Cindy's assessment plan includes asking the children to find *O*s in the "October" poem by coming up to the chart and asking the children which words have an *O*. One way she could strengthen her assessment plan is to work one-on-one with each student. She could create a checklist for each student in her effort to individually assess each student's ability to recognize words and the /o/ sounds. This is called an authentic assessment because she is assessing each student's performance within the instructional setting. A second way Miss Cindy could assess her objectives is to work with small groups of children. She could read the "October" poem out loud and listen more carefully to individual students as they repeat the lines after the teacher. Echo reading is an excellent strategy to improve student fluency. In addition, repeat reading of predictable texts, such as *Chicken Soup with Rice,* supports phonemic awareness.

2. **Suggested content:** Two key strengths of Miss Cindy's lesson are her use of a <u>quality text</u> to teach reading and her <u>use of multimedia</u>, specifically the sound recording. *Chicken Soup with Rice* is a <u>predictable</u>, <u>authentic text</u> that invites young readers to read and reread. The <u>repetition and rhyme</u> makes reading fun and also helps to develop <u>phonemic awareness</u>. Children can listen for the rhyme and identify the words that have the /o/ sound. The specific poem she uses for this lesson, "October," provides additional <u>content information</u> about seasons and months of the year. Allowing children not only to read the text, but also to <u>hear the text</u>, allows children who learn best through their <u>musical intelligence</u> to succeed in remembering the text and being able to retell.

Instructional Scenario II

3. **Suggested content:** Although Annie has many strengths, such as her interest in animals and in counting objects, her <u>leadership strength</u> is the one that I will discuss in this response. Annie is well liked by her peers and has a strong ability to lead her peers. Miss Lisa can capitalize on Annie's strength as a leader by <u>assigning Annie as the leader</u> of the work group during a group project, such as a <u>literature circle</u>. Miss Lisa could teach Annie <u>positive strategies for leading the group, asking questions</u>, and <u>checking on the progress of the group</u>. Annie benefits from leading a literature circle because she has to stay on task herself, ask <u>higher-level questions</u>, and know the directions. Another instructional activity that would meet Annie's learning style is the <u>field trip</u>. Annie also could be her group leader in this setting. Field trips also offer Annie the opportunity to <u>learn by doing</u>—meeting the needs of her preference for <u>kinesthetic activities</u>. Both of these activities lead Annie to be intrinsically motivated to learn and to use her leadership abilities in positive ways.

4. **Suggested content:** Annie is an active student who can be a positive or negative class leader. Miss Lisa must plan her classroom-management strategies to <u>set up Annie for success</u>, not <u>power struggles</u>. One strategy that Miss Lisa can use is to choose Annie as a <u>special helper</u>. This affords Annie the chance to lead, <u>satisfying her attention needs</u>, and gives her the <u>chance to move about the room</u> or school building more frequently, <u>satisfying her need to move to learn</u>. A second strategy that Miss Lisa can use is to offer <u>positive reinforcement</u> for Annie's efforts and successes. Both of these strategies offer Annie recognition for her successes and provide her an opportunity to lead in the classroom in positive ways.

Time: 2 hours

70 multiple-choice questions and 4 constructed-res___se questions

Multiple-Choice Question___

Directions: For each multiple-choice question, sel___ best answer and mark the corresponding letter space on your answer sheet.

1. Madison has been having difficulty at reces___ time on the playground. She used to like to ___ with her friends and to play tag, but recent___ has taken an interest in playing kickball wi___ new set of children. At first, she just stood ___ the sidelines to watch the game, secretly h___ she would be invited to play. When this di___ happen, Madison lodged a complaint with ___ teacher that one of the children playing ki___ had intentionally thrown the ball at her. E___ Erikson suggested that children in elemen___ and middle school (ages 6 to 12) work to ___ which of the following conflicts that Mad___ appears to be struggling with at this time?

   A. Identity vs. role confusion
   B. Preoperational vs. operational think___
   C. Generativity vs. stagnation
   D. Competence vs. inferiority

2. Steven enjoys talking with his sixth-grad___ friends as well as listening to popular mu___ takes pride in his new sneakers—an expe___ popular brand—and his hooded sweatsl___ a skateboarding company. Which of the ___ following needs would Abraham Maslo___ suggest Steven is striving to meet?

   A. Esteem needs
   B. Self-actualization needs
   C. Love and belongingness needs
   D. Physiological needs

3. Which of the following theorists sugge___ people possess multiple intelligences, s___ intrapersonal, interpersonal, and musi___ intelligences?

   A. Gardner
   B. Howarth
   C. Epstein
   D. Binet

--- CUT HERE ---

4. Sean is a kindergartener who enjoys working with clay, playing catch to learn letters, and making things. Which of the following modalities is Sean's preferred way to learn?

   A. Tactile
   B. Visual
   C. Musical
   D. Auditory

5. Mark is making patterns with counters shaped like teddy bears. His teacher asks him questions as he works, such as, "How many teddy bears are yellow?" and "What kind of pattern are you making?" Mark also notes that some teddy bears are not yellow. He tells his teacher that there are blue and green teddy bears, too. Which of the following instructional strategies is Mark's teacher using to help Mark better understand patterns?

   A. Summarizing
   B. Identifying similarities and differences
   C. Cause and effect
   D. Providing recognition and reinforcing effort

6. Nishita is a gifted second-grader who accurately and thoroughly completes her assignments 30 minutes earlier than her peers. Recently, Nishita appears to be bored with her schoolwork and is spending time visiting classmates while they are trying to complete their work. Nishita also has started to forget to hand in her classwork. Which of the following instructional strategies may be most helpful to Nishita?

   A. Cooperative learning
   B. Jigsaw
   C. Chunking curriculum
   D. Curriculum compacting

7. Mrs. Horton is teaching a reading lesson to her second-grade students. She already has discussed the story's beginning, middle, and end, and next she would like her students to be able to identify the main characters, the setting, and the basic plot elements of the story. Which of the following graphic organizers would be most helpful in Mrs. Horton's lesson?

   A. Sequence chart
   B. Story map
   C. Hierarchical array
   D. Venn diagram

8. The primary purpose of using mnemonic devices, such as imagery and acronyms, is to help students

   A. make a connection between the new information to be memorized.
   B. build prior knowledge.
   C. make notes in a way to be memorized.
   D. build upon active thinking and new information.

9. Teachers must follow their school district's code of ethics, which guides professional responsibilities, EXCEPT under which of the following circumstances?

   A. Collaborating with student's caregivers
   B. Following U.S. laws
   C. Providing information unrelated to employment
   D. Committing to lifelong learning for all

10. Corporal punishment is not unconstitutional, but it may be _____ and administered only according to the laws of the state.

    A. illegal
    B. ineligible
    C. punishment
    D. punitive

11. Students have limited freedom of speech in schools. For example, student newspapers supported solely by the school may be edited by school personnel. School newspapers supported solely by student groups

    A. may be edited by school personnel.
    B. may be limited to distribution in school only.
    C. may not be distributed to student groups at other schools.
    D. may not be edited by school personnel.

12. In 1957, a group of African-American students asserted their right to attend the local high school. They were met with racial slurs, a mob mentality among some of the bystanders, and a cascade of rocks and bottles thrown at them. Federal soldiers had to escort the children through the doors of the school. The courageous students who advanced the civil rights movement became known as the

    A. Little Rock 9.
    B. Black Panthers.
    C. Memphis 5.
    D. Montgomery Bus Riders.

13. Which of the following is a federal law prohibiting discrimination on the basis of a person's disability for all services, programs, and activities made available by state or local governments?

    A. Race to the Top
    B. Section 504
    C. ADA
    D. P.L. 94-142

14. Madison is a fourth-grader who enjoys school, especially when the teacher uses films, graphic organizers, or the computer-projection machine during lessons. Which of the following learning modalities best describes Madison?

    A. Auditory learner
    B. Visual learner
    C. Tactile learner
    D. Kinesthetic learner

Question 15 is based on the following passage.

Jamie is a sixth-grader who dislikes mathematics but is assigned to an honors-level mathematics class. She has set a goal to get a B in the class so that she can be placed in the honors-level track at the middle school. She completes course requirements that are graded, but she does not offer any additional effort if her grade is not at stake. Jamie rarely completes the extra-credit opportunities and spends little time studying for tests and quizzes in this math class.

15. Based on the principles of teaching and learning, which of the following best describes Jamie's motivation in this class?

   A.   Extrinsic
   B.   Self-centered
   C.   Intrinsic
   D.   Achievement

16. Which of the following theorists suggests that females are socialized to highly value social relationships and to take responsibility for the well-being of others?

   A.   Hoffman
   B.   Gilligan
   C.   Kohlberg
   D.   Piaget

17. Mr. Ellson, a third-grade teacher, likes to have his students work in groups to complete projects together. He also tends to use the overhead projector to display examples of student work or specific examples of high-quality projects. Which of the following theorist's work influences Mr. Ellson's practice?

   A.   Erikson
   B.   Dewey
   C.   Bandura
   D.   Maslow

18. Survey, Question, Read, Recite, and Review (SQ3R) is a method used most often in which of the following strategies?

   A.   Phonemic awareness
   B.   Cooperative learning
   C.   Nonlinguistic representations
   D.   Summarizing and note taking

19. Which of the following cooperative-learning activities involves a "home team" of heterogeneously grouped students who then work in small groups to become experts on a portion of the content to be learned? After the students become "experts," they return to the home team to share important information.

   A.   Think-pair-share
   B.   STAD
   C.   Numbered heads together
   D.   Nonlinguistic representation

20. Mrs. Basel, a sixth-grade science teacher, assigns at least three lab experiments to her students each week. She highly values an inquiry-based approach to teaching science and believes that her students more deeply understand when she uses which of the following instructional approaches?

   A.   Sequencing and repetition
   B.   Generating and testing hypotheses
   C.   Standardized-based instruction
   D.   Differentiated instruction

21. Before a student can be suspended or expelled, he or she must be afforded a

   A.   meeting with the teacher.
   B.   trial.
   C.   due process hearing.
   D.   lawyer.

22. Jennifer Smith is a fifth-grade teacher who strives to meet the needs of all her students, and she persists when faced with challenging teaching or learning circumstances. She possesses an awareness of her own culture and those of her students. Her principal describes Jennifer as a

   A.   beginning teacher.
   B.   master teacher.
   C.   reflective practitioner.
   D.   collaborative educator.

23. Which of the following reports, issued in the 1980s, suggested that current education majors and those in the teaching force were not all highly academically qualified to teach, especially in the content areas?

    A. A Nation at Risk
    B. No Child Left Behind
    C. Report of the National Reading Panel
    D. Elementary and Secondary Education Report

24. The Stanford Achievement Test and the Stanford-Binet intelligence tests were introduced by Lewis Terman, who used a scientific approach to determine and classify student ability. Terman's work is considered by many to have started the _____ in the United States.

    A. Scientific period
    B. Intelligence period
    C. Performance movement
    D. Testing movement

25. Mrs. Manning has regular class meetings to discuss classroom rules, procedures, and policies. If students are having difficulty following a rule or if a policy seems too strict, the meeting is a place where the students and teacher can review concerns and come up with alternate solutions. Mrs. Manning's class meeting is grounded in

    A. Canter's assertive-discipline theory.
    B. Kounin's with-it-ness theory.
    C. Glasser's choice theory.
    D. Jones's time-on-task theory.

26. Mrs. Benton likes to have a friendly relationship with her students and brings a *laissez-faire* approach to classroom management. For example, she prefers that the students take charge of the classroom procedures, and she allows them to go to the restroom, use the office phone, or visit the school nurse or another teacher's classroom whenever the students want to. Between teaching lessons, Mrs. Benton uses the Internet to order from catalogs and to check her e-mail while the students work on seat work. Based on this situation, which of the following is NOT a strength of Mrs. Benton's teacher professionalism?

    A. Understanding her role as a teacher
    B. Viewing diversity as positive and enriching
    C. Understanding her own culture
    D. Valuing the importance of empowering learners

Question 27 is based on the following passage.

   Michelle enjoys school, especially this fourth-grade school year, because she is learning more about U.S. history, geometry, and earth science. She asks many questions of her teacher and often talks to her family about the things she has learned at school. Yesterday, Michelle brought a drawing of 3-D objects to school that she had made at home.

27. Which of the following describes Michelle's motivation in fourth grade?

    A. Teacher centered
    B. Parent centered
    C. External
    D. Intrinsic

28. The primary purpose of a school-to-work program is to

    A. help students choose a college.
    B. prepare students for future living.
    C. prepare students for graduation.
    D. help students engage in community service.

29. Mr. Murray has planned a health lesson in which his third-grade students must write a summary on a health-related article found in a magazine or on the Internet. He has planned for an assessment that looks at the overall quality of the students' work. This type of assessment plan is called

    A. norm-referenced scoring.
    B. achievement scoring.
    C. holistic scoring.
    D. objective scoring.

30. The sixth-grade teachers at North Central Elementary have their students switch classes in order to prepare them for the changing of classes and teachers next year at the middle school. For example, one sixth-grade teacher teaches science, another teaches language arts, and another teaches social studies. The teachers have written a unit of study collaboratively in order to help students make connections between classes and content areas. This type of unit is known as

    A. interdisciplinary.
    B. content planning.
    C. thematic.
    D. standards based.

31. Mrs. Eberly, a fifth-grade teacher, looks to which of the following professional associations for standards and best practice in mathematics instruction?

    A. National Accreditation of Mathematics Programs
    B. Addison and Wellesley
    C. National Association of Mathematics Instruction
    D. National Council of Teachers of Mathematics

32. Miss Whitman likes to involve her students in the process of exploring the natural world in an effort to help students better understand science and the natural world. Recently, she had her students build a cardboard model house with four rooms and then wire the home with electricity to light it. Which of the following approaches is Miss Whitman using in her teaching of science?

    A. Inquiry model
    B. Hypothesis model
    C. Scientific process
    D. Standards-based approach

33. This professional association was formed in 1916. Its motto is "Democracy in Education and Education for Democracy." Which of the following associations is being described here?

    A. Democratic Teachers for American Education
    B. National Education Association
    C. Congress of Teachers and Industrial Organization
    D. American Federation of Teachers

34. Miss Southwick is a first-year teacher of fifth grade who is planning a new unit for her social studies class. She is unsure what her students must know and be able to do at this age level and in this content area. She has looked at the district curriculum guide, but it is outdated and not helpful. Which of the following will best aid Miss Southwick when planning this lesson?

    A. Teachers' union
    B. Teacher assistants
    C. Content standards
    D. School handbook

35. Which of the following laws advanced education as a social responsibility, not just a parental responsibility?

    A. Massachusetts Laws of Education 1642 and 1647
    B. No Child Left Behind and ESEA
    C. P.L. 94-142 and Section 504 of the Rehabilitation Act
    D. ADA and *Brown v. Board of Education*

36. Which of the following school positions is rooted in Horace Mann's concept of a teacher leader and started in the secondary schools, years later spreading to the primary schools?

    A. Head teacher
    B. Superintendent
    C. Principal
    D. Teacher assistant

37. Zachary is a third-grader who is working on a science experiment that involves balance and weights of objects. With his group at his side, Zachary places a lump of green clay on one pan of the balance and a lump of red clay on the other pan. His group notes that the lumps nearly balance the scale, and they decide that each lump of clay weighs almost the same amount.

Then the teacher asks the group to flatten the green lump of clay and roll it into a "snake." She asks the children to predict which will weigh more now: the green or the red clay. Zachary is convinced that the red lump that has not been flattened and rolled will definitely weigh more. According to Piaget, which of the following stages best captures the level of Zachary's thinking?

    A. Deductive
    B. Preoperational
    C. Concrete operational
    D. Sensorimotor

38. Lee is a third-grade student whose family has had a difficult time making ends meet. His dad works third shift as a security guard, and his mom has been laid off from her position at the local jewelry factory. Lee and his two sisters and two brothers try to help out around the house while also keeping up with their schoolwork. Lee's mom has shared her concern that they may not be able to pay the rent next month. Based on Maslow's hierarchy of needs, which of the following may need to be met to ensure Lee's sense of security in school and at home?

    A. Esteem needs
    B. Physiological needs
    C. Basic needs
    D. Belongingness needs

Questions 39–40 are based on the following passage.

Dmitri is a third-grader in Mrs. Kendall's classroom. Holly is a third-grader in the same classroom. Dmitri is an outgoing, musically talented, and happy child. His favorite subjects are music and science. Holly is a quiet girl who likes to wear her long bangs over her eyes. She is insightful and sensitive, as noted during a lesson on butterflies and the life cycle. Holly worked hard to care for the butterflies and made careful observations of them in her science notebook. Holly's favorite subjects are science and art.

39. According to Gardner's theory of multiple intelligences, which of the following multiple intelligences might Dmitri possess?

    A. Interpersonal and musical intelligences
    B. Visual-spatial and linguistic intelligences
    C. Intrapersonal and musical intelligences
    D. Linguistic and logical-mathematical intelligences

40. According to Gardner's theory of multiple intelligences, which of the following multiple intelligences might Holly possess?

    A. Visual-spatial and logical-mathematical intelligences
    B. Intrapersonal and naturalist intelligences
    C. Interpersonal and naturalist intelligences
    D. Bodily-kinesthetic and linguistic intelligences

41. Mr. McGillivray is preparing for an evaluation by his principal. He wants to more carefully focus on his ability to carefully plan a lesson and then assess student progress. He should work on which of the following to improve his lesson implementation in these areas?

    A. Creating standards-based units and gathering resources
    B. Opening the lesson and modeling
    C. Setting objectives and providing feedback
    D. Correcting student papers and giving homework

42. Mr. Bell is teaching a lesson on writing a lab report. He has set clear goals and objectives for the lab report and is presenting the parts of the report in small, attainable increments to make certain his students meet success on this assignment. Which of the following instructional methods is Mr. Bell using?

    A. Cooperative learning
    B. Demonstration
    C. Sequencing
    D. Direct instruction

43. Mrs. Rainy is using the book *The Three Little Pigs* to teach her students about a story's beginning, middle, and end. She has read the book aloud to the children and had them role-play the key scenes in the story. Next, she would like to have her students write one sentence about the beginning, a second sentence about the middle, and a third sentence about the end of the story. What type of graphic organizer might help her achieve her objective?

    A. Venn
    B. Sequence
    C. Cause and effect
    D. Brainstorm

44. Joshua excitedly arrives home from school to tell his dad about the "trip" his fourth-grade class is taking across the United States. Joshua is working with three other classmates to plan their route and pack their belongings so that they're the first "car" in the class to make the coast-to-coast trip out West. Joshua's dad teasingly asks how much this field trip will cost, and Joshua tells his dad that it's not a real trip the class is going on, that this is _____ in his social studies class.

    A. a simulation
    B. a lesson plan
    C. an experiment
    D. a standards-based objective

45. This group wrote a report calling for changes to liberalize the American high school. They called for eight years of elementary education and four years of secondary education. What is the name of this group?

    A. National Reading Panel
    B. National Coalition of Schools
    C. NEA Committee of Ten
    D. High School Reform Committee

46. Mr. Monroe is concerned about one of his second-grade students who is having difficulty in his classroom. His student, Charles, is frequently absent or tardy. When he is present, he is often shy or withdrawn. Mr. Monroe has tried several ways to address his concerns for Charles and to help Charles to be successful in the second grade. He has called Charles's parents on several occasions; he has met with the teacher support team about Charles; and he has tried to get to know Charles individually through small talk and focused attention on him. Which of the following characteristics of a reflective educator best describes Mr. Monroe?

    A. Reflective educators show persistence.
    B. Reflective educators attend professional development.
    C. Reflective educators have good interpersonal skills.
    D. Reflective educators possess an awareness of culture.

47. Miss Florence is a first-year principal at San Martin Elementary. She has learned that her state laws allow paddling of students with permission of the child's parents and with good reason. Paddling involves choosing an appropriate size paddle (smaller for younger students and larger for older students), requiring the child to lean over a desk, and striking the child on the backside three times with force. Although she is uncomfortable with this type of discipline, Miss Florence is required to paddle students if they repeatedly violate school rules. Paddling, in this scenario, is also known as

    A. assertive discipline.
    B. control theory.
    C. negative reinforcement.
    D. corporal punishment.

48. Mrs. Denham has been a classroom teacher for two years and is missing the learning-filled environment of her university classes. She would like to stay current on best instructional practices, current education research, and up-to-date children's book lists. Which of the following professional development resources is most likely to be helpful to Mrs. Denham?

    A. School library
    B. Professional workshops
    C. Her principal
    D. Workshop

49. Mr. Wiley asks questions that begin with *why, how does,* and *in what ways* so that his students are able to analyze and integrate information. Which of the following is the type of thinking Mr. Wiley is fostering?

    A. Divergent thinking
    B. Preoperational thinking
    C. Creative thinking
    D. Convergent thinking

50. Tory is a student who seems made for school. She is organized, uses her time wisely, works well with other students, and completes tasks with attention to detail. Her teachers all say she has a positive _____ for learning.

    A. attribute
    B. behavior
    C. conscience
    D. disposition

51. Jimmy stops and makes connection about what he reads, especially when he is interested in the topic or when he is having difficulty understanding. The metacognitive thinking process Jimmy is using is called _____?

    A. self-regulation
    B. self-assessment
    C. authentic assessment
    D. reciprocal thinking

52. _____ is the part of memory that holds and actively processes a limited amount of information for a short amount of time.

    A. Working memory
    B. Long-term memory
    C. Synapse
    D. Cortex

53. Mrs. Little is writing a new unit plan for social studies. She refers to her state's _____ to set the grade-level expectations and how her students will show what they know and are able to do.

    A. content standards
    B. common core state standards
    C. performance standards
    D. cognitive standards

54. In planning her social studies unit, Mrs. Little uses a three-step process known as backward design. Which one of the following is NOT one of the three parts of backward design?

    A. Asking what students need to know and what they need to be able to do
    B. Planning the scope and sequence of the unit
    C. Planning how to assess what students know and are able to do
    D. Planning the lessons

55. In curriculum development, the _____ of the unit involves the material or skill to be taught.

    A. sequence
    B. scope
    C. assessment
    D. planning

56. The broad goals of a school district, state, or school provide subject-specific outlines of course content, standards, and performance expectations is known as _____.

    A. a curriculum framework
    B. an emergent curriculum
    C. an evidenced-based unit plan
    D. a sequential outline

57. Mary is a fourth-grade child who is tested and achieves a raw score of 10 points. Children near the end of first grade (at the ninth month) on average earn a raw score of 10 points. Mary is assigned _____ of 1–9 (sometimes written 1.9).

    A. a stanine score
    B. a grade-equivalent score
    C. an aptitude score
    D. a raw score

58. Teachers, social workers, school psychologists, behavioral specialists, reading specialists, speech/language specialists, occupational therapists, nurses, administrators, and parents all are people who are eligible to serve on a child's _____ team.

    A. FERPA
    B. CAST
    C. IEP
    D. CAP

59. Gabe is a 9-year-old boy who has begun thinking logically about concrete events but has difficulty understanding abstract or hypothetical concepts. Piaget would say Gabe is thinking in what stage?

    A. Preoperational
    B. Formal operational
    C. Sensorimotor
    D. Concrete operational

60. Students' school records are maintained with care and confidentiality in the school's main office. Only the child's teacher, parent, school personnel who have permission to view the file, and the child have the right to access this academic record. The law that outlines student records confidentiality is known as _____.

    A. IEP
    B. P.L. 94-142
    C. FERPA
    D. Section 504

61. New and original behavior, which creates a culturally appropriate product is known as _____.

    A. problem solving
    B. giftedness
    C. creativity
    D. inquiry

62. Mrs. Horton believes children learn by observing others. In the classroom, this may occur through teacher modeling, peer discussions, or learning vicariously through others' experiences. Mrs. Horton is using _____ theory to guide her instructional practice.

    A. social-learning
    B. information-processing
    C. behaviorist
    D. Freudian

63. Mr. Simonelli breaks down a unit's content into smaller units to provide support and frequent feedback to his student. After the student demonstrates understanding of each section of important information, he introduces the next section. This process is known as _____.

    A. curriculum compacting
    B. curriculum chunking
    C. curriculum development
    D. curriculum frameworking

64. Hunter suggested a model of instruction that involves the following parts of an effective lesson: objectives, standards of performance, anticipatory set or advance organizer, teaching (which includes modeling, student input, directions, and checking for understanding), guided practice and monitoring, and lesson closure and practice. This instructional process is known as _____ instruction.

    A. cooperative
    B. reciprocal
    C. indirect
    D. direct

65. Mrs. Kennedy enjoys teaching her unit on the Westward Movement in which students experience a WebQuest and activities that involve her students in actively learning about the lives of the settlers—the places they traveled and their experiences. This type of instructional process is best known as _____.

    A. inquiry
    B. distance learning
    C. simulation
    D. independent learning

66. Mr. Keefe uses a cooperative-learning structure to actively engage his students in learning information by working with small groups of students who have been grouped randomly. The structure that best fits this description is called _____.

    A. SQ3R
    B. STAD
    C. round table
    D. numbered heads together

67. During a social studies unit on explorers, Madison was surprised and startled to learn that not all explorers treated native peoples with respect and dignity, sometimes killing villages of people and taking over their land. Madison had always thought explorers were good people, seeking new lands to discover and share with one another. Education psychologists would best describe Madison's discomfort as

    A. conditional knowledge.
    B. cognitive dissonance.
    C. critical thinking.
    D. correlation coefficients.

68. Educating children with disabilities in a classroom with students without disabilities is best known as

    A.   homogenous grouping.
    B.   pullout.
    C.   team teaching.
    D.   inclusion.

69. The reliability of a test tells educators which of the following?

    A.   How the test aligns to the Common Core State Standards
    B.   Whether the test may be used for placement decisions
    C.   Whether the test measures learning consistently
    D.   How the test measures aptitude

70. Which of the following is NOT an example of an authentic assessment?

    A.   Multiple-choice test
    B.   Portfolio
    C.   Role play
    D.   Student-project display

Constructed-Response Questions

Directions: The following questions require you to write short answers, or "constructed responses." You are not expected to cite specific theories or texts in your answers; however, your knowledge of specific principles of learning and teaching will be evaluated. Be sure to answer all parts of the question. Write your answers in the space provided.

Instructional Scenario I

Scenario: Miss Egan

Miss Celia Egan is a fifth-grade teacher who has just introduced a science lesson on cloud formation to her students. The children are excited about the lesson because it involves hands-on learning and setting up an experiment to see how clouds actually form. In addition, Miss Egan has planned for a television celebrity—Katie King, the local weatherperson—to answer the students' questions about clouds and weather at the end of the unit. As part of her school system's evaluation process, Miss Egan will be observed by the assistant principal, Mrs. Kathy Brown. Miss Egan has prepared her lesson plan (Document 1) and shared it with her assistant principal in preparation for the observation.

Document 1: Observing Cloud Formations

Objective

The students will summarize orally and in writing the key concept of the lesson, that clouds are formed when warm, humid air rises and cools, which causes water vapor in the air to condense.

Resources

- 4 clean mayonnaise-size jars
- 4 zip-seal sandwich-size plastic bags
- Ice
- 4 liquid measuring cups
- Warm water
- 4 pieces of black construction paper
- Tape
- 4 flashlights
- Matches (for adult use only)
- 4 parent volunteers to support instruction and to light matches
- VCR/TV
- TV film clip of Katie King from a day that was cloudy
- Water-cycle diagram
- Science journal and pencil

Procedures

1. Motivation—film clip and discussion
2. Warm-up
3. Preview
4. Teach

5. Experiment/discuss
6. Independent practice—write summary

Motivation

Show students the film clip of Katie King, the local TV weatherperson. Discuss the weather for that day (cloudy) and probe for background knowledge on how clouds are formed.

Warm-Up

Observe types of cloud formations and discuss the prefixes and meanings of cloud types to help students understand cloud formations (for example, *cirrus* means curly or fibrous; *cumulus* means lumpy or piled).

Preview

Show a water-cycle diagram/poster depicting cloud formation, water vapor, condensation, and heat source (the sun).

Teach

1. Teacher divides the class into four groups and asks parent volunteers to work with each of the groups. He or she then demonstrates procedures for setting up the experiment.
2. Students place black construction paper on the back of the mayonnaise-size jar.
3. Students place 1 cup of warm water in the jar.
4. Adults light match, hold it at the mouth of the jar for a few moments, and then drop match in the water.
5. Quickly have students place a sandwich bag full of ice over the mouth of the jar.
6. Students observe cloud formation.
7. Students write down observations in science journals.

Assessment

The teacher informally checks the student science journals for participation and effort in the observation process. Next, the teacher formally assesses the homework summaries using the following criteria for an exemplary summary:

- Clear and concise summary of cloud formation process; no intrusive errors in mechanics or spelling
- Paragraph format with main idea sentences, three to five detail sentences, and a closing sentence
- Accurate science content that contains definitions of *condensation, water vapor,* and *heat source*
- Work completed on time, either neatly handwritten or typewritten copy

Independent Work

For homework, students will write a summary that shows their understanding of the cloud-formation process.

After the lesson, Miss Egan was disappointed with many of her students' ability to stay focused during the experiment. Miss Egan felt that she had lost control of the classroom's management at several points in the lesson, including the showing of the film clip of Katie King and demonstrating the procedures of the experiment. Two groups had to repeat the experiment because they did not follow the sequence. In addition, one parent volunteer expressed frustration that two girls were continuously bickering over whose turn it was to manipulate the science materials. Mrs. Brown not only noted similar issues in her observation, but also added that the students' independent work on writing summaries of their understanding of the content of the lesson were below school standards for mechanics and spelling, as well as for content knowledge.

1. Suggest TWO ways that Miss Egan could improve her classroom management of this science lesson. Be certain to base your suggestions on the principles of instruction and assessment, as well as best communication techniques in the classroom.

2. Suggest TWO ways Miss Egan can look to Mrs. Brown, her assistant principal, for professional development and guidance in her efforts to grow as a teacher. Be certain to base your answer on the principles of teacher professionalism.

Preview
film clip
(go over expectations)
preview + prepare
volunturs
(um taxing, etc.

Professional literature
professional workshops

Instructional Scenario II

Scenario: Miss Arrighie

Miss Arrighie is a third-grade teacher in an urban elementary school that has been cited by the board of education as needing improvement. Her school has not been making Adequate Yearly Progress (AYP). Document 1 shows the third-grade students' reading achievement scores for the last three school years.

Document 1

Woonton School					
Grade 3	School Year	Above Standard	Meets Standard	Nearly Achieved Standard	Below Standard
Reading for high-level comprehension	2007–08	1%	10%	25%	64%
	2008–09	3%	10%	30%	57%
	2009–10	2%	7%	40%	51%
Reading for basic understanding	2007–08	25%	15%	41%	19%
	2008–09	36%	21%	42%	1%
	2009–10	38%	24%	38%	0%
Vocabulary	2007–08	5%	13%	33%	49%
	2008–09	6%	15%	37%	42%
	2009–10	2%	21%	29%	48%

Presently, Miss Arrighie has a diverse group of students. For example, 89 percent of her students receive free or reduced lunch; 76 percent of her students are Hispanic, 13 percent are African American, 6 percent are Caucasian, and 5 percent are Native American; 37 percent of her students receive special-education services; and 61 percent of her students spoke another language before learning English (PLNE).

Miss Arrighie has been attending several professional-development workshops and courses to better understand the diverse needs of her students and to learn strategies to improve her students' reading achievement, particularly in the areas of vocabulary and higher-level comprehension. She has tried reading in small groups, guided reading, and phonics programs, but she knows she needs to add more effective instructional methods to her teaching repertoire.

3. Suggest TWO strategies or methods for improving her students' vocabulary. Be sure to base your response on the principles of students as learners and the instructional process.

4. Discuss the pattern of student reading achievement in the area of "Reading for High Level Comprehension" for the past three years at Woonton School and suggest TWO strategies to improve high-level reading comprehension for Miss Arrighie's third-graders. Be sure to base your response on the principles of assessment and instructional process.

graphic organizers (continum) key words inferred

direct instruction on comprehension strategies use RTI

Answers and Explanations

Multiple-Choice Questions

Answer Key

Question	Answer	Content Category	Where to Get More Help
1	D	Students as Learners	Chapter 7
2	C	Students as Learners	Chapter 7
3	A	Students as Learners	Chapter 7
4	A	Students as Learners	Chapter 7
5	B	Instructional Process	Chapter 8
6	D	Instructional Process	Chapter 8
7	B	Instructional Process	Chapter 8
8	A	Instructional Process	Chapter 8
9	C	Professional Development, Leadership, and Community	Chapter 10
10	A	Professional Development, Leadership, and Community	Chapter 10
11	D	Professional Development, Leadership, and Community	Chapter 10
12	A	Professional Development, Leadership, and Community	Chapter 10
13	C	Students as Learners	Chapter 7
14	B	Students as Learners	Chapter 7
15	A	Students as Learners	Chapter 7
16	B	Students as Learners	Chapter 7
17	C	Instructional Process	Chapter 8
18	D	Instructional Process	Chapter 8
19	C	Instructional Process	Chapter 8
20	B	Instructional Process	Chapter 8
21	C	Professional Development, Leadership, and Community	Chapter 10
22	C	Professional Development, Leadership, and Community	Chapter 10
23	A	Professional Development, Leadership, and Community	Chapter 10
24	D	Professional Development, Leadership, and Community	Chapter 10
25	C	Students as Learners	Chapter 7
26	A	Students as Learners	Chapter 7
27	D	Students as Learners	Chapter 7
28	B	Students as Learners	Chapter 7
29	C	Assessment	Chapter 9
30	A	Instructional Process	Chapter 8
31	D	Instructional Process	Chapter 8
32	A	Instructional Process	Chapter 8
33	D	Professional Development, Leadership, and Community	Chapter 10
34	C	Professional Development, Leadership, and Community	Chapter 10
35	A	Professional Development, Leadership, and Community	Chapter 10

Question	Answer	Content Category	Where to Get More Help
36	C	Professional Development, Leadership, and Community	Chapter 10
37	C	Students as Learners	Chapter 7
38	B	Students as Learners	Chapter 7
39	A	Students as Learners	Chapter 7
40	B	Students as Learners	Chapter 7
41	C	Instructional Process	Chapter 8
42	D	Instructional Process	Chapter 8
43	B	Instructional Process	Chapter 8
44	A	Instructional Process	Chapter 8
45	C	Professional Development, Leadership, and Community	Chapter 10
46	A	Professional Development, Leadership, and Community	Chapter 10
47	D	Professional Development, Leadership, and Community	Chapter 10
48	B	Professional Development, Leadership, and Community	Chapter 10
49	D	Students as Learners	Chapter 7
50	D	Students as Learners	Chapter 7
51	A	Students as Learners	Chapter 7
52	A	Students as Learners	Chapter 7
53	C	Instructional Process	Chapter 8
54	B	Instructional Process	Chapter 8
55	B	Instructional Process	Chapter 8
56	A	Instructional Process	Chapter 8
57	B	Assessment	Chapter 9
58	C	Professional Development, Leadership, and Community	Chapter 10
59	D	Students as Learners	Chapter 7
60	C	Students as Learners	Chapter 7
61	C	Students as Learners	Chapter 7
62	A	Students as Learners	Chapter 7
63	B	Instructional Process	Chapter 8
64	D	Instructional Process	Chapter 8
65	C	Instructional Process	Chapter 8
66	D	Instructional Process	Chapter 8
67	B	Students as Learners	Chapter 7
68	D	Instructional Process	Chapter 8
69	C	Assessment	Chapter 9
70	A	Assessment	Chapter 9

Answer Explanations

1. **D** Madison appears to be struggling with her sense of competence versus her sense of inferiority, which Erikson suggests children in elementary and middle school (ages 6 to 12) work to resolve. In this stage, students strive to master sets of skills, which can lead either to a sense of competence or to feelings of inferiority.

2. **C** Maslow's levels or hierarchy of needs include the love and belongingness needs in which people need to belong to groups, such as churches or social organizations. Steven's interest in talking with friends, listening to popular music, and wearing clothing associated with sports teams all show Steven's attempts to fit into a particular peer group and to receive recognition or "love" from them.

3. **A** Gardner is the theorist who suggested multiple intelligences. There are eight multiple intelligences, according to Gardner's theory: bodily-kinesthetic, interpersonal, intrapersonal, linguistic, logical-mathematical, musical, naturalist, and spatial.

4. **A** There are four learning modalities: auditory, kinesthetic, tactile, and visual. Sean appears to be a tactile learner, one who prefers to learn by touching or feeling something.

5. **B** Mark is working on identifying similarities and differences in his work with patterns and teddy-bear counters.

6. **D** Of the choices offered, Nishita would benefit most from curriculum compacting, which is determining the key components of the curriculum that must be met and offering a compacted version of the work. Students like Nishita may become bored or even develop discipline problems when the work is too easy and not challenging. Choice C, curriculum compacting, is not a correct method for Nishita, as this instructional technique requires the teacher to check in more frequently with students having difficulty with the content being studied. Choice B, jigsaw, is a cooperative-learning method that might be beneficial to Nishita, but it is not the best choice among the four. When a teacher jigsaws curriculum, he or she offers a portion of information to be learned by an individual student, who then reports the information learned to a small group; the group discusses and learns the material together to complete the jigsawed puzzle of information.

7. **B** A story map is the best graphic organizer to present information such as characters, plot, and setting, which also are known as story elements or story grammar. Choice A, sequence chart, is best used to support instruction about the beginning, middle, and ending events in the story. Choice C, hierarchical array, shows the relationship between a concept/term and its related elements, which are presented below the concept or term. Choice D, Venn diagram, is best used to show the similarities and differences among elements in a story.

8. **A** Mnemonic devices help students make a connection between the new information to be memorized. Encouraging students to connect prior knowledge to new information can help students retain this new information.

9. **C** Teachers have the right to withhold information unrelated to employment, such as marital status, sexual preference, and number of children. Choices A (collaborating with student's caregivers), B (following U.S. laws), and D (committing to lifelong learning for all) are common elements in a district's code of ethics for teachers.

10. **A** Corporal punishment is not unconstitutional, but it may be illegal in the state in which you teach.

11. **D** Student periodicals, such as newspapers, yearbooks, or magazines, may not be edited by school personnel if they are fully supported by student groups.

12. **A** The Little Rock 9 was comprised of nine African-American students from Little Rock, Arkansas, who nonviolently and bravely decided to challenge their right to attend the all-white Rock Central High in Little Rock, Arkansas.

13. **C** The Americans with Disabilities Act (ADA) is a federal law that prohibits discrimination on the basis of a person's disability for all services, programs, and activities provided by state and local governments. Choice A, Race to the Top, is the reauthorization of the Elementary and Secondary Education Act (ESEA). Choice B, Section 504 (of the Rehabilitation Act of 1973), is a civil-rights law prohibiting discrimination against individuals with disabilities by federally assisted programs or activities. Choice D, P.L. 94-142, passed in 1975, is now codified as the Individuals with Disabilities Education Act (IDEA).

14. **B** Madison's preferred learning modality is visual learning, learning by seeing. Visual learners are more successful when teachers use methods such as film, PowerPoint presentations, overheads, notes on a chalkboard, or notes on a whiteboard.

15. **A** Jamie appears to be motivated by extrinsic rewards for learning, not the intrinsic reward of learning for learning's sake.

16. **B** Gilligan's work questions the male-centered personality, psychology, and moral development theorists. She suggests three stages in the ethic of care: pre-conventional, in which the goal is individual survival; conventional, in which the goal is self-sacrifice to achieve goodness; and post-conventional, in which the goal is to uphold principles of nonviolence.

17. **C** Bandura's social-learning theory suggests that children learn by observing others. In the classroom, this may occur as modeling or learning vicariously through others' experiences.

18. **D** Survey, Question, Read, Recite, and Review (SQ3R) is an instructional routine students can use to summarize and take notes effectively.

19. **C** Numbered heads together is a cooperative-learning strategy in which activities involve a "home team" of heterogeneously grouped students who work in small groups to become experts on a portion of the content to be learned. After the students become experts, they return to the home team to share important information.

20. **B** Generating and testing hypotheses has become known as one of the "9 essential strategies." When using this strategy, students more deeply understand concepts being taught and must clearly explain their hypotheses and conclusions.

21. **C** Students must be offered a hearing as part of due process established in the *Goss v. Lopez* case of 1971. Students facing suspension or expulsion must be afforded a hearing before their rights to an education are denied.

22. **C** In challenging teaching situations, reflective practitioners show persistence, along with an understanding of their own and others' cultures. There are several other attributes of a reflective practitioner, such as a willingness to collaborate, good interpersonal skills, and an ability to critically analyze his or her own practice.

23. **A** The Nation at Risk report was issued during the Reagan Administration and called for the creation of teaching, teacher education, and education standards.

24. **D** The testing movement in U.S. education is thought to have begun with Terman's introduction of the Stanford-Binet intelligence test in 1916, along with other tests, such as the Stanford Achievement Test.

25. **C** Glasser's choice theory calls for regular class meetings to discuss classroom rules and procedures in a collaborative and problem-solving setting. In this context, students and teacher co-negotiate their learning environment, building ownership and responsibility for all in the learning community.

26. **A** Mrs. Benton appears to be having difficulty enacting and understanding the importance of her role as a teacher. Although a *laissez-faire* approach to the classroom can be effective for several teachers, Mrs. Benton's attempts to befriend her students, rather than teach them, shows her lack of professionalism and misguided priorities in the classroom.

27. **D** Michelle's motivation is intrinsic—from within. She learns for the sake of learning and does not appear to need external rewards for learning.

28. **B** The primary purpose of a school-to-work program is to help prepare students for future living.

29. **C** Holistic scoring is a way to assess the overall quality of a student's work. The teacher does not evaluate each individual part; instead, he or she focuses on providing feedback about the whole piece of work.

30. **A** A unit that incorporates content areas, such as science and language arts as described in this situation, is considered interdisciplinary. The goal of an interdisciplinary unit is to help students make connections between content areas and classes in hopes that the student will transfer learning beyond the classroom walls.

31. **D** Mrs. Eberly will look to the National Council of Teachers of Mathematics for professional standards for teachers of mathematics.

32. **A** Miss Whitman is using an inquiry model of instruction to help her students discover science concepts and how things work in science. In an inquiry-model approach, the teacher provides hands-on experiences for the students to discover meaning. The teacher does not lecture or tell in this instructional model.

33. **D** The American Federation of Teachers was formed in 1916 with the motto "Democracy in Education and Education for Democracy."

34. **C** Content standards are more likely than the school handbook to guide Miss Southwick's instruction in this scenario. School handbooks usually contain school policies and sometimes contain brief outlines of what is taught at each grade level. Miss Southwick will get more reliable information about content she can teach from the content standards of her professional association.

35. **A** The Massachusetts Laws of Education 1642 and 1647 established social responsibility to teach children to read and write.

36. **C** Horace Mann established the role of the principal as a teacher leader and instructional leader.

37. **C** Zachary is showing his level of development at the concrete-operational level when he does not recognize the principle of conservation of weight. According to Piaget, concrete-operational thinkers have an ability to formulate and test hypotheses. In addition, concrete-operational thinkers often try to confirm or disprove a hypothesis by changing two or more variables.

38. **B** According to Maslow's hierarchy of needs, Lee's physiological needs must be met or he will have difficulty with higher-level needs, such as love, sense of belonging, and esteem needs.

39. **A** According to Gardner's theory of multiple intelligences, Dmitri shows strengths in the areas of musical and interpersonal intelligences.

40. **B** According to Gardner's theory of multiple intelligences, Holly shows strengths in the areas of naturalist and intrapersonal intelligences.

41. **C** Mr. McGillivray should focus on setting objectives and providing feedback to his students in his efforts to strengthen his lesson planning.

42. **D** Mr. Bell is using direct instruction, which is an overarching method that involves carefully planned lessons presented in small, attainable increments with clearly defined goals and objectives.

43. **B** Mrs. Rainy would use a sequence diagram to best teach her students how to note a story's beginning, middle, and end.

44. **A** Joshua seems to really enjoy the simulation his teacher is using in social studies class. A simulation involves students actively experiencing real-life situations through scenarios and dramatization of events.

45. **C** The NEA Committee of Ten created the report, which resulted in the U.S. education school configuration of eight years of elementary education and four years of secondary education.

46. **A** In this situation, Mr. Monroe shows his professionalism through his persistence in helping to find a way to assist his student.

47. **D** Corporal punishment is that which involves striking a child. Corporal punishment is considered constitutional according to federal laws, but it may be considered illegal in schools according to state laws.

48. **B** Mrs. Denham would most likely benefit from attending a professional development series of workshops to expose her to new ideas outside of her building and to new colleagues with whom she could build relationships.

49. **D** Convergent thinking is a process of gathering several pieces of information to solve a problem.

50. **D** Disposition is a person's natural tendency to approach learning or problem solving in certain ways. A student's disposition is an important factor to consider and attempt to shape, if needed, so that the student can succeed in complex or challenging learning tasks.

51. **A** Self-regulation the process of taking control of one's own learning or behavior.

52. **A** Working memory is the part of memory that holds and actively processes a limited amount of information for a short amount of time.

53. **C** Performance standards set the level of performance expectation for student groups (for example, first-graders or 5- to 7-year-olds). Performance standards generally are set at the state and local level and can generally be found on your state's department of education website or your local school district's website.

54. **B** Jay McTighe and Grant Wiggens suggest that teachers use a backward design when planning for standards-based instruction. In the past, educators typically sought materials or the content to teach to students, planned the lesson, and then designed an assessment to measure student progress. With backward design, teachers are encouraged to begin with the student's learning needs first, plan the assessment next, and finally plan the rest of the lesson activities and select materials. Educators now know we need to start with the students' needs first, plan assessments next, and then finalize our lesson plan. These are three questions to ask yourself as you use backward design to plan instruction:

    1. What do students need to know and be able to do?

    2. How will I assess what students know and are able to do?

    3. How will I plan the lesson?

55. **B** Scope, as it relates to curriculum, is the material or skill to be taught. For example, during my fourth-grade dinosaur unit, the scope of what I was teaching was measurement—specifically, length and distance in U.S. standard and metric systems.

56. **A** Curriculum frameworks list the broad goals of a school district, state, or school and provide subject-specific outlines of course content, standards, and performance expectations.

57. **B** Grade-level equivalents demonstrate the grade and month of the school year to which a student score can be compared. For example, a score of 5.1 would indicate that a student is performing at a fifth-grade, first-month level.

58. **C** Members of a student's Individualized Education Plan (IEP) team consist of a variety of professionals such as teachers, social workers, school psychologists, behavioral specialists, reading specialists, speech/language specialists, occupational therapists, nurses, administrators, and parents. These educational partners come together to create and revise an IEP for a student with special needs.

59. **D** Children approximately ages 7 to 11 think in logical terms, not in abstract terms, which is known as concrete-operational thinking. Students in this age range require hands-on experiences to learn concepts and manipulate symbols logically.

60. **C.** The Family Educational Rights and Privacy Act (FERPA) is legislation passed in 1974 that gives students and parents access to school records, and limits access to records by others.

61. **C** Creativity is new and original behavior, which creates a culturally appropriate product.

62. **A** Social-learning theory suggests that children learn by observing others. In a classroom setting, this may occur through modeling or learning vicariously through others' experiences. One important concept from social-learning theory is distributed cognition, in which a person is able to learn more with another or in a group than he or she might be able to do alone.

63. **B** Curriculum chunking involves breaking down a unit's content into smaller units or chunks and provides support and frequent feedback to the student as he or she demonstrates understanding of each chunk of information.

64. **D** Direct instruction is an overarching method for teaching students that includes carefully planned lessons presented in small, attainable increments with clearly defined goals and objectives. Direct-instruction methods tend to be more teacher centered and include specific instructional strategies, such as lecture, demonstration, mastery learning, review of student performance, and student examination.

65. **C** Simulations help students become immersed in the content being studied. For example, in an interdisciplinary unit of study on the Westward Movement in the United States, students are grouped into wagons and wagon trains and provided with realistic scenarios to consider during each day of the simulation. Computer and video technology offers teachers many opportunities for simulations.

66. **D** Numbered heads together is a cooperative-learning structure in which students are heterogeneously grouped into a "home team." Then each student is assigned a number so that he or she can join all the students with the same number to become an "expert" on assigned materials. For example, all the students who were assigned the number five read about and discuss music from the Harlem Renaissance. Once each of the numbered group has had time to learn the assigned materials, the students return to their home team and teach their peers the content they have learned.

67. **B** Cognitive dissonance is a discomfort experienced when one's beliefs do not match new information being learned. Madison's beliefs came into question and created cognitive dissonance in her mind when she learned of some explorers' mistreatment of native peoples.

68. **D** Inclusion is a special-education practice in which students with and without disabilities are taught together in the classroom, often with a team-teaching (Choice C) pair consisting of a special-education and regular-education teacher. Choice A, homogenous grouping, is the instructional practice of grouping students with similar abilities or interests. Choice B, pullout, is a phrase often used to connote the opposite of inclusion—pulling students with special needs from the regular-education classroom to work with a special-education teacher and a small group of students who also have special needs.

69. **C** Test reliability is defined as the consistency with which the test measures something.

70. **A** Multiple-choice assessments, like this one, are considered traditional assessments. Authentic assessments (choices B, C, and D), on the other hand, are those in which students are asked to replicate real-life tasks that demonstrate meaningful knowledge and skills.

Constructed-Response Questions

Instructional Scenario I

1. **Suggested content:** Miss Egan taught a lesson on cloud formations that was not implemented well, primarily because of classroom-management issues. Two suggestions for Miss Egan are: preview film clip and prepare volunteers. To more thoroughly prepare students for the purpose of viewing the film clip of Katie King, Miss Egan should clearly state the objectives of her lesson and review appropriate behaviors when viewing the film. She could create a simple graphic organizer for students to write on while they view the film or immediately after. This will hold each student individually accountable for the viewing, and it helps students know that watching the film is purposeful. If Miss Egan spent a bit more time preparing the classroom volunteers on how to demonstrate the procedures of the experiment and how to manage the materials of the experiment, the students may have more effectively taken turns and completed the experiment successfully. Although this may take a bit more planning time than conducting this experiment for the whole group with only the teacher demonstrating, it is worth the effort because of safety (matches were in use) and also because the students are more able to observe closely in small groups.

2. **Suggested content:** Miss Egan can seek the expertise, advice, and support of her assistant principal, Mrs. Brown, by asking her to suggest professional reading and professional development ideas about classroom management. Professional literature can offer ideas to Miss Egan on her own time and can provide a variety of models and theories to guide her to discover what is right for her and her class. Mrs. Brown may even have a few specific titles from her own professional library to loan to Miss Egan. Miss Egan also can ask her assistant principal to support her efforts to locate and attend professional-development workshops on the topic of classroom management. Mrs. Brown may know of local, statewide, or national opportunities for professional development and can advocate for the release time—and also possibly for the funds—for Miss Egan to attend.

Instructional Scenario II

3. **Suggested content:** Miss Arrighie has a diverse group of third-grade students, and she wants to improve her vocabulary instruction. One method to do this is to use graphic organizers such as a continuum. The continuum graphic organizer is a horizontal line with an arrow at either end. Near one end of the continuum, the teacher places a word, such as *sad,* and near the other end of the continuum the teacher places a word with the opposite meaning, such as *happy.* With the students' help, the teacher places other words that are synonymous with happy and sad, and they place the words along the continuum. Miss Arrighie can keep this graphic organizer posted in the classroom and remind students to use exciting words instead of *happy* and *sad* in their written and spoken language. A second method to improve students' vocabulary development is the key-word method. The teacher selects target words to teach students, those that are central to understanding the meaning of the text. Then the teacher uses morphemes, rhymes, or word parts to help students to remember the meaning of the word. For example, if Miss Arrighie was trying to teach the word citizen, she would think of a smaller word or sound within *citizen,* such as *city.* Then the teacher would draw a city and a person in the city, whose name is Zen. She would draw the following on the whiteboard:

CITIZEN

City + Zen = drawing of the city and a stick figure named Zen

4. **Suggested content:** The pattern of "Reading for High-Level Comprehension" is improving in some areas and not improving in other areas. For example, in 2007–08, 1 percent of the students were reading above the standard in this area and, during 2008–09, 3 percent of the students were reading above the standard. In 2009–10, this same area dropped to 2 percent. More dramatically, in 2007–08, 64 percent of the students were not achieving the standard, but by 2008–09 the percentage of students reading below the standard had reduced to 51 percent. Although there has been some improvement at Woonton School, clearly more students need to meet or exceed the standard for reading for high-level comprehension. One method to use is to provide direct instruction on specific comprehension strategies, such as making inferences and summarizing. The teacher offers many specific lessons on these strategies with models and then lots of guided practice to scaffold support for students. A second approach to improve students' reading achievement is to use the Response to Intervention process to plan a targeted intervention for students who need to improve their reading achievement. Miss Arrighie could collaborate with the reading specialist to plan the evidence-based approaches that could be tried with students for six to eight weeks. After this period of time, the teacher would then reassess students to see if they have made progress, and if they have not, Miss Arrighie would consider a Tier 2 targeted intervention.

This full-length PLT Grades 5–9 practice test (0623) is designed to give you an overall sense of the test's format and to help you determine the content areas you need to focus on in your studies. You may want to practice your pacing while taking the full-length practice test. You will have a total of two hours to complete the entire PLT test, which consists of 70 multiple-choice questions and 4 constructed-response questions.

After you complete the full-length practice test, score your answers and use the explanations to self-diagnose content areas to study in Part III of this guide. You also may want to complete the other practice tests in Chapters 11, 12, and 14 to aid you in determining which content areas to study. Even though these additional practice tests are written for other PLT test grade levels, the question topics (Students as Learners; Instructional Process; Assessment; and Professional Development, Leadership, and Community) remain the same.

CUT HERE

(Remove these sheets and use them to mark your answers to the multiple-choice questions.)

Answer Sheet

1 Ⓐ Ⓑ Ⓒ ●		41 Ⓐ ● Ⓒ Ⓓ
2 ● Ⓑ Ⓒ Ⓓ		42 Ⓐ Ⓑ ● Ⓓ
3 Ⓐ Ⓑ ● Ⓓ		43 Ⓐ ● Ⓒ Ⓓ
4 Ⓐ ● Ⓒ Ⓓ		44 ● Ⓑ Ⓒ Ⓓ
5 Ⓐ Ⓑ ● Ⓓ		45 Ⓐ Ⓑ ● Ⓓ
6 ● Ⓑ Ⓒ Ⓓ		46 Ⓐ Ⓑ ● Ⓓ
7 Ⓐ Ⓑ Ⓒ ●		47 Ⓐ Ⓑ ● Ⓓ
8 ● Ⓑ Ⓒ Ⓓ		48 ● Ⓑ Ⓒ Ⓓ
9 ● Ⓑ Ⓒ Ⓓ		49 Ⓐ ● Ⓒ Ⓓ
10 Ⓐ Ⓑ ● Ⓓ		50 Ⓐ ● Ⓒ Ⓓ
11 Ⓐ Ⓑ ● Ⓓ		51 Ⓐ Ⓑ Ⓒ ●
12 ● Ⓑ Ⓒ Ⓓ		52 Ⓐ Ⓑ ● Ⓓ
13 Ⓐ ● Ⓒ Ⓓ		53 ● Ⓑ Ⓒ Ⓓ
14 Ⓐ Ⓑ ● Ⓓ		54 Ⓐ Ⓑ Ⓒ ●
15 Ⓐ ● Ⓒ Ⓓ		55 Ⓐ Ⓑ ● Ⓓ
16 ● Ⓑ Ⓒ Ⓓ		56 Ⓐ Ⓑ ● Ⓓ
17 Ⓐ Ⓑ Ⓒ ●		57 Ⓐ Ⓑ ● Ⓓ
18 Ⓐ ● Ⓒ Ⓓ		58 ● Ⓑ Ⓒ Ⓓ
19 Ⓐ Ⓑ ● Ⓓ		59 Ⓐ Ⓑ ● Ⓓ
20 ● Ⓑ Ⓒ Ⓓ		60 Ⓐ Ⓑ Ⓒ ●
21 Ⓐ ✗ ● Ⓓ		61 Ⓐ Ⓑ Ⓒ ●
22 Ⓐ ● Ⓒ Ⓓ		62 ● Ⓑ Ⓒ Ⓓ
23 Ⓐ Ⓑ Ⓒ ●		63 Ⓐ ● Ⓒ Ⓓ
24 ● Ⓑ Ⓒ Ⓓ		64 Ⓐ ● Ⓒ Ⓓ
25 Ⓐ ● Ⓒ Ⓓ		65 Ⓐ ● Ⓒ Ⓓ
26 Ⓐ Ⓑ ● Ⓓ		66 Ⓐ Ⓑ Ⓒ ●
27 Ⓐ Ⓑ ● Ⓓ		67 Ⓐ ● Ⓒ Ⓓ
28 Ⓐ Ⓑ Ⓒ ●		68 Ⓐ Ⓑ Ⓒ ●
29 Ⓐ ● Ⓒ Ⓓ		69 Ⓐ Ⓑ ● Ⓓ
30 ● Ⓑ Ⓒ Ⓓ		70 Ⓐ ● Ⓒ Ⓓ
31 Ⓐ Ⓑ ● Ⓓ		
32 Ⓐ Ⓑ Ⓒ ●		
33 Ⓐ ● Ⓒ Ⓓ		
34 ● Ⓑ Ⓒ Ⓓ		
35 Ⓐ Ⓑ ● Ⓓ		
36 ● Ⓑ Ⓒ Ⓓ		
37 Ⓐ ● Ⓒ Ⓓ		
38 ● Ⓑ Ⓒ Ⓓ		
39 Ⓐ Ⓑ ● Ⓓ		
40 Ⓐ Ⓑ Ⓒ ●		

or D

Time: 2 hours

70 multiple-choice questions and 4 constructed-response questions

Multiple-Choice Questions

Directions: For each multiple-choice question, select the best answer and mark the corresponding letter space on your answer sheet.

1. Celia and Alyssa are in the sixth grade at Wakeland Elementary School. Both girls take pride in looking their best at school and often seek the approval of their peers. Which of the following best describes the girls' stage of moral development according to Lawrence Kohlberg?

   A. Over-conventional
   B. Pre-conventional
   C. Post-conventional
   D. Conventional

2. Mr. Conlin, a fifth-grade teacher, prefers instructional methods that enable his students to discover meaning. For example, in his recent lesson on measurement, he asked his students to plan and then enact their plan to draw three dinosaurs to scale on the school playground. He provided the materials and resources to help students learn more about the actual size of each dinosaur; otherwise, Mr. Conlin let his students discover their own solutions to the challenge of drawing such large animals. A guiding principle behind Mr. Conlin's practice is his educational philosophy about which of the following?

   A. Constructivism
   B. Behaviorism
   C. Nonviolence
   D. Self-actualization

Questions 3–4 are based on the following passage.

Phyllis is a fifth-grader who is making slower-than-average progress in her gross-motor, fine-motor, and language development. She has difficulty with handwriting, physical-education activities, and speaking in class. Phyllis is receiving special services from the resource teacher, the speech-language pathologist, and the occupational/physical therapist.

3. Phyllis's learning differences may be described as which of the following?

   A. Attention deficit disorder
   B. Autism
   C. Developmental delays
   D. Mental retardation

4. Which of the following federal laws protects Phyllis's rights and prohibits discrimination on the basis of her disability?

   A. Section 504 of the Rehabilitation Act
   B. Americans with Disabilities Act (ADA)
   C. P.L. 94-142
   D. IEP

5. Mrs. Whitman, a seventh-grade teacher, has planned a cooperative-learning activity in which her students count off 1-2-3-4 to four work groups. When all the children who counted off the number 1 get together, they read and discuss the first section of the social studies text chapter and answer the questions for section 1. When all the children who counted off the number 2 get together, they read and discuss the second section of the social studies text chapter and answer the questions for section 2. In a similar pattern, groups 3 and 4 read and complete questions for sections 3 and 4, respectively. After the groups complete their reading and questions, the children return to their regular seats, which are placed in groups of four, and share their "expertise" on the assignment. This cooperative-learning structure is known as which of the following?

   A. Think-pair-share
   B. STAD
   C. Numbered heads together
   D. Advance organizers

6. Mrs. Brown strives to respond to the wide range of abilities of her fifth-grade learners by using methods such as tiered instruction and flexible grouping. Mrs. Brown is

    A. differentiating instruction.
    B. sequencing instruction.
    C. directing instruction.
    D. demonstrating instruction.

7. Miss Wade is teaching vocabulary and shades of meaning. She uses the following graphic organizer to help her students learn a variety of ways to express feelings of happiness and anger.

    furious   angry   frustrated   okay
            content   happy   ecstatic

    Which of the following types of graphic organizers best describes the "feelings visual" that Miss Wade is using?

    A. Venn diagram
    B. Sequence chart
    C. Matrix
    D. Continuum

8. One approach to classroom management centers on effective lesson planning as the best way to manage classroom behavior. The teacher begins the lesson with an "anticipatory set" to help the students connect their background knowledge and experiences with the new information in the lesson. Next, the teacher models and provides guided practice for the new information to be learned. At the close of the lesson, the teacher provides opportunities for independent and extended practice. This approach is known as

    A. Hunter's model. _Madeline_
    B. Canter's model.
    C. Glasser's model.
    D. Jones's model.

9. In a report established by the Clinton Administration and continued in the George W. Bush Administration, officials established that all students will start school ready to learn; high-school graduation rates will meet or exceed 90 percent; and teachers will have access to high-quality professional development. Which of the following reports is described?

    A. Goals 2000
    B. No Child Left Behind
    C. National Reading Panel Report
    D. A Nation at Risk

10. Teaching professionals who are working to build positive relationships with families ensure that they use which of the following?

    A. Empowerment of learners
    B. Advocacy for learners
    C. Respectful communication with caregivers
    D. Discrimination of students

11. Which of the following reports demonstrates the merits of a classical curriculum and was supported by those with a conservative view of education?

    A. No Child Left Behind
    B. Yale Report of 1828
    C. Morrill Report of 1862
    D. Goals 2000

12. The U.S. Supreme Court has ruled that the First Amendment of the U.S. Constitution requires public-school officials to be neutral in their treatment of religion. In other words, schools can show neither favoritism nor hostility toward acts of religious expression, such as which of the following?

    A. Symbols
    B. Ministers
    C. Priests
    D. Prayer

13. Effective classroom managers have a keen sense of awareness about all that is going on in the classroom simultaneously. Jacob Kounin calls this ability teacher

    A. perception.
    B. with-it-ness.
    C. professionalism.
    D. behavior modification.

14. When a teacher plans a lesson, he or she should be aware of factors of the learning environment that he or she can control, such as _____, which may influence student achievement.

    A. school location
    B. classroom location
    C. seating arrangement
    D. class size

Questions 15–16 are based on the following passage.

Josiah is a seventh-grader who is having difficulty in school, primarily because of his limited vocabulary and poor reading habits. His social studies teacher, Mr. Enright, is concerned about Josiah's ability to pass the seventh grade and has asked for a meeting of the Teacher Support Team (TST) to discuss Josiah.

15. Mr. Enright's primary concern is most likely Josiah's

    A. health history.
    B. prior-year instruction.
    C. family background.
    D. readiness to learn.

16. Mr. Enright is concerned that Josiah may not have had the experiences, both learning and social, to have a vocabulary typically expected of a seventh-grader. Mr. Enright believes that if he helps Josiah develop his _____ for the social studies content, his vocabulary and understanding of the social studies content may improve.

    A. schema
    B. test-taking skills
    C. homework
    D. family

17. Mrs. Burt likes to use short speeches by famous people in history, as well as historical photographs from reputable websites. These materials are known as which of the following?

    A. Sound clips
    B. Historical media
    C. Original websites
    D. Primary sources

18. In a unit of study on African-American folktales, Mrs. Pates asks her class, "What are the features of African-American folktales?" On Bloom's Taxonomy, this question is at which of the following levels?

    A. Literal level
    B. Analysis level
    C. Evaluation level
    D. Literature-connection level

19. "The student will list and explain three causes of World War II" is known as which of the following in a lesson plan?

    A. Goal
    B. Behavioral objective
    C. Assessment
    D. Preview

20. Which of the following assessments measures a student's ability to develop or acquire skills and knowledge?

    A. Aptitude test
    B. Criterion-referenced test
    C. Standardized test
    D. Diagnostic test

21. Which of the following legal cases ruled that all students can be required to attend public *or* private schools?

    A. *Brown v. Board of Education*
    B. *Roe v. Wade*
    C. *Pierce v. Society of Sisters*
    D. *Plessy v. Ferguson*

22. An attendance act passed in Massachusetts in 1852 was the first general law to control the conditions for children. It was the start of which of the following in the United States?

    A. National Education Association
    B. Compulsory education
    C. Separate but equal education
    D. Normal school education

23. Which of the following provided the foundation for vocational education in the United States and was seen as an enhancement to the traditional high-school curriculum?

    A. Cardinal Principles of Secondary Education
    B. Progressive-education movement
    C. No Child Left Behind
    D. Manual-training movement

24. Which of the following dramatically changed U.S. education after October 4, 1957?

    A. Soviet launching of *Sputnik*
    B. U.S. launching of *Apollo*
    C. A Nation at Risk
    D. *Brown v. Board of Education*

25. Jessica tends to make decisions based on which actions will please others, especially her teachers and her peers. She places a lot of emphasis on maintaining relationships with others and listens carefully to others' views when making decisions. According to Kohlberg's theory, which of the following best describes Jessica's level of moral development?

    A. Post-conventional
    B. Pre-conventional
    C. Anti-conventional
    D. Conventional

26. Maddie works in the resource classroom for her writing and mathematics instruction as stated in her IEP. Maddie's resource teacher often helps Maddie see the real-life purpose behind the writing or math lesson and helps her see when and where she can use this lesson again in another learning situation. Her classroom teacher and her resource teacher communicate about Maddie's progress and frequently share materials and lesson plans to help Maddie do which of the following?

    A. Master skills
    B. Exit from special education
    C. Transfer learning
    D. Satisfy state and federal requirements

Questions 27–28 are based on the following passage.

Carrie is a seventh-grader with delayed speech who dislikes being touched and has difficulty following simple directions. She also has a limited vocabulary and is quite distractible.

27. Which of the following special education labels most closely matches Carrie's learning and developmental behaviors?

    A. Learning disabled
    B. Functionally mentally retarded
    C. Autistic
    D. Gifted

28. Carrie is eligible to receive instruction in her _____ as mandated by federal special-education laws.

    A. neighborhood school
    B. private school
    C. self-contained classroom
    D. least restrictive environment (LRE)

29. Which of the following measures of central tendency is defined as the midpoint of a set of numbers, such as scores from a classroom?

    A. Mode
    B. Median
    C. Mean
    D. Average

30. Which of the following is most likely to be read by a teacher but not corrected for spelling, grammar, or mechanics?

    A. Free-response journal
    B. Science-lab report
    C. Reader-response entry
    D. Summative essay

31. Mrs. McGuire reads aloud to her students every day after lunch. She chooses a book that is beyond the instructional reading level for the majority of her students, with rich vocabulary and many personal connections for her students. Which group formation would most likely be most effective for reading aloud to her class?

    A. Jigsaw
    B. Flexible group
    C. Whole group
    D. Cooperative group

32. Mrs. Faella has asked Paul and Denise to read together. She has instructed Paul to read the first passage and for Paul to ask Denise questions. When they are done discussing the first passage, Denise then reads aloud and then asks Paul questions about the text. Which of the following best describes this instructional routine?

    A. Fluency reading
    B. Echo reading
    C. Scaffolded teaching
    D. Reciprocal teaching

33. Mrs. Josephson enjoys learning from the diverse experiences of her students, and her peers see her as a highly professional and reflective teacher. Mrs. Josephson most likely holds which of the following views?

    A. Diversity is a challenge that she can overcome.
    B. Diversity is a positive, enriching aspect of teaching.
    C. Diversity is a necessary evil in teaching.
    D. Diversity is a problem in American schools today.

34. Which of the following landmark cases found that "separate educational facilities are inherently unequal"?

    A. *Brown v. Board of Education*
    B. Oregon School Case of 1925
    C. Land Ordinance of 1785
    D. *Lau v. Nichols*

35. A founding father of America advanced formal education by establishing a plan for an English-language grammar school. This school would teach not only Latin but also English. Which of the following founding fathers created this plan for schools (which never was fully enacted in his lifetime)?

    A. Thomas Jefferson
    B. George Washington
    C. Benjamin Franklin
    D. John Hancock

36. Which of the following colleges was established in 1636 to ensure that the leaders of the church, state, and judicial systems were well prepared and learned?

    A. Harvard College
    B. Colgate College
    C. Simmons College
    D. Providence College

37. Which of the following theorists' work focuses on children learning by observing others?

    A. Kohlberg
    B. Bandura
    C. Maslow
    D. Jones

38. Which of the following theorists suggested that children learn through two complementary processes called assimilation and accommodation?

    A. Small
    B. Piaget
    C. Glasser
    D. Freud

Questions 39–40 are based on the following passage.

Maria is an eighth-grader who is learning about the Harlem Renaissance in her English class. Her teacher has set up opportunities for the students to read and learn more about this period in small groups by using quality websites. Maria shares her enthusiasm when she finds an excellent source of information on the Internet and explains to her teacher, "As I think back about my reading, I realize it was like I was there in Harlem! I could hear Nora Zeale Hurston and Langston Hughes reading their recent works. In my mind, I was thinking that this was the birth of the Jazz Age and the Beat Poets. What a great website, and what a great time in history!"

39. Which of the following describes Maria's thinking about her own reading of this website?

   A. Reciprocal
   B. Rote
   C. Metacognitive
   D. Literal

40. Maria's teacher most likely set up the students in peer groups to research the Harlem Renaissance for which of the following reasons based on principles of learning and teaching?

   A. To be sure that each student had a chance on the computer
   B. To help each student complete a worksheet on the assignment
   C. To minimize classroom disruption
   D. To help each student find his or her zone of proximal development

41. Which of the following study strategies involves surveying text, questioning, and then reading, reciting, and reviewing the text to better comprehend it?

   A. 4 MAT
   B. SQ3R
   C. Summarizing and note taking
   D. Cooperative learning

42. Bobby is having difficulty completing his homework and practice activities in mathematics. He makes several errors in his work and has worked more slowly than his peers. Which of the following instructional modifications might help Bobby complete his math work with more success?

   A. Curriculum compacting
   B. Rote learning
   C. Curriculum chunking
   D. Jigsaw

43. Mr. Matthews likes to immerse his students in the social studies content that he teaches. During a recent unit on Westward Expansion, the students took a covered-wagon ride, and then they read and reenacted a story from this period and charted their course across the country. Which of the following methods is Mr. Matthews employing?

   A. Simulation
   B. Whole language
   C. Project-based learning
   D. Demonstration

44. At the end of the school year, Mrs. Lahiri provided which of the following evaluations to her supervisor to demonstrate her progress toward her professional goals?

   A. Summative evaluation
   B. Formative evaluation
   C. Diagnostic evaluation
   D. Remedial evaluation

45. Mrs. Basel modifies her teaching practice to meet the unique needs of several of her seventh-grade students. For example, she incorporates a basketball-like game into studying for a unit test in science. In addition, Mrs. Basel attends meetings about those of her students who are struggling academically, socially, or emotionally. Which of the following best describes Mrs. Basel's reason for her teaching practice?

   A. She wants to receive good evaluations.
   B. She likes to play games.
   C. She advocates for all students.
   D. She wants more free time to plan.

46. If a teacher could reasonably have foreseen a negative teaching situation, or if a teacher acted differently from the way a reasonable teacher placed in a similar situation would have acted, then which of the following is true of this teacher?

    A. The teacher can freely associate with whomever he or she chooses.
    B. The teacher can be recommended for tenure.
    C. The teacher cannot be fired.
    D. The teacher can be sued and found liable for negligence.

47. The National Council of Teachers of English, the International Reading Association, and the National Science Teachers Association are all

    A. seminars.
    B. journals.
    C. conferences.
    D. professional associations.

48. Which of the following federal laws prohibits discrimination on the basis of a person's disability for all services, programs, and activities provided or made available by state or local governments?

    A. ADA
    B. P.L. 94-142
    C. IEP Act
    D. No Child Left Behind

49. The following measurable verbs are all found on the _____ domain of Bloom's Taxonomy: describe, analyze, identify, judge, and define.

    A. affective
    B. cognitive
    C. effective
    D. psychomotor

50. Which of the following is NOT a type of knowledge that information-processing theorists suggest we foster in students?

    A. Analytical
    B. Declarative
    C. Procedural
    D. Conditional

51. One's belief that one is capable is known as _____.

    A. self-concept
    B. self-handicapping
    C. self-fulfilling prophesy
    D. self-efficacy

52. Miss Hattoy regularly uses graphic organizers, concrete objects, and PowerPoint presentations to best meet the needs of which type of learner?

    A. Musical learners
    B. Kinesthetic learners
    C. Verbal-linguistic learners
    D. Visual learners

53. **A cooperative-learning structure in which** students are assigned to heterogeneously grouped teams of four or five members who collaborate on worksheets designed to provide extended practice on instruction given by the teacher is best known as _____.

    A. STAD
    B. jigsaw
    C. numbered heads together
    D. think-pair-share

54. In this evidence-based teaching method, the teacher and the student engage in a discussion of the text. Both the student and the teacher question and respond to the text in an effort to improve the student's comprehension of the material.

    A. Peer tutoring
    B. Mentoring
    C. Differentiated instruction
    D. Reciprocal teaching

55. A key goal in teaching is for students not only to learn the knowledge and skills during the lesson but also to _____ the knowledge and skills in a new situation, so that learning is placed in long-term memory.

    A. judge
    B. transfer
    C. analyze
    D. define

56. Units that give students a chance to work at their own pace under the teacher's leadership or guidance can be particularly beneficial for students who need course material modified to be more challenging or simplified. This type of instruction is called an _____.

A. interdisciplinary unit
B. independent-study unit
C. emergent-curriculum unit
D. understanding-by-design unit

57. This type of assessment scoring allows one to compare student performance to typical students in that same age group. Which of the following best defines this assessment scoring?

A. Grade-equivalent scoring
B. Multiage scoring
C. Age-equivalent scoring
D. Age-norm-referenced scoring

58. After Bryan continued to gaze out the classroom window and not complete assigned tasks for several days in a row, Mrs. Petit decided to observe Bryan for 10 full minutes in one-minute intervals during the instructional period. Then, after class ended, Mrs. Petit reflected on her observations of Bryan in a process best known as _____.

A. incident analysis
B. reflective cycle
C. special-education referral
D. psychological inquiry

59. A process of learning and adopting the customs and values of another culture is best known as _____.

A. modifaction
B. accommodation
C. acculturation
D. immersion

60. Which of the following factors is most likely to place a student at risk for academic success in school?

A. Gender
B. Age of parents
C. Demographics
D. Low socioeconomic status

61. Children who show difficulty in mixing with other children, prefer to be alone, have an aloof manner, have difficulty expressing their needs, and use gestures or pointing instead of words show symptoms of which learning difference?

A. Learning disability
B. Mental retardation
C. Reynaud's syndrome
D. Autism-spectrum disorder

62. Children who are able to read widely and have large vocabularies at an early age, learn basic skills more quickly and with less practice than peers, and are better able to construct and handle abstractions at an early age show behavioral characteristics of _____.

A. giftedness
B. relatedness
C. helpfulness
D. constructivism

63. A teacher assistant aiding a student learning the 9s multiplication table through teaching patterns to help the student recall the facts is an example of which theory?

A. Zone of proximal development
B. Constructivist theory
C. Behaviorist theory
D. Operant conditioning

64. Theorists who are concerned with learning that can be observed are most likely which of the following?

A. Constructivists
B. Behaviorists
C. Psychomotorists
D. Optometrists

65. Mr. Fournier uses _____ sparingly in the classroom to decrease the frequency of the student response it follows.

A. punishment
B. rewards
C. contingency contracts
D. sticker charts

66. McTigue and Wiggins suggest teachers create units of instruction based on what students need to know and be able to do, by assessing student learning, and then by thoroughly selecting materials and planning a series of lessons. This unit-planning process is best known as _____.

    A. universal design
    B. emergent-curriculum development
    C. frameworks for learning
    D. Understanding by Design

67. What is the key difference between holistic and analytic scoring?

    A. Holistic scoring provides a rubric; analytic scoring provides a checklist.
    B. Holistic scoring provides a single score; analytic scoring evaluates various aspects of student performance separately.
    C. Holistic scoring evaluates various aspects of student performance separately; analytic scoring provides a single score.
    D. Holistic scoring is based on authentic assessments; analytic scoring is based on standardized assessments.

68. A criterion-referenced assessment is designed to

    A. demonstrate a student's attitude in a specific content area.
    B. establish criteria for grading in reference to other students.
    C. indicate how a student performs compared to peers.
    D. show what students know and are able to do based on predetermined criteria or standards.

69. This type of anxiety is usually low level and often enhances student performance on classroom tasks and assessments.

    A. Trait anxiety
    B. Debilitating anxiety
    C. Facilitating anxiety
    D. Hot anxiety

70. After several warnings to Weston about talking out of turn in class, Mrs. Colao keeps Weston after school for detention. This consequence is best known as

    A. removal punishment.
    B. presentation punishment.
    C. corporal punishment.
    D. intermittent punishment.

Constructed-Response Questions

Directions: The following questions require you to write short answers, or "constructed responses." You are not expected to cite specific theories or texts in your answers; however, your knowledge of specific principles of learning and teaching will be evaluated. Be sure to answer all parts of the question. Write your answers in the space provided.

Instructional Scenario I

Scenario: Ms. Manning

Ms. Manning is an eighth-grade English teacher at Broad Leaf Middle School. Several of her students have documented IEPs for learning disabilities in the area of reading, and two of her students have been diagnosed with attention deficit hyperactivity disorder (ADHD). One of her students receives English as a second language (ESL) services from the ESL teacher, and 10 of her 25 students receive free or reduced lunch.

As required by her teacher contract, Ms. Manning must create a professional portfolio containing clear evidence that she is achieving her professional goals. Later this month, Ms. Manning will be evaluated by her principal.

Document 1

Professional Goals

- Create effective bridges between students' experiences and the eighth-grade curriculum goals.
- Improve classroom discussions to help students share their thinking at a variety of levels for a variety of purposes.
- Develop and utilize active partnerships with parents, colleagues, and school leaders.

Document 2

Unit Goals

- Students will analyze the qualities of a good friend.
- Students will read about a variety of friendships, from destructive to healthy, and make connections between literature and real-life experiences.
- Students will write a comparative essay about the similarities and differences between healthy and destructive friendships.

Document 3

Project Directions

A primary assignment in Ms. Manning's friendship unit involves students responding to two texts: *Give a Boy a Gun* by Todd Strasser and *Freak the Mighty* by Rodman Philbrick. The friends in *Give a Boy a Gun* have a destructive relationship that culminates in a school shooting and massacre. The friends in *Freak the Mighty* are an unlikely pair that shares a mutually rewarding friendship, even though they are very different. After reading and discussing each of the texts from a variety of perspectives and critical-thinking levels, the students are given an assignment to analyze the characters' relationships, to reflect on the life lessons in the literature and to write a series of five to seven interview questions to ask a peer and a family member about friendships—both destructive and healthy ones.

Document 4

Project Assessment Rubric

Ms. Manning established the following guidelines for an exemplary comparative essay:

- Three to four in-text citations about *Freak the Mighty* and *Give a Boy a Gun* that use quotation marks and other punctuation properly and include a page number.
- Your interpretation of or personal connection to each in-text citation and an explanation of why you included these specific quotes.
- Five to seven interview questions that pursue deeper, higher-level understanding of destructive and healthy friendships.
- Conducted interviews with a family member and a peer (evidence of interview notes attached).
- Typewritten, double-spaced, two-paragraph comparative essay. The first paragraph describes the nature of healthy friendships with details/supports from the texts and interviews. The second paragraph describes the nature of destructive friendships with details/supports from the texts and interviews.

1. Identify TWO instructional methods Ms. Manning could use to help her students achieve the eighth-grade curriculum objectives. Be sure to base your response on principles of instruction and assessment.

2. Suggest TWO teaching methods that Ms. Manning could implement to stimulate discussion about friendships among her diverse learners. Be sure to base your response on principles of best communication techniques and instructional methods.

[Handwritten notes: • Visualize good friend • questioning techniques • Literature circles • higher-level questioning]

$$\frac{10}{25} = \frac{x}{100} \quad 40\%$$

[Handwritten calculations: 100 × 10 = 1000; 25)1000 = 40]

Instructional Scenario II

Scenario: Miss Kelly

Miss Kelly knows that the upcoming school year will be fraught with challenges, so she has started planning her long-term and short-term goals for her sixth-grade students. Miss Kelly's neighborhood elementary school has been consolidated with another elementary school in the district because of declining school enrollments and school budgets. Miss Kelly is used to knowing many of her new students' parents and siblings, as she has been at the same neighborhood school for several years. This year, she will know only 2 of her 25 families. In addition, Miss Kelly's school district has adopted a new mathematics series that promotes the use of complex problem solving, algebra, and higher-level thinking. Her new principal has decided to analyze data on student performance in mathematics this school year. Miss Kelly is a bit anxious about all these changes in the upcoming teaching year.

Miss Kelly plans to focus her efforts on helping her students meet or exceed standards in mathematics problem solving. She has obtained and carefully read the teacher's manual for the new mathematics series and has attended two full days of professional development about implementing the new series.

Miss Kelly's long-term goals include the following:

- Students will meet or exceed sixth-grade mathematics standards in problem solving.
- Each student will become a friend to a younger buddy to help build a sense of school community.

Miss Kelly's short-term goals include the following:

- Students will use the problem-solving strategy to find a pattern.
- Students will know how to locate important places and people in the school building.
- Students will meet with a buddy to establish relationships and to discuss mathematics problem-solving strategies.

3. Suggest TWO instructional methods that will support Miss Kelly's short-term instructional goals. Be sure to cite principles of best practice in assessment and instruction.

4. Identify TWO ways that Miss Kelly can approach the changes in her school district and teaching situation as a teaching professional. Be sure to base your response on principles of teacher professionalism and effective communication techniques.

3.-guest speakers
Scavenger hunt w/ map to locate speakers
extrinsic rewards
respectful
-do strategy herself + examine thinking process   wait time
4. professional association NCTE   (metacognition)
  keep up to date

communicate w/ colleagues
use I messages

Answers and Explanations

Multiple-Choice Questions

Answer Key

Question	Answer	Content Category	Where to Get More Help
1	D	Students as Learners	Chapter 7
2	A	Students as Learners	Chapter 7
3	C	Students as Learners	Chapter 7
4	B	Students as Learners	Chapter 7
5	C	Instructional Process	Chapter 8
6	A	Instructional Process	Chapter 8
7	D	Instructional Process	Chapter 8
8	A	Instructional Process	Chapter 8
9	A	Professional Development, Leadership, and Community	Chapter 10
10	C	Professional Development, Leadership, and Community	Chapter 10
11	B	Professional Development, Leadership, and Community	Chapter 10
12	D	Professional Development, Leadership, and Community	Chapter 10
13	B	Students as Learners	Chapter 7
14	C	Students as Learners	Chapter 7
15	D	Students as Learners	Chapter 7
16	A	Students as Learners	Chapter 7
17	D	Instructional Process	Chapter 8
18	B	Instructional Process	Chapter 8
19	B	Instructional Process	Chapter 8
20	A	Assessment	Chapter 9
21	C	Professional Development, Leadership, and Community	Chapter 10
22	B	Professional Development, Leadership, and Community	Chapter 10
23	D	Professional Development, Leadership, and Community	Chapter 10
24	A	Professional Development, Leadership, and Community	Chapter 10
25	D	Students as Learners	Chapter 7
26	C	Students as Learners	Chapter 7
27	A	Students as Learners	Chapter 7
28	D	Students as Learners	Chapter 7
29	B	Assessment	Chapter 9
30	A	Instructional Process	Chapter 8
31	C	Instructional Process	Chapter 8
32	D	Instructional Process	Chapter 8
33	B	Professional Development, Leadership, and Community	Chapter 10
34	A	Professional Development, Leadership, and Community	Chapter 10
35	C	Professional Development, Leadership, and Community	Chapter 10

Question	Answer	Content Category	Where to Get More Help
36	A	Professional Development, Leadership, and Community	Chapter 10
37	B	Students as Learners	Chapter 7
38	B	Students as Learners	Chapter 7
39	C	Students as Learners	Chapter 7
40	D	Students as Learners	Chapter 7
41	B	Instructional Process	Chapter 8
42	C	Instructional Process	Chapter 8
43	A	Instructional Process	Chapter 8
44	A	Assessment	Chapter 9
45	C	Professional Development, Leadership, and Community	Chapter 10
46	D	Professional Development, Leadership, and Community	Chapter 10
47	D	Professional Development, Leadership, and Community	Chapter 10
48	A	Professional Development, Leadership, and Community	Chapter 10
49	B	Students as Learners	Chapter 7
50	A	Students as Learners	Chapter 7
51	D	Students as Learners	Chapter 7
52	D	Students as Learners	Chapter 7
53	A	Instructional Process	Chapter 8
54	D	Instructional Process	Chapter 8
55	B	Instructional Process	Chapter 8
56	B	Instructional Process	Chapter 8
57	C	Assessment	Chapter 9
58	A	Professional Development, Leadership, and Community	Chapter 10
59	C	Students as Learners	Chapter 7
60	D	Students as Learners	Chapter 7
61	D	Students as Learners	Chapter 7
62	A	Students as Learners	Chapter 7
63	A	Instructional Process	Chapter 8
64	B	Instructional Process	Chapter 8
65	A	Instructional Process	Chapter 8
66	D	Instructional Process	Chapter 8
67	B	Assessment	Chapter 9
68	D	Assessment	Chapter 9
69	C	Students as Learners	Chapter 7
70	A	Instructional Process	Chapter 8

Answer Explanations

1. **D** Celia and Alyssa are on the conventional level of moral development. According to Kohlberg, this level is characterized by seeking the approval of others or doing what will gain approval. This behavior is typical of many middle-school and some high-school students. Choice A, over-conventional, is a distracter. Choice B, pre-conventional, is seen in some school students and is characterized by punishment avoidance and exchanging favors, neither of which is depicted in this scenario. Choice C, post-conventional, is rarely seen before college and is indicated by an understanding of the larger social contract and universal ethical principles.

2. **A** Mr. Conlin's practice is grounded in constructivism, a theory of learning that emphasizes a student's ability to solve real-life problems and make new meaning by reflecting on the learning experience. Practice grounded in behaviorism (Choice B) centers on students' response to stimuli. Choices C (nonviolence) and D (self-actualization) are distracters.

3. **C** Although some of her behaviors may be found in other answer choices, Phyllis's learning differences are appropriately called developmental delays in this situation.

4. **B** The ADA prohibits discrimination against Phyllis based on her disabilities and protects her rights.

5. **C** This cooperative activity is known as numbered heads together.

6. **A** Tiered instruction is an instructional method to differentiate instruction in which the teacher plans tasks of varying complexity, but all with the same high standards and content expectations.

7. **D** The diagram that Miss Wade uses is a continuum, which helps reveal the subtle shades of meaning of vocabulary words.

8. **A** Hunter's model is an approach to classroom management that centers on the teacher's planning for good lessons, not managing an individual child's behavior. Created by Madeline Hunter, lessons in this model include an anticipatory set, modeling, guided practice, independent practice, and extended practice.

9. **A** Goals 2000 calls for all students to start school ready to learn, for high-school graduation rates to meet or exceed 90 percent, and for all teachers to have access to high-quality professional development. (There are additional recommendations in this report that are not mentioned in the question.)

10. **C** Teaching professionals are expected to use respectful communication with children's caregivers. Choices A (empowerment of learners) and B (advocacy for learners) are not specific to working with caregivers. Choice D (discrimination of students) is a distracter.

11. **B** The Yale Report of 1828 praises the merits of a classical curriculum.

12. **D** According to the U.S. Supreme Court, schools must remain neutral on issues involving school prayer as religious expression. The school can neither promote school prayer nor punish it.

13. **B** Kounin calls a teacher's ability to be aware of all that is going on in a classroom simultaneously as with-it-ness. (Some folks think that teachers are born with eyes in the backs of their heads, too!)

14. **C** A teacher should plan for the classroom environmental factors that he or she can control, such as seating arrangement. For lessons involving the use of the chalkboard, all students must have a clear visual path to the chalkboard. For lessons involving conversation, student must face one another and sit in close enough proximity to be able to converse. Choices A (school location), B (classroom location), and D (class size) are factors typically beyond a teacher's control.

15. **D** Based on the passage, Josiah is showing a lack of readiness to learn the content of seventh grade. Mr. Enright is most likely concerned about this and is seeking ideas to help Josiah. Although Josiah's health history (Choice A), prior-year instruction (Choice B), and family background (Choice C) may be factors affecting Josiah's performance, these responses are too narrow to the question regarding the teacher's primary concern.

16. **A** Mr. Enright is going to try to develop Josiah's background knowledge or schema for the seventh-grade social studies content to help Josiah learn and remember the content.

17. **D** Speeches and photographs are known as primary sources. Choices A (sound clips) and C (original websites) are too narrow, naming places one might find primary sources. Choice B (historical media) is a distracter.

18. **B** According to Bloom's Taxonomy, Mrs. Pate's question is at the analysis level, a higher-level question.

19. **B** A behavioral objective focuses on observable student behaviors and is measurable.

20. **A** An aptitude test measures a student's ability to develop or acquire skills and knowledge.

21. **C** *Pierce v. Society of Sisters,* also known as the Oregon Case of 1925, established that the state of Oregon could not require all students to attend public school, because doing so violates a child's Fourteenth Amendment rights of personal liberty. This case established that all students can be required to attend public *or* private schools, but not one or the other.

22. **B** Compulsory education was started in the United States after a ruling in 1852 in Massachusetts that was the first general law to attempt to control the conditions for children.

23. **D** The manual-training movement provided the foundation of vocational education in U.S. schools today.

24. **A** On October 4, 1957, the Soviet Union successfully launched *Sputnik,* which catapulted the United States into a space race to prove that the United States was more powerful than any other nation. This event also launched a major reform of mathematics and science education in the United States.

25. **D** Jessica is operating at the conventional level, according to Kohlberg's theory of moral development, which involves making decisions that please others and establishing, as well as maintaining relationships. Choice A, post-conventional, typically is not seen before college age and involves making choices for the great social contract and universal ethical principles. Choice B, pre-conventional, centers on punishment avoidance and an exchange of favors. Choice C (anti-conventional) is a distracter.

26. **C** Maddie's teachers are striving to help Maddie transfer learning from one classroom to another and beyond the classroom walls; this scenario encapsulates the definition of *transfer.* Choice A (master skills) is too narrow. Choice B (exit from special education) is too broad. Choice D (satisfy state and federal requirements) is not the implicit or explicit purpose for teaching Maddie the way her teachers do in this scenario.

27. **A** Carrie's behaviors are indications of a student who may have learning disabilities. It is important for a teacher to note such observations and report them to a TST or another specialist in the school, but not to "label" the student as learning disabled. Teachers teach and report observations; diagnosticians and other specialists establish diagnoses.

28. **D** Federal law mandates that children are to be educated in their least restrictive environment (LRE).

29. **B** The midpoint in a set of numbers is known as the median.

30. **A** A free-response journal is intended to be used for rough drafts and short bits of writing that are not corrected for grammar, mechanics, or conventions. Choice A is the credited response because it is most likely not going to be corrected for errors. All other choices in this question may or may not be graded for grammar, mechanics, or conventions depending on a teacher's or a school's preference.

31. **C** Reading aloud in this scenario is most effective when done as a whole group. This setup helps build community, offers a common text to discuss, and settles students for an afternoon of schoolwork.

32. **D** Mrs. Faella is using an instructional strategy known as reciprocal teaching in which one student (or adult) reads aloud a portion of text and asks questions of another, and then the roles reverse. Choices A (fluency reading) and C (scaffolded teaching) are distracters. Echo reading (Choice B) is a method in which a more capable reader reads first, and a less capable reader repeats the same reading passage.

33. **B** To be considered a teacher with professionalism, Mrs. Josephson must see and believe that diversity is a positive, enriching aspect of teaching. All other choices do not value diversity in the classroom.

34. **A** *Brown v. Board of Education* established that the long-held contention that separate but equal schools is inherently unequal. This case was a pivotal one in U.S. education history and advanced the integration and rights of all children in public schools.

35. **C** Benjamin Franklin had the foresight to create a plan for schools that teach English-language grammar, not only Latin, as was the standard in schools of his time. Franklin's plan for an English-language grammar school was never fully accepted or enacted during his lifetime, but the idea certainly influenced schools of today.

36. **A** Harvard College was established in 1636 to ensure that the leaders of the church, state, and judicial systems were learned and well prepared for their vocations.

37. **B** Bandura's work focuses on children's ability to learn by observing others; he is a key theorist in the social-cognitive theoretical perspective on learning. Kohlberg (Choice A) offered theories on moral reasoning. Maslow (Choice C) contributed understanding of the hierarchy of human needs. Jones (Choice D) offered specific classroom-management approaches.

38. **B** Piaget suggested that children learn through two complementary processes called assimilation and accommodation.

39. **C** Maria is showing her teacher that she is a metacognitive reader when she describes her awareness of her own reading process. Metacognition is the ability to think about one's own thinking, which is depicted in this scenario about Maria.

40. **D** Maria's teacher was optimizing Vygotsky's theory of a zone of proximal development, in which a more able peer (or teacher) helps a student learn something too challenging to learn alone. This practice embraces a social-constructivist view of teaching.

41. **B** SQ3R is a study strategy that helps students take notes on and learn new information.

42. **C** Bobby would benefit from curriculum chunking. His teacher can offer smaller, more manageable amounts of homework practice for Bobby. This way, the teacher can offer more frequent check-ins and support as needed. When Bobby demonstrates that he can handle more information with success, the teacher can offer more work. Curriculum compacting (Choice A) is a method used for students who are easily achieving objectives and need more challenging work. Rote learning (Choice B) is a method to teach a learner to memorize facts, which is too narrow of a response to this situation. Jigsaw (Choice D) is a cooperative learning structure in which portions of information are assigned to small groups of students and then information is shared with the whole class.

43. **A** Mr. Matthews is using simulation to teach his students during this social studies unit.

44. **A** Mrs. Lahiri provided a summative evaluation, or an evaluation that reviews progress to date. A summative evaluation occurs at the end of a period and may not necessarily be used to inform practice or instruction.

45. **C** Mrs. Basel is demonstrating her professional desire to meet the needs of all her students and advocate for all her students as learners.

46. **D** In this case, the teacher could be sued and found liable for negligence.

47. **D** Professional associations offer leadership and guidance to a group of professionals. Every content area taught in public schools has a professional association to guide it. Find out about your area's professional association as soon as you finish studying for this test!

48. **A** The ADA, also known as Title II, prohibits discrimination on the basis of a person's disability for all services, programs, and activities provided or made available by state or local governments.

49. **B** Bloom's cognitive domain involves the mind and skills or strategies one uses, and is organized into six levels from lowest order to higher order: knowledge, comprehension, application, analysis, synthesis, and evaluation.

50. **A** Analytical knowledge is the only choice not present in the information-processing theoretical perspective. Information-processing theorists helped us know that in order to acquire knowledge, one must develop declarative knowledge (knowledge of "what is"; Choice B), procedural knowledge (knowledge of "how to"; Choice C), and conditional knowledge (knowledge of "when again"; Choice D).

51. **D** Self-efficacy is one's belief that one is capable. Self-concept (Choice A) involves the mental images one has about strengths, areas of weaknesses, and so on. Self-handicapping (Choice B) is an action or choice to ensure that one is not responsible for his or her failures or shortcomings. Self-fulfilling prophesy (Choice C) involves a prediction of failure or success, which directly or indirectly contributes to the outcome.

52. **D** Visual learners process information through seeing. They learn through visual displays, films, illustrated books, handouts, graphic organizers, bulletin boards, and so on. Choices A (musical learners) and C (verbal-linguistic learners) are too narrow. Kinesthetic learners (Choice B) learn by doing, such as in experiments, role play, or simulations, which this scenario does not include.

53. **A** Student Teams Achievement Divisions (STAD) is a cooperative-learning structure in which students are assigned to heterogeneously grouped teams of four or five members who collaborate on worksheets designed to provide extended practice on instruction given by the teacher.

54. **D** Reciprocal teaching is an evidenced-based teaching method in which the teacher and the student engage in a discussion of the text. Both the student and the teacher question and respond to the text in an effort to improve the student's comprehension of the material.

55. **B** When students transfer learning they are able to use previously learned material in a new situation or context. Teachers can promote students' ability to transfer learning experiences to new situations by developing "conditional knowledge" or helping students know when and how they might use the learned information in a new setting. Transfer of learning often is supported in the closing of the lesson and during extended practice opportunities.

56. **B** Independent-study units give students a chance to work at their own pace under the teacher's leadership or guidance. Independent-study units can be particularly beneficial for students who need course material modified to be more challenging or simplified.

57. **C** Age-equivalent scoring allows one to compare student performance to typical students in that same age group.

58. **A** In a concerns-based reflection model, as suggested by Fred Korthagen, the teacher deeply thinks about one particular teaching or learning event that concerns him or her, which is known as incident analysis. The teacher looks back to his or her thoughts, feelings, and the event from multiple perspectives, trying to reveal what is the central issue in this situation.

59. **C** Acculturation is a process of learning and adopting the customs and values of another culture.

60. **D** Research indicates that children from low-SES households and communities develop academic skills more slowly compared to children from higher-SES groups. Young children from low-SES households tend to have lower pre-academic skills. School systems in low-SES communities often are under-resourced, which negatively affects students' academic progress. Low-SES children tend to have fewer resources to help with their academic achievement, such as materials and someone to help with homework or to read to them. In addition, they tend to have suffered from the effects of their families' unemployment, a high level of migration of the best qualified teachers in their schools, and the effects of limited access to healthcare. Gender (Choice A) and age of parents (Choice B) are not research-based factors that are likely to place a student at risk. Choice C (demographics) is too broad.

61. **D** Autism-spectrum disorders may include autism, Asperger's syndrome, and other pervasive developmental delays (PDDs). Students with these disorders have difficulty socializing and communicating. Asperger's syndrome is a form of autism in which the person has normal intelligence and language development, but has marked difficulties with social skills and social cognition. Choice A, learning disability, is too broad. Mental retardation (Choice B) is indicated by a lack of normal development of intellectual functioning. Reynaud's syndrome (Choice C) is a medical condition in which a person's extremities are more susceptible to cold temperatures.

62. **A** Giftedness is considered significantly higher than usual ability or aptitude in one or more areas.

63. **A** Lev Vygotsky's notion of zone of proximal development suggests that the teacher or a more capable peer is capable of helping the students learn something just beyond his or her intellectual reach with cognitive support. In this scenario, the teacher assistant aiding a student learning the 9s multiplication table demonstrates an effort to teach in a student's zone of proximal development with the guidance of a more capable person. Choice B, constructivist theory, is too broad. Behaviorist theory (Choice C) and operant conditioning (Choice D) are not correct because the emphasis is not on shaping stimuli and responses.

64. **B** Behaviorism is a theoretical perspective on learning that focuses on what can be observed and measured in learning—people's behaviors (responses) and events in the environment that promote behavior (stimuli). Constructivists (Choice A) are most concerned with how learners construct, rather than absorb, information. Choices C (psychomotorists) and D (optometrists) are distracters.

65. **A** Punishment in the classroom is meted out to decrease the frequency of the response it follows. For example, after a student continually talks during the lesson, the teacher keeps him in for recess in order to decrease his talking in class. Rewards (Choice B) and stickers charts (Choice D) are typically used to increase positive students learning behaviors. Contingency contracts (Choice C) is too narrow of a choice; this approach is an agreement made in advance with a student about the rewards and consequences of actions.

66. **D** State-of-the-art curriculum and unit planning involves a process known as Understanding by Design (UbD), suggested by McTighe and Wiggins. UbD uses the principles of backward design that we've covered previously in this chapter to design a unit of instruction based on what students need to know and be able to do, how we will assess student learning, and then planning a series of lessons. Universal design (Choice A) involves establishing a learning environment that is accessible to all. Choices B (emergent-curriculum development) and C (frameworks for learning) are distracters.

67. **B** Holistic scoring summarizes a student's performance and provides a single score; whereas analytic scoring evaluates various aspects of student performance separately to offer more detailed information. Choice B is the opposite definition of holistic and analytical scoring. Choices A and D are distracters.

68. **D** Criterion-referenced assessments are designed to demonstrate what students know and are able to do based on predetermined criteria or standards, usually based on the school curriculum. Choice C (indicate how a student performs compared to peers) refers to a norm-referenced assessment. Choices A (demonstrate a student's attitude in a specific content area) and B (establish criteria for grading in reference to other students) are distracters.

69. **C** Facilitating anxiety is low-level anxiety that often enhances a student's performance on classroom tasks or assessments. Debilitating anxiety (Choice B) is high-level anxiety that usually detracts from student's ability to perform tasks well. Choice A, trait anxiety, is a response to nonthreatening situations with anxiety. Choice D, hot anxiety, is a distracter.

70. **A** Punishment in the classroom is meted out to decrease the frequency of the response it follows. For example, after Weston continually talks during the lesson, Mrs. Colao keeps him after school for detention in order to decrease his talking in class; this is known specifically as removal punishment. Presentation punishment (Choice B) is a form of punishment in which the teacher adds, or presents, a stimulus in an effort to decrease student behavior (for example, giving more homework to punish a student for not doing the previous homework assignment). Corporal punishment (Choice C) involves striking or spanking the learner. Choice D, intermittent punishment, is a distracter.

Constructed-Response Questions

Instructional Scenario I

1. **Suggested content:** Ms. Manning is teaching a unit on friendships using two books, *Freak the Mighty* and *Give a Boy a Gun.* One way that she could create an effective bridge between her students and the literature is to open the lesson by asking the students to <u>visualize</u> a good friend and then discuss that friend's character traits. After the students have a chance to widely respond, the teacher could <u>write down a list of character traits</u> of a friend. Finally, the teacher could give a <u>brief overview of each book</u>, highlighting the characters that have the same character traits of the students' friends or the ones who have traits opposite to their friends. This practice <u>activates and builds upon students' schema</u> of a friend and <u>motivates</u> students <u>intrinsically</u> to read and learn.

   A second method Ms. Manning could use is <u>questioning techniques</u>. She could plan questions using the <u>cognitive and affective domains of Bloom's Taxonomy</u> to help her students recall factual information, <u>think critically</u> at higher levels, and <u>make personal connections</u> to the texts. Ms. Manning would want to use wait time to allow students time to think and would also want to use <u>all pupil-response techniques</u>, such as polling the students after a question. She would want to <u>respect all students' responses</u> and <u>handle incorrect answers diplomatically</u>, without dismissing the contributions of the students who made an error.

2. **Suggested content:** Ms. Manning is teaching two quality trade books to help her students more deeply comprehend text and better understand positive and destructive friendships. One way that she could have her students discuss the books' themes is to <u>organize her class into literature circles</u>. In this method, the teacher sets up groups of four to six students to discuss a literature selection. Each student has a <u>role</u> to play in the discussion (for example, <u>leader, word finder, summarizer, illustrator</u>, and so on), and each student is <u>active in the discussion</u>.

   A second discussion method that Ms. Manning could use is <u>higher-level questioning techniques</u>. For example, she could ask questions about the <u>main themes</u> in the book, ask the students to analyze the meaning of a portion of text, or ask them to <u>draw conclusions</u> about a character's motive. It is important for Ms. Manning to create a <u>supportive environment</u> for discussion and allow for <u>alternative viewpoints</u>.

Instructional Scenario II

3. **Suggested content:** Miss Kelly has three instructional goals and has several instructional options to help her students achieve them. One of Miss Kelly's short-term goals is that students will be able to locate important people and places in the school building. One way that she could help her students achieve this objective is to plan a series of <u>guest speakers</u> in the classroom and then mark that guest speaker's location in the school. After all the speakers' visits, the students could go on a <u>scavenger hunt</u> in small groups to follow the school map and locate these important people and places in the building. Miss Kelly could offer <u>extrinsic rewards</u> for students who complete the map successfully, use the best hallway behavior, or use the most <u>respectful manners</u> while visiting important people in the school. Another short-term goal is to have her sixth-grade students use "find a pattern" to solve word problems. One method she could use is to know how "find a pattern" problem solving works by trying this strategy herself and examining her thinking process, or <u>metacognition</u>, while using this strategy. Then Miss Kelly could use a think-aloud to explain how she approached a word problem. After the think-aloud, Miss Kelly could cue her students' thinking using both verbal and <u>nonverbal cues</u>. If she used <u>wait time</u> and <u>reflective listening</u> statements, she would be reinforcing the types of thinking required when using "find a pattern" and also would be reinforcing important mathematical vocabulary.

4. **Suggested content:** Miss Kelly is facing a challenging, changing school year that she can embrace professionally. One way that she can get support is to turn to her <u>professional association, such as the National Council of Teachers of Mathematics,</u> to learn about problem solving and mathematics. This association offers <u>workshops, conferences, and professional journals</u> to provide a variety of supports to flexibly meet her learning needs. Keeping up-to-date with the professional reading and practices in her field

not only will be beneficial to Miss Kelly's sense of <u>professionalism</u>, but also will pay off for her students and their <u>mathematical achievement</u>. Professional workshops offer Miss Kelly the opportunity to <u>learn directly from educators in her field</u> and allow her to build her professional network.

Another way Miss Kelly can approach her professional changes is to work on improving her communication skills as a teaching professional. For example, she could set <u>clear professional goals</u> and <u>seek out colleagues and administrators</u> to help her achieve them. When conflicts occur, she can use <u>I messages</u> to let others know her perspective and can use paraphrasing to demonstrate that she is a <u>careful and attentive listener</u>.

Chapter 14

PLT Grades 7–12 Practice Test

This full-length PLT Grades 7–12 practice test (0624) is designed to give you an overall sense of the test's format and to help you determine the content areas you need to focus on in your studies. You may want to practice your pacing while taking the full-length practice test. You will have a total of two hours to complete the entire PLT test, which consists of 70 multiple-choice questions and 4 constructed-response questions.

After you complete the full-length practice test, score your answers and use the explanations to self-diagnose content areas to study in Part III of this guide. You also may want to complete the other practice tests in Chapters 11, 12, and 13 to aid you in determining which content areas to study. Even though these additional practice tests are written for other PLT test grade levels, the question topics (Students as Learners; Instructional Process; Assessment; and Professional Development, Leadership, and Community) remain the same.

CUT HERE

(Remove these sheets and use them to mark your answers to the multiple-choice questions.)

Answer Sheet

1 Ⓐ Ⓑ Ⓒ Ⓓ	41 Ⓐ Ⓑ Ⓒ Ⓓ	
2 Ⓐ Ⓑ Ⓒ Ⓓ	42 Ⓐ Ⓑ Ⓒ Ⓓ	
3 Ⓐ Ⓑ Ⓒ Ⓓ	43 Ⓐ Ⓑ Ⓒ Ⓓ	
4 Ⓐ Ⓑ Ⓒ Ⓓ	44 Ⓐ Ⓑ Ⓒ Ⓓ	
5 Ⓐ Ⓑ Ⓒ Ⓓ	45 Ⓐ Ⓑ Ⓒ Ⓓ	
6 Ⓐ Ⓑ Ⓒ Ⓓ	46 Ⓐ Ⓑ Ⓒ Ⓓ	
7 Ⓐ Ⓑ Ⓒ Ⓓ	47 Ⓐ Ⓑ Ⓒ Ⓓ	
8 Ⓐ Ⓑ Ⓒ Ⓓ	48 Ⓐ Ⓑ Ⓒ Ⓓ	
9 Ⓐ Ⓑ Ⓒ Ⓓ	49 Ⓐ Ⓑ Ⓒ Ⓓ	
10 Ⓐ Ⓑ Ⓒ Ⓓ	50 Ⓐ Ⓑ Ⓒ Ⓓ	
11 Ⓐ Ⓑ Ⓒ Ⓓ	51 Ⓐ Ⓑ Ⓒ Ⓓ	
12 Ⓐ Ⓑ Ⓒ Ⓓ	52 Ⓐ Ⓑ Ⓒ Ⓓ	
13 Ⓐ Ⓑ Ⓒ Ⓓ	53 Ⓐ Ⓑ Ⓒ Ⓓ	
14 Ⓐ Ⓑ Ⓒ Ⓓ	54 Ⓐ Ⓑ Ⓒ Ⓓ	
15 Ⓐ Ⓑ Ⓒ Ⓓ	55 Ⓐ Ⓑ Ⓒ Ⓓ	
16 Ⓐ Ⓑ Ⓒ Ⓓ	56 Ⓐ Ⓑ Ⓒ Ⓓ	
17 Ⓐ Ⓑ Ⓒ Ⓓ	57 Ⓐ Ⓑ Ⓒ Ⓓ	
18 Ⓐ Ⓑ Ⓒ Ⓓ	58 Ⓐ Ⓑ Ⓒ Ⓓ	
19 Ⓐ Ⓑ Ⓒ Ⓓ	59 Ⓐ Ⓑ Ⓒ Ⓓ	
20 Ⓐ Ⓑ Ⓒ Ⓓ	60 Ⓐ Ⓑ Ⓒ Ⓓ	
21 Ⓐ Ⓑ Ⓒ Ⓓ	61 Ⓐ Ⓑ Ⓒ Ⓓ	
22 Ⓐ Ⓑ Ⓒ Ⓓ	62 Ⓐ Ⓑ Ⓒ Ⓓ	
23 Ⓐ Ⓑ Ⓒ Ⓓ	63 Ⓐ Ⓑ Ⓒ Ⓓ	
24 Ⓐ Ⓑ Ⓒ Ⓓ	64 Ⓐ Ⓑ Ⓒ Ⓓ	
25 Ⓐ Ⓑ Ⓒ Ⓓ	65 Ⓐ Ⓑ Ⓒ Ⓓ	
26 Ⓐ Ⓑ Ⓒ Ⓓ	66 Ⓐ Ⓑ Ⓒ Ⓓ	
27 Ⓐ Ⓑ Ⓒ Ⓓ	67 Ⓐ Ⓑ Ⓒ Ⓓ	
28 Ⓐ Ⓑ Ⓒ Ⓓ	68 Ⓐ Ⓑ Ⓒ Ⓓ	
29 Ⓐ Ⓑ Ⓒ Ⓓ	69 Ⓐ Ⓑ Ⓒ Ⓓ	
30 Ⓐ Ⓑ Ⓒ Ⓓ	70 Ⓐ Ⓑ Ⓒ Ⓓ	
31 Ⓐ Ⓑ Ⓒ Ⓓ		
32 Ⓐ Ⓑ Ⓒ Ⓓ		
33 Ⓐ Ⓑ Ⓒ Ⓓ		
34 Ⓐ Ⓑ Ⓒ Ⓓ		
35 Ⓐ Ⓑ Ⓒ Ⓓ		
36 Ⓐ Ⓑ Ⓒ Ⓓ		
37 Ⓐ Ⓑ Ⓒ Ⓓ		
38 Ⓐ Ⓑ Ⓒ Ⓓ		
39 Ⓐ Ⓑ Ⓒ Ⓓ		
40 Ⓐ Ⓑ Ⓒ Ⓓ		

Time: 2 hours

70 multiple-choice questions and 4 constructed-response questions

Multiple-Choice Questions

Directions: For each multiple-choice question, select the best answer and mark the corresponding letter space on your answer sheet.

1. Mr. Craig is a first-year teacher of tenth-grade social studies. He feels successful in his knowledge of content, his ability to plan lessons, and his interactions with colleagues. He has reflected on his instruction and realizes that his students frequently talk off-task, especially during independent seat work. Which of the following suggestions would be most helpful to Mr. Craig in this situation?

   A. Call the students' parents, speak with the principal, and offer after-school help.
   B. Offer after-school help, give students detention, and speak individually with students.
   C. Create incentive systems, speak with the principal, and use more wait time.
   D. Give the teacher "look," create incentive systems, and provide individual help.

2. According to Erik Erikson's theory of human development, adolescents ages 12 through 18 work to resolve which of the following conflicts?

   A. Peers vs. parents
   B. Identity vs. role confusion
   C. Social vs. academic
   D. Guilt vs. isolation

3. Mr. Sanderson believes that students need clear guidelines and expectations for homework. He does not allow any late homework, although he allows students to show him their homework the next day for no credit. For students who complete homework on time, he gives full credit. In addition, students who complete homework receive one extra-credit point for every five homework assignments completed. Which of the following principles of learning and teaching guides Mr. Sanderson's practice?

   A. Intrinsic motivation
   B. Operant conditioning
   C. Rewards
   D. Structure

4. Mrs. Gagliardi and her eleventh-grade English students enjoy their discussions of the King Arthur legend. Mrs. Gagliardi prefers to help her students come to their own interpretations and meaning of the text through open-ended questions and through exposing her students to a variety of viewpoints on the legend's meaning. Mrs. Gagliardi is using which of the following theories to guide her educational practice?

   A. Constructivism
   B. Behaviorism
   C. Authoritarianism
   D. Moral development

Questions 5–6 are based on the following scenario.

Ms. Salvatore is a special-education resource teacher who provides services identified with Individualized Education Plans (IEPs) in Mrs. Keen's heterogeneously grouped seventh-grade English classroom. Mrs. Keen has just completed a lesson on S. E. Hinton's *The Outsiders* and has asked her students to complete a character-analysis activity in small groups. Ms. Salvatore helps any student who needs the support but pays particular attention to the students identified as having special needs. One student, Jeffrey, appears to be having difficulty getting along with the students in his group and quickly becomes angry. Jeffrey has been diagnosed with an emotional problem and has a Behavior Intervention Plan (BIP) to support him.

5. Ms. Salvatore and Mrs. Keen's work together is known as

   A. an individualized program.
   B. a resource room.
   C. an inclusion program.
   D. a self-contained room.

6. Students with identified emotional problems usually benefit from which of the following supports?

   A. Self-contained classrooms and strict rules
   B. A supportive environment and unlimited choices
   C. A strict environment and no-tolerance policies
   D. Structured choices and a positive environment

7. If a teacher wants to ask higher-level questions, which of the following types of questions from Bloom's Taxonomy would he or she use?

   A. Comprehension and discussion
   B. Analysis and synthesis
   C. Knowledge and literal
   D. Open-ended and reflective

8. Which of the following types of tests are written for a variety of subjects and levels designed to measure a student's knowledge of or proficiency in an area that was learned or taught?

   A. Achievement tests
   B. Aptitude tests
   C. Criterion-referenced tests
   D. Essay tests

9. Mrs. Audette is a new tenth-grade social studies teacher at Central High School. Recently, she has been experiencing personal problems related to the breakup of her marriage. The police have visited her home on several occasions, and charges of domestic assault have been filed by both Mrs. Audette and her estranged spouse. Reports of these personal problems have been published in the police logs of the local newspaper. She has neither shared her personal problems at work nor missed any days of school. Which of the following teachers' rights pertain to Mrs. Audette's circumstances?

   A. She can be fired because of the charges.
   B. She can be suspended during a civil or criminal trial.
   C. She cannot be fired because she did not commit domestic assault.
   D. She cannot be fired unless her behavior interferes with her teaching effectiveness.

10. In 1918, secondary education was reorganized to include the following: health education, basic skills, good relationships, vocations, civic education, worthy use of leisure time, and ethical behavior. Which of the following is the name for this reorganization?

    A. American Federation of Teachers
    B. Manual-Training Movement
    C. Testing Movement of Secondary Education
    D. Cardinal Principles of Secondary Education

11. Which of the following public laws mandates the regulation and formulation of IEPs for students with identified learning differences?

    A. ADA
    B. NCLB
    C. P.L. 94-142
    D. Section 504 of the Rehabilitation Act

12. The Progressive period of U.S. education is marked by an influence of which of the following revolutions?

    A. Industrial Revolution
    B. American Revolution
    C. Spanish Revolution
    D. New England Revolution

13. Pedro is a student who is new to the United States and just recently began to speak English. Spanish is his native language. Which of the following behaviors does a student often engage in when thought and language first come together?

    A. Babbling
    B. Self-talk
    C. Simultaneous play
    D. Zone of proximal development

14. Which of the following is the process through which social activities evolve into mental activities?

    A. Inner speech
    B. Internalization
    C. Tertiary activities
    D. Assimilation

15. Josh's family situation—living with a single mom who is dependent on alcohol and drugs—makes it difficult for him to be successful in school. Josh is the provider for this family at the young age of 13, and he is the authoritative voice for his younger siblings. Josh helps his siblings complete homework; he fixes dinner; he organizes all the school papers and even signs permission slips. Josh has a difficult time in school when he is treated "like a baby" and is told what to do by teachers and other authority figures. Which of the following best describes Josh's difficulty in school?

    A. Josh may have learning disabilities.
    B. Josh has a behavior problem.
    C. Josh is from a minority ethnic group.
    D. Josh has a cultural mismatch between home and school.

16. Mrs. Xavier plans her lessons so that her students work heterogeneously on similar assignments, but with varying levels of support. For example, she tiers the instruction of a summary writing assignment to provide more support and direction for the students who are still struggling with this type of writing, and she offers more creativity and freedom for the same assignment to the students who have mastered this style of writing. Which of the following best describes Mrs. Xavier's instructional practice?

    A. Grade-equivalent instruction
    B. Sequential instruction
    C. Differentiated instruction
    D. Scope and sequence instruction

17. Which of the following is an important comprehension strategy that involves teaching students to use a double-entry notebook or SQ3R to comprehend written materials that can be incorporated into lessons in the early grades through adulthood?

    A. Reinforcing and providing recognition
    B. Identifying similarities and differences
    C. Summarizing and note taking
    D. Nonlinguistic representations

18. Which of the following strategies helps students tap into their natural curiosity to understand concepts more deeply?

    A. Generating and testing hypotheses
    B. Anchored instruction
    C. Tiered instruction
    D. Compacted instruction

19. 1) Anticipatory set, 2) Modeling, 3) Guided practice, and 4) _____. Which of the following comes next in Hunter's model of lesson planning?

    A. Motivation
    B. Independent practice
    C. Assessment
    D. Preview

20. Which of the following guides a teacher's instruction to ensure that he or she is following district requirements, as well as not repeating content from a previous grade level?

   A. Unit plans
   B. Lesson plans
   C. Book lists
   D. Curriculum frameworks

21. Which of the following people is considered a founding father of the Progressive period (1880–1920) of American education?

   A. Gardner
   B. Piaget
   C. Dewey
   D. Mann

22. Which of the following reports provided evidence that education in the United States, particularly in secondary schools, was falling behind that in other countries?

   A. No Child Left Behind
   B. A Nation at Risk
   C. First Year Studies
   D. ESEA

23. Which of the following reports was written during the Clinton Administration and included such issues as schools being drug free and schools promoting partnerships to increase parental involvement?

   A. Goals 2000
   B. National Reading Panel Report
   C. NEA Committee of Ten Report
   D. Title I Report

24. Mr. and Mrs. Smith attended a recent parent/teacher conference with Mrs. Rodrigues, their child's sixth-grade teacher. The Smiths are frustrated that their daughter is still not reading at grade level and blame the schools, teachers, and administration for her lack of success in this area. Mrs. Rodrigues used which of the following to show her professionalism and willingness to listen to the Smiths' concerns?

   A. Open communication
   B. Closed communication
   C. Multicultural communication
   D. Respectful communication

25. Maria is participating in a classroom taught entirely in English even though she has just moved to the United States from Central America. Her lessons are offered in simplified English so that she can learn both English and the academic content. Which of the following best describes the type of instruction Maria is receiving?

   A. Primary language not English (PLNE) instruction
   B. Ebonics
   C. English as a second language (ESL) instruction
   D. English-immersion instruction

26. Stewart and Sarah are visual and auditory learners who also show multiple intelligences in the verbal-linguistic and musical areas. Which of the following instructional resources would most likely meet Stewart and Sarah's learning styles?

   A. Multimedia/technology
   B. Books
   C. Whiteboard and markers
   D. Art supplies

27. Which of the following theories espouses offering adequate support or scaffolding to enable students to perform challenging tasks with success?

   A. Behaviorist theory
   B. Social-learning theory
   C. Motivation theory
   D. Classical theory

28. Boys usually enter adolescence at age _____; girls usually enter adolescence at age _____.

   A. 10; 12
   B. 12; 10
   C. 15; 13
   D. 14; 12

29. Which of the following assessment types helps inform a teacher's day-to-day instruction with students?

   A. Summative assessment
   B. Norm-referenced assessment
   C. Formative assessment
   D. Achievement assessment

30. Which of the following types of assessment helps inform curriculum and school progress toward goals?

   A. Summative assessment
   B. Formative assessment
   C. Diagnostic assessment
   D. Behavior assessment

31. Which of the following is typically an effective behavior reinforcer for students in grades 6–8?

   A. Colorful stickers for a job well done
   B. Short periods of free time with peers
   C. Classroom duties, such as leader or office helper
   D. Position in class lineup

32. Which of the following is usually an effective instructional modification for students with learning disabilities?

   A. Setting strict routines and rules
   B. Setting up homogeneous groups
   C. Setting clear but flexible limits
   D. Setting conflict-resolution guidelines for the class

33. Which of the following is the federal document that establishes the responsibility for public education?

   A. *Brown v. Board of Education*
   B. *Plessy v. Ferguson*
   C. First Amendment
   D. U.S. Constitution

34. Which of the following states that it is legal for an employer to hire from underrepresented groups, but that an employer cannot dismiss a person from an underrepresented group by using this guideline?

   A. Civil rights
   B. Discrimination on the basis of race
   C. Discrimination on the basis of age
   D. Reverse discrimination

35. Which of the following entities is legally responsible for education in the United States?

   A. Federal government
   B. States
   C. School district
   D. U.S. Constitution

36. Teachers and students have legal rights. The U.S. courts have placed limits on a teacher's ability to disrupt the curriculum or the functioning of a school. Which of the following best describes teachers' and students' rights in this situation?

   A. Freedom of speech
   B. Freedom of religion
   C. Freedom to bear arms
   D. Freedom of the press

37. According to Lawrence Kohlberg, what moral behavior do adolescents usually exhibit in the conventional stage?

   A. Antisocial behaviors
   B. Deep levels of reflection
   C. Attempts to gain approval from peers
   D. Conformity to rules

38. According to Jean Piaget, what cognitive-development behaviors do adolescents exhibit in the formal-operational stage?

   A. Inability to separate and control variables
   B. Ability to demonstrate and develop concepts without concrete materials or images
   C. Inability to test multiple hypotheses
   D. Ability to depend on concrete reality to develop concepts

39. Ricky is a ninth-grade student who shows many at-risk behaviors for dropping out of high school. Even though Ricky has a history of academic failure, which of the following must the teacher do in Ricky's situation?

   A. Send Ricky to the school guidance counselor.
   B. Submit a referral for counseling for Ricky.
   C. Assign extra homework to help Ricky catch up.
   D. Communicate high expectations for Ricky's success.

40. Mrs. Martinez strives to understand her own culture and the culture of her students in her effort to meet all of her students' educational needs. Which of the following levels of culture will Mrs. Martinez better understand if she learns about the social roles in her students' home lives, their home languages, their nonverbal communication behaviors, and their family structures?

    A. Behavioral level
    B. Emotional level
    C. Cultural norms
    D. Concrete level

41. Which of the following correlates most highly with scores from norm-referenced assessments?

    A. At-risk behaviors
    B. Learning disability
    C. Academic achievement
    D. Socioeconomic status

42. When a teacher is working with a small group of students, which of the following classroom-environment factors should the teacher consider most?

    A. Ability to hear the whole class
    B. Ability to see the small group
    C. Ability to see the whole class
    D. Ability to use the chalkboard

43. Which of the following is a formative assessment?

    A. Pretest
    B. Hearing screening
    C. SAT I
    D. California Achievement Test

44. Ms. Weeks is an eleventh-grade social studies teacher who recently learned that she is pregnant. Which of the following is her right as a teacher?

    A. She has the right to choose her substitute teacher.
    B. She must take maternity leave for six weeks.
    C. She must return to work immediately after the child's birth.
    D. She has the option to take maternity leave.

45. Brian is a freshman with Down's syndrome at Central High School. Brian receives his English, mathematics, and science instruction in a self-contained special-education room. He attends regular-education classes with his grade-level peers for all other subjects, including physical education and lunch. Which of the following describes the instructional setting for Brian's educational programming?

    A. Self-contained classroom
    B. Least restrictive environment (LRE)
    C. Private-school setting
    D. School-to-work program

46. A student with documented learning disabilities who has been found eligible for special-education service must have an

    A. individual education process.
    B. independent education evaluation.
    C. individualized education plan.
    D. independent education program.

47. One of the predominant leaders during the Early National period of U.S. education was

    A. Ulysses S. Grant.
    B. Benjamin Franklin.
    C. John Dewey.
    D. Horace Mann.

48. During the late 1800s, the laws of Massachusetts required students to attend school in an effort to control and improve the living conditions for children. By 1918, all U.S. states had regulations about students' school attendance. Which of the following is the term for required attendance in public schools?

    A. Mandatory requirements
    B. Truancy education
    C. Tardy education
    D. Compulsory education

49. Theorist most concerned with storage, retrieval, working memory, and long-term memory are which of the following?

    A. Information-processing theorists
    B. Cognitive-behavioral theorists
    C. Choice theorists
    D. Constructivist theorists

50. Thought of as the grandfather of behaviorism, this researcher conducted many of the experimental research studies that form the basis of behavioral-learning theory. His theory of operant conditioning is based on the idea that learning is a function of change in observable behavior. Changes in behavior are the result of a person's response to events (stimuli). When a stimulus-response is reinforced (rewarded), the individual becomes conditioned to respond. This is known as *operant conditioning*.

    A. Jean Piaget
    B. Howard Gardner
    C. B. F. Skinner
    D. Lev Vygotsky

51. When a learner responds to a new event or object by changing an existing scheme or creating a new scheme, this is best known as _____.

    A. equilibrium
    B. articulation
    C. learning
    D. accommodation

52. Manuel's understanding of the civil war in his home country helped him better understand the U.S. Civil War. This is an example of _____.

    A. negative reinforcement
    B. positive reinforcement
    C. positive transfer
    D. negative transfer

53. The high school teachers at Central High School used their common planning time to collaboratively plan and coordinate a series of lessons in three content areas: social studies, art, and English. This is best known as _____.

    A. a thematic-unit plan
    B. an interdisciplinary-unit plan
    C. an emergent-unit plan
    D. a criterion-referenced unit plan

54. Well-written lesson objectives should have three parts that include which of the following components?

    A. Conditions, cognitive verb, and rubrics
    B. What students will understand, know, and be able to do
    C. Measurable verb, conditions, and criteria
    D. Assessment, measurable verb, and standards

55. Which of the following standards were created in an unprecedented effort to establish clear and consistent goals for learning that will prepare America's children for success in college and work?

    A. Common Core State Standards
    B. Content Standards
    C. Performance Standards
    D. New Standards

56. Mr. Greene does not use the lecture method to teach about how to play volleyball. Instead, he uses a method in which he actively shows students the basics of the game, such as setting and volleying. Mr. Greene is most likely using which instructional process?

    A. Demonstration
    B. Direct instruction
    C. Reciprocal teaching
    D. Peer coaching

57. At the end of the chapter, Mrs. Fogarty duplicates the chapter quizzes provided by the test publisher. Which of the following best describes the type of assessment Mrs. Fogarty is using?

    A. Norm-referenced test
    B. Standards-based test
    C. Evidence-based test
    D. Criterion-referenced test

58. Which of the following can best be described as a documented statement of a teacher's responsibilities, philosophy, goals, and accomplishments as a teaching professional?

    A. Résumé
    B. Teaching portfolio
    C. Cover letter
    D. Curriculum vita

59. A specific object or event that positively or negatively influences a person's learning or behavior is best known as a _____.

   A. response
   B. condition
   C. stimulus
   D. cue

60. James is trying to remember a list of 12 words his teacher has shown him. He glances at the list, reads it, mentally classifies the words into categories—such as clothing, furniture, and food—and then recalls many of the 12 words aloud to his teacher. This example shows that James has a strong _____.

   A. working memory
   B. ability to memorize
   C. long-term memory
   D. recitation memory

61. Which of the following classroom-management approaches involves the teacher focusing on students' behavior, not students, when resolving classroom conflicts and negotiating classroom rules and consequences with student input?

   A. Pavlov's control theory
   B. Glasser's choice theory
   C. Jones's say-see-do approach
   D. Canter's assertive-discipline approach

62. Maria has the tendency to be a passive learner who is dependent on others for guidance and decision making. Which of the following best describes Maria's behavior?

   A. Self-determination
   B. Self-fulfillment
   C. Learned helplessness
   D. Learning disability

63. Mr. Fogleman opens class with an open-ended question about erosion. He then invites students to conduct a variety of experiments to more deeply understand erosion. Finally, the students and Mr. Fogleman discuss their discoveries. Which of the following instructional methods best describe Mr. Fogleman's approach?

   A. Teacher-practitioner model
   B. Peer-assisted tutoring model
   C. Independent-instructional model
   D. Inquiry model

64. Mrs. Lacoste's Block Island, Rhode Island, eleventh-grade students engage in Skype discussions with eleventh-grade students on the mainland in Westerly, Rhode Island, as part of a _____ course of instruction in which students do not share the same classroom but learn together.

   A. simulation
   B. discovery
   C. distance-learning
   D. university

65. A sophomore at the East Bay MET School spends six hours a week at a fire station studying forensic science as part of her high-school coursework. Back in the classroom, she studies the mathematics, communication, and science skills required to be successful as a criminal-science investigator. Which of the following best describes the instructional process at work in this example?

   A. Experiential education
   B. Experimental education
   C. Site-based management
   D. Traditional education

66. Groups of students who work together to collaboratively complete a task and who authentically need one another in order to get the work done are experiencing which of the following central tenets of cooperative learning?

   A. Positive interdependence
   B. Simultaneous task management
   C. Jigsaw
   D. STAD

67. Teachers have each of the following rights, EXCEPT

   A. the right to withhold information unrelated to employment.
   B. the right to the Individuals with Disability Act.
   C. the right not to take maternity/family leave.
   D. the right to free speech.

68. If you were especially interested in how an adolescent's culture affects his or her cognitive development, which theorist's contributions would you find most helpful?

    A. Dewey
    B. Pavlov
    C. Piaget
    D. Vygotsky

69. When a test has a norm group, the teacher knows that the test results can be

    A. compared to criterion-referenced results.
    B. disaggregated.
    C. compared to those of peers.
    D. used to make graduation decisions.

70. Teachers should view lesson planning as a

    A. guideline to support instruction that can be changed during lesson implementation.
    B. procedure that will lead to successful teaching.
    C. framework that has one specific, correct way to complete.
    D. requirement for teacher certification.

Constructed-Response Questions

Directions: The following questions require you to write short answers, or "constructed responses." You are not expected to cite specific theories or texts in your answers; however, your knowledge of specific principles of learning and teaching will be evaluated. Be sure to answer all parts of the question. Write your answers in the space provided.

Instructional Scenario I

Scenario: Miss Matthews

Miss Matthews is a first-year eighth-grade teacher at Curtis Junior High School. She has planned a lesson on problem solving for her principal to observe as part of the district's teacher-evaluation procedure. Document 1 shows the plans that Miss Matthews submitted to the principal prior to the lesson.

Document 1

Lesson plan

Problem of the Day

Objective

The student will solve a two-step mathematics problem by using the guess-and-check strategy.

The student will know the formulas for the volumes of cones, cylinders, and spheres and use them to solve real-world and mathematical problems (Common Core State Standards 8 G.9).

Resources

- "Problem of the day" slips of paper
- Math notebooks
- Pencils with erasers
- Calculators

Motivation

Miss Matthews will read the problem of the day aloud and ask students to visualize this situation in their minds.

Procedures

Warm-Up

Students will play a game of guess-and-check using mental math and then calculators. Miss Matthews will display math problems on the overhead projector. The students will discuss their strategies for solving problems.

Preview

Miss Matthews will tell the students that they will use the problem-solving strategy of guess-and-check to solve a problem.

Teach

1. A student distributes the problem of the day.
2. The students glue the problem into their math notebooks.
3. Miss Matthews asks a volunteer to read the problem aloud to the class.
4. She asks students to brainstorm ways to approach the problem; once the guess-and-check strategy is identified, Miss Matthews requires students to try this approach.
5. The students solve the problem independently in their math notebooks.

Assessment

Miss Matthews asks students to peer-review problems for accuracy and use of the guess-and-check strategy.

- The student earns a 3 if he or she solved the problem accurately and used guess-and-check.
- The student earns a 2 if he or she solved the problem accurately but did not use guess-and-check or did not solve the problem accurately but did use guess-and-check.
- The student earns a 1 if he or she attempted to solve the problem but did not solve it accurately and did not use guess-and-check.
- The student earns a 0 if he or she did not turn in the work or turned in incomplete work.

Independent Work

The homework assignment is a similar problem requiring the use of guess-and-check.

Evaluation

When the principal came to visit Miss Matthews's math class, she saw evidence of excellent planning but poor classroom management. Miss Matthews clearly knew her content; set clear expectations in the written assignment; and designed a good, standards-based math problem for students to solve. The problem was implementation. When Miss Matthews asked a student to pass out the problems at the beginning of the lesson, the student acted silly and pretended to be a "problem of the day fairy" as she passed out the papers. Several students enjoyed the performance, and the class became noisy with laughter. Miss Matthews nervously laughed with the students and thanked the girl for handing out the papers with such drama and flair. Next, when the students were supposed to be brainstorming ways to solve the problem, several students were talking in the back of the class. Two students asked to go to their lockers for their forgotten math notebooks, and Miss Matthews allowed them to do so. When Miss Matthews collected the students' in-class responses, she noted a wide range of scores, from 3s to 0s. Several students who were present did not even hand in their classwork.

1. Identify TWO classroom-management strategies for Miss Matthews to implement in her math classroom. Be sure to base your response on principles of teaching and communication techniques.

2. Suggest TWO ways that Miss Matthews can involve her students more appropriately and actively in the lesson. Be sure to base your answer on principles of student learning and instruction.

Instructional Scenario II

Scenario: Colin

Colin is a kind, athletic tenth-grader who loves music, spending time with friends, talking online, and attending Spanish class. A tutor helps him get average grades in science and mathematics. His tutor has noticed that Colin has organizational problems and needs a lot of help breaking down information when studying for tests. The tutor reports the following areas of strength and weakness for Colin:

- Strengths:
  - Visual learner
  - Excellent memory
  - Aptitude with languages
- Weaknesses:
  - Study habits
  - Attention span
  - Concentration when reading

Recently, Colin has started to skip classes and go to a local breakfast spot with friends. He seems to be prioritizing his social life above his academic life, and he is having a difficult time finding a balance between the two. His mother, a single parent, tries to help with Colin's schoolwork, but she works many hours at the local bank, so Colin often is responsible for completing his homework on his own.

Colin's guidance counselor, Mr. Sweeney, asked to speak to Colin about his goals and progress in tenth grade. Colin stated that everything was fine, but Mr. Sweeney was not convinced and decided to set up a meeting with Colin's mother and teachers.

3. Suggest TWO ways that Colin's teachers or guidance counselor can collaborate with others to provide supports for him. Be sure to base your response on principles of communication and teacher professionalism.

4. Identify ONE area of learning difference that could explain Colin's learning behavior at school and with his tutor. Suggest TWO teaching methods to support his learning needs. Be sure to base your response on principles of student learning and instruction.

Answers and Explanations

Multiple-Choice Questions

Answer Key

Question	Answer	Content Category	Where to Get More Help
1	D	Students as Learners	Chapter 7
2	B	Students as Learners	Chapter 7
3	B	Students as Learners	Chapter 7
4	A	Students as Learners	Chapter 7
5	C	Instructional Process	Chapter 8
6	D	Instructional Process	Chapter 8
7	B	Instructional Process	Chapter 8
8	A	Assessment	Chapter 9
9	D	Professional Development, Leadership, and Community	Chapter 10
10	D	Professional Development, Leadership, and Community	Chapter 10
11	C	Professional Development, Leadership, and Community	Chapter 10
12	A	Professional Development, Leadership, and Community	Chapter 10
13	B	Students as Learners	Chapter 7
14	B	Students as Learners	Chapter 7
15	D	Students as Learners	Chapter 7
16	C	Students as Learners	Chapter 7
17	C	Instructional Process	Chapter 8
18	A	Instructional Process	Chapter 8
19	B	Instructional Process	Chapter 8
20	D	Instructional Process	Chapter 8
21	C	Professional Development, Leadership, and Community	Chapter 10
22	B	Professional Development, Leadership, and Community	Chapter 10
23	A	Professional Development, Leadership, and Community	Chapter 10
24	D	Professional Development, Leadership, and Community	Chapter 10
25	D	Students as Learners	Chapter 7
26	A	Students as Learners	Chapter 7
27	B	Students as Learners	Chapter 7
28	B	Students as Learners	Chapter 7
29	C	Assessment	Chapter 9
30	A	Instructional Process	Chapter 8
31	B	Instructional Process	Chapter 8
32	C	Instructional Process	Chapter 8
33	D	Professional Development, Leadership, and Community	Chapter 10
34	D	Professional Development, Leadership, and Community	Chapter 10
35	B	Professional Development, Leadership, and Community	Chapter 10

Question	Answer	Content Category	Where to Get More Help
36	A	Professional Development, Leadership, and Community	Chapter 10
37	C	Students as Learners	Chapter 7
38	B	Students as Learners	Chapter 7
39	D	Students as Learners	Chapter 7
40	A	Students as Learners	Chapter 7
41	D	Assessment	Chapter 9
42	C	Instructional Process	Chapter 8
43	A	Assessment	Chapter 9
44	D	Instructional Process	Chapter 8
45	B	Professional Development, Leadership, and Community	Chapter 10
46	C	Professional Development, Leadership, and Community	Chapter 10
47	B	Professional Development, Leadership, and Community	Chapter 10
48	D	Professional Development, Leadership, and Community	Chapter 10
49	A	Students as Learners	Chapter 7
50	C	Students as Learners	Chapter 7
51	D	Students as Learners	Chapter 7
52	C	Students as Learners	Chapter 7
53	B	Instructional Process	Chapter 8
54	C	Instructional Process	Chapter 8
55	A	Instructional Process	Chapter 8
56	A	Instructional Process	Chapter 8
57	D	Assessment	Chapter 9
58	B	Professional Development, Leadership, and Community	Chapter 10
59	C	Students as Learners	Chapter 7
60	A	Students as Learners	Chapter 7
61	B	Students as Learners	Chapter 7
62	C	Students as Learners	Chapter 7
63	D	Instructional Process	Chapter 8
64	C	Instructional Process	Chapter 8
65	A	Instructional Process	Chapter 8
66	A	Instructional Process	Chapter 8
67	B	Professional Development, Leadership, and Community	Chapter 10
68	D	Students as Learners	Chapter 7
69	C	Assessment	Chapter 9
70	A	Instructional Process	Chapter 8

Answer Explanations

1. **D** Mr. Craig can attempt to handle this discipline problem within the classroom first; therefore, Choice D is the credited response. The teacher can first try to give a "look," or a stern glance; create incentive systems; and provide additional help when a student is talking off-task. Other answer choices suggest that Mr. Craig should go beyond the classroom walls to turn around student talking, such as calling the student's parents (Choice A), giving detention (Choice B), and speaking with the principal (Choice C). Each of these options would be acceptable after Mr. Craig tries to remedy the student talking during class time.

2. **B** According to Erikson's stages of human development, adolescents ages 12 through 18 work to resolve the conflict of identity vs. role confusion. Adolescents consider the roles they play in the adult world and initially experience a sense of role confusion. Eventually, most adolescents achieve a sense of identity— better understanding of who they are and how they can contribute to the adult world.

3. **B** Mr. Sanderson's practice is guided by an understanding of B. F. Skinner's theory of operant conditioning. Operant conditioning is a form of learning in which a learning response increases in frequency when followed by reinforcement.

4. **A** Constructivism is a theoretical perspective on learning that suggests learners create or construct knowledge from their experiences. In Mrs. Gagliardi's classroom students come to their own interpretations of literature, a hallmark of constructivism.

5. **C** An inclusion program for special-education students typically provides supports for students in as many general-education classes as possible, such as this scenario with Ms. Salvatore and Mrs. Keen's class. Usually, the special-education teacher works in the general-education teacher's classroom to provide supports to students with IEPs and to offer expertise and assistance within the classroom.

6. **D** Students with emotional and/or behavioral problems usually respond well to structured choices and a positive, supportive classroom environment. The teacher must strive to maintain a balanced perspective about the student and focus on the student's efforts at self-control and self-discipline. Choices A (self-contained classrooms and strict rules), B (a supportive environment and unlimited choices), and C (a strict environment and no-tolerance policies) all suggest a level of control and rigidity, which often results in an escalation of the student's emotional or behavioral issues rather than the more desirable de-escalation of behavior problems in the classroom.

7. **B** Higher-level questions in Bloom's Taxonomy include analysis and synthesis questions.

8. **A** Achievement tests are written for a variety of subjects and levels and are designed to measure student knowledge or proficiency in the areas that were learned.

9. **D** Mrs. Audette cannot be fired unless her behavior interferes with her teaching effectiveness. This is one of several rights that teachers have.

10. **D** The Cardinal Principles of Secondary Education reorganized secondary schools to include health education, basic skills, good relationships, vocations, civic education, worthy use of leisure time, and ethics.

11. **C** P.L. 94-142 mandates the regulation and formulation of Individualized Education Plans (IEPs) for students with identified learning differences.

12. **A** The Progressive period in U.S. education was influenced by the Industrial Revolution.

13. **B** Self-talk is a behavior that students often engage in when thought and language first come together. Secondary teachers may see this behavior in students who are learning a language for the first time, such as English language learners (ELLs). Choices A (babbling) and C (simultaneous play) are distracters related to infancy. Zone of proximal development (Choice D) is related to the next "just right" skill or concept to teach a learner with assistance from a teacher or a more capable peer.

14. **B** Internalization is the process through which social activities evolve into mental activities.

15. **D** Josh may be experiencing a cultural mismatch between home and school. At home, he is playing the role of an adult, being the caregiver for his mother and siblings. At school, he is required to switch to a more age-appropriate role but one that is not a part of Josh's cultural experiences. Although the other choices are possibly true, each is too narrow and not the best description of the key issue affecting Josh—a cultural mismatch.

16. **C** Mrs. Xavier differentiates her lesson instruction to meet the needs of individual students while maintaining high expectations for all students.

17. **C** Summarizing and note taking are essential instructional strategies that teach students to better comprehend materials. SQ3R requires students to survey the chapter prior to reading, ask questions while reading, read, recite, and review. The double-entry notebook requires students to take notes, make connections, and summarize. Choice A (reinforcing and providing recognition) is not a comprehension strategy.

18. **A** Generating and testing hypotheses strategies help students tap into their natural curiosity, study real-life problems, and understand concepts more deeply.

19. **B** Hunter's model is a classroom-management strategy that focuses on planning instruction. The next step in lesson planning, according to Hunter's model, is independent practice.

20. **D** Curriculum frameworks help guide a teacher's instruction to help him or her follow the district requirements.

21. **C** Dewey is considered the father of progressive education.

22. **B** A Nation at Risk, published in the 1980s, suggested that U.S. schools were falling behind those in other countries.

23. **A** Written during the Clinton Administration, Goals 2000 was a report on U.S. education that included recommendations for improving schools.

24. **D** Mrs. Rodrigues is using respectful communication with Mr. and Mrs. Smith. Respectful communication is a key behavior of teaching professionals. Open communication (Choice A) is a term used more typically in business to indicate a form of communication between peers. Although Choice A may possibly be correct, Choice D is the credited response because the scenario more closely defines respectful communication. Choice C (multicultural communication) is a distracter.

25. **D** English-immersion instruction consists of classroom discourse conducted in English only, even if students speak other languages. The teacher offers simplified English so that Maria can learn both English and academic content.

26. **A** Auditory learners benefit from the use of instructional resources that require listening, such as multimedia and technology.

27. **B** Social-learning theory focuses on the concept that people learn from observing others.

28. **B** Boys usually enter adolescence at age 12, and girls usually enter adolescence at age 10.

29. **C** Formative assessment is used before or during instruction to inform instructional planning and enhance student achievement. Summative assessment (Choice A) provides information at the close of instruction. Norm-referenced assessment (Choice B) and achievement assessment (Choice D) usually take days to administer and then score; therefore, these choices are incorrect.

30. **A** Summative assessment is used after instruction or teaching to evaluate a student's or teacher's achievement at the end of a period of instruction.

31. **B** Students in grades 6–8 generally respond well to the reward of short periods of free time with peers. All other choices are typically more appropriate for elementary-school students.

32. **C** Students with learning disabilities generally respond well to teachers setting clear but flexible limits. Choice A (setting strict routines and rules) is opposite to this; therefore, it is incorrect. Research does not support placing students in homogenous groups (Choice B), or similar-ability groups; instead,

learning-disabled students should work with a range of grade-level peers. Choice D (setting conflict-resolution guidelines for the class) is too broad and related more to classroom management in general.

33. **D** The U.S. Constitution establishes the responsibility of public education.

34. **D** Equal-opportunity policies state that it is legal to hire underrepresented groups, but that an employer cannot dismiss a person from an underrepresented group based on reverse-discrimination policy.

35. **B** The U.S. Constitution establishes that the legal responsibility for education in the United States falls on each of the states.

36. **A** Teachers and students have the right to freedom of speech according to the U.S. Constitution.

37. **C** According to Kohlberg's stages of moral development, adolescents usually attempt to gain the approval of peers during the conventional stage. Choice A (antisocial behaviors) is a distracter. Deep levels of reflection (Choice B) are more often seen during the post-conventional stage. Conformity to rules (Choice D) usually is seen at Kohlberg's pre-conventional level of moral reasoning.

38. **B** Piaget suggests that in the formal-operational stage, adolescents show the ability to demonstrate and develop concepts without the use of concrete materials or images. Choices A (inability to separate and control variables) and C (inability to test multiple hypotheses) are abilities, not inabilities, of adolescents in the formal-operational developmental stage. Choice D (ability to depend on concrete reality to develop concepts) is a distracter.

39. **D** Teachers must communicate high expectations for Ricky's success in an effort to teach all children and do so professionally. All other choices are options for the teacher to offer to support Ricky's progress in school.

40. **A** According to Hidalgo's theory on the three levels of culture, the behavioral level of culture is comprised of people's social roles, home languages, nonverbal communication behaviors, and family structures.

41. **D** Norm-referenced assessment scores correlate most highly with socioeconomic status.

42. **C** In an effort to manage the entire classroom environment and ensure the safety of students, the teacher should have the ability to see the whole class when working with a small group.

43. **A** A pretest is a type of formative assessment that helps the teacher determine students' prior knowledge and plan instruction accordingly. Choice B (hearing screening) is a screening exam. Choices C (SAT I) and D (California Achievement Test) are norm-referenced examinations.

44. **D** A teacher who is pregnant has the right to take a maternity leave that is not counted as sick time.

45. **B** Brian is receiving instruction in his least restrictive environment (LRE). Brian needs a higher level of support in English, mathematics, and science; therefore, he attends a self-contained classroom for these lessons. He does not need as much support in other subjects, so he attends these classes with his grade-level peers.

46. **C** As legally guided in P.L. 94-142, students with documented learning disabilities who have been found eligible for special education must have an Individualized Education Plan (IEP).

47. **B** Benjamin Franklin was a predominant leader, as well as a leader in education, during the Early National period of U.S. education.

48. **D** Compulsory education began in the late 1800s in an effort to require students to attend school in order to control and improve the conditions of children.

49. **A** Information-processing theorists focus more on what happens inside the learner's mind, considering the processes of learning, memory, and performance. Some theorists believe that the human mind works a lot like a computer processor; therefore, they contributed terms such as *storage, retrieval, working memory,* and *long-term memory.*

50. **C** B. F. Skinner is thought of as the grandfather of behaviorism, because he conducted much of the experimental research that is the basis of behavioral-learning theory. His theory of operant conditioning is based on the idea that learning is a function of change in observable behavior. Changes in behavior are the result of a person's response to events (stimuli). When a stimulus-response is reinforced (rewarded), the individual becomes conditioned to respond. This is known as operant conditioning.

51. **D** Accommodation is responding to a new event or object by changing an existing scheme or creating a new scheme. For example, after my refrigerator leaked the sixth time, I called the repairperson again but referred to my paperwork to see when my repair contract would end and began to search sales circulars for new refrigerators.

52. **C** Positive transfer is involved when something is learned at one point that facilitates learning or performance in another situation. Negative transfer (Choice D) occurs when something learned interferes with the learning or performance in another situation.

53. **B** Interdisciplinary-unit instruction incorporates information from two or more content areas (for instance, science, mathematics, physical education, technology, and literacy) to help students see the connections and real-life links across the disciplines. A thematic-unit plan (Choice A), on the other hand, centers on one theme, rather than the connections among disciplines.

54. **C** Objectives should have three parts: measurable verb, conditions, and criteria (also known as your assessment plan).

55. **A** Many states have adopted the Common Core State Standards (CCSS) in English Language Arts/ Literacy and Mathematics to guide curriculum development and student assessment in K–12 schools. The CCSS were developed by the National Governors' Association and the Council of Chief State School Officers to establish clear and consistent goals for learning that will prepare America's children for success in college and work. Choice B (Content Standards) is incorrect because it is too broad of a choice.

56. **A** Teacher demonstrations involve explicitly showing students what something is or how to do something. For example, a science teacher might demonstrate the proper use of a Bunsen burner in a lab, or, as in this scenario, the physical education teacher demonstrates a series of volleyball moves. Choice D (peer coaching) is a distractor. Choices B (direct instruction) and C (reciprocal teaching) involve teacher-centered instructional methods of cognitive skills or concepts.

57. **D** Criterion-referenced tests determine how well a student performs on an explicit objective relative to a predetermined performance level, such as grade-level expectations or mastery. Criterion-referenced tests do not help teachers compare student results to those of other test takers. An example of a criterion-referenced test is a teacher-made or publisher-made exam at the end of a social studies text chapter.

58. **B** A teaching portfolio often contains evidence of teaching effectiveness and professional development, such as lesson plans, recommendation letters, student artifacts, photos, and reflections. A résumé (Choice A), cover letter (Choice C), and curriculum vita (Choice D) *may* contain all the items in the question stem, but they may not.

59. **C** A specific object or event that positively or negatively influences a person's learning or behavior is a stimulus.

60. **A** Working memory is the part of memory that holds and actively processes a limited amount of information for a short amount of time. Choice B (ability to memorize) is not a part of the memory. Long-term memory (Choice C) may not necessarily have been developed in this scenario. Choice D (recitation memory) is a distracter.

61. **B** Glasser's choice theory is a classroom-management approach in which teachers focus on students' behavior, not on the students themselves, when resolving classroom conflicts. Teachers who subscribe to control theory use class meetings to change behavior in the classroom. Students who have a say in the rules, curriculum, and environment of the classroom have greater ownership of their learning. Glasser's approach emphasizes creating a safe space to learn—"our space to learn"—and is designed to promote intrinsic motivation to learn and to behave in the classroom.

62. **C** A tendency for a person to be a passive learner who is dependent on others for guidance and decision making is learned helplessness.

63. **D** An inquiry approach to teaching involves students in the process of exploring the natural and/or material world in an effort to help them discover meaning. In social studies, a teacher might have students listen to the music of the Civil War to examine the themes and issues raised in the lyrics. In science, a teacher might have students experiment with a variety of soil types to see which absorb more water. In mathematics, a teacher might have students use tiles to create tessellations to discover patterns and relationships among the geometric shapes.

64. **C** Distance learning focuses on teaching methods integrated with technology, delivering instruction to students who are at their computers, not in a traditional classroom. Choice A (simulation) is too narrow. Choice B (discovery) is too broad. Choice D (university) is a distracter.

65. **A** Experiential educational approaches tie information to an "anchor" and also may be known as anchored instruction. In other words, the student uses concrete applications of the concept being taught (the anchor) to connect what he or she is learning to a concrete experience.

66. **A** Positive interdependence is a key tenet of cooperative learning, in which the teacher ensures the students must work together to successfully accomplish a task.

67. **B** Teachers do not have a right to the Individuals with Disability Act (IDEA). IDEA is a federal statute made up of several grant programs focused on helping states educate students with disabilities. Choices A (the right to withhold information unrelated to employment), C (the right not to take maternity/family leave), and D (the right to free speech) are all rights that teachers have.

68. **D** Vygotsky contributed to the sociocultural theoretical perspective and suggested that a learner's culture plays a significant role in learning. Dewey (Choice A) contributed to a philosophy of pragmatism in education and is considered the father of progressive education. Pavlov (Choice B) contributed to the behaviorist theoretical perspective through his experiments with animals. Piaget (Choice C) contributed to the constructivist theoretical perspective, providing information about learners' cognitive development.

69. **C** Results from tests that have norm groups can be compared to the results of peers. This is also known as norm-referenced testing. Choices B (disaggregated) and D (used to make graduation decisions) are too broad. Choice A (compared to criterion-referenced results) is a distracter.

70. **A** Lesson planning is a guideline that helps teachers successfully prepare for instruction, which should be adapted, modified, or even abandoned if it is not helping students learn during instruction. Choice B (procedure that will lead to successful teaching) is too broad. Choice C (framework that has one specific, correct way to complete) is incorrect because there is not one correct way to prepare a successful lesson plan. Choice D (requirement for teacher certification) is a distracter.

Constructed-Response Questions

Instructional Scenario I

1. **Suggested content:** Miss Matthews is a math teacher who is teaching a problem-solving lesson to her eighth-grade students but is having difficulty controlling some student behaviors. One classroom-management strategy that Miss Matthews can implement is Canter's <u>assertive-discipline approach</u>. With this approach, the teacher sets <u>clear expectations</u> for student behavior and <u>follows through consistently and fairly</u> with <u>consequences</u>. This approach is based on the tenet that students have a <u>choice</u> to follow the rules or face the <u>natural consequences</u>. One common sequence of consequences involves marking checks on the chalkboard or whiteboard:

   - 1 check = warning
   - 2 checks = detention
   - 3 checks = call home and detention
   - 4 checks = meeting with the principal, detention, and possible suspension

A second approach Miss Matthews can try is to use positive and negative reinforcement as indicated by student behaviors. At first, she could positively reinforce on-task, appropriate class behaviors by giving frequent, genuine, positive feedback. She could involve students more actively in the instructional decisions, such as whether they want to solve the problem alone or with a partner. Finally, Miss Matthews can sparingly use negative reinforcement, such as letting the students know that those students who solve their problems correctly, quickly, and quietly will not have to take the quiz on guess-and-check on Friday. This will motivate the student who is passing out papers to act appropriately, to pass out papers efficiently, and to remain on task during the lesson.

2. **Suggested content:** Miss Matthews can involve her students actively and appropriately in the lesson in two ways:

- Allow the students to model the problem solving by using the overhead projector during the warm-up section of the lesson.
- Pair up the students to solve the problem in Step 5 of the teach portion of her lesson plan.

When Miss Matthews's students demonstrate their problem-solving abilities to open the lesson, the tone of the lesson—this is a serious class where we work hard to learn—is set, providing a strong context for the lesson to come. Allowing the students to work in pairs for the independent-practice portion of the lesson supports students' social needs to talk and work together, a central tenet in social-learning theory. It also offers students who may still be learning the problem-solving strategy an appropriate scaffold of instruction and offers students who are strong in this concept or skill the opportunity to strengthen their understanding by teaching.

Instructional Scenario II

3. **Suggested content:** Colin is a tenth-grader who is losing focus on the purpose of his studies. He is having a hard time finding a balance between his academic and social priorities. Colin's guidance counselor, teachers, and mother could work together in several ways to provide more structure and support for Colin. One way to do so is to require Colin to use an assignment planner and write down each of his tests, quizzes, and homework assignments. After Colin writes down an assignment, he is responsible for asking the teacher to review his planner and sign it. When Colin goes home to do his homework independently, he has a clear idea of what his assignments are. When his mother gets home, she can look at the planner, review Colin's completed homework, and then sign the planner. This home/school/student communication system provides supports for Colin without shifting the responsibility of the work from Colin.

A second way they could work together is to work collaboratively to develop an action plan. Colin's teacher and guidance counselor could facilitate a meeting between Colin, his mother, and any other important stakeholders in Colin's school and personal life, such as his guitar teacher, his older sister, and his neighbor, with whom Colin spends lots of time each day. Together they would set a few clear and measurable goals to be achieved over a short time frame, such as one month. They would set up an action plan for Colin, a self-monitoring system, and supports, if needed, during the month. At the end of the month, they would meet again to assess Colin's progress and to communicate the next steps to support Colin's educational and personal goals.

4. **Suggested content:** Colin's tutor has noticed his strengths, as well as his weaknesses. His tutor reports that Colin has poor study habits, a short attention span, and poor concentration when reading. Colin's behavior could indicate attention deficit disorder (ADD). Based on these observations, the teacher could try two instructional strategies to help Colin with his academics. The first is to use graphic organizers to help Colin organize and synthesize information visually. Colin is a visual learner, so graphic organizers may be very helpful for him when studying for tests or trying to learn lots of information.

The second strategy is to break down the assignments into two or three smaller parts—known as curriculum chunking—to provide more support, positive reinforcement, and instruction for Colin if needed.